T0300137

Redefining Success

Redefining Success: Integrating Sustainability into Management Education advocates incorporating sustainability concepts that go beyond the financial 'bottom line' into management education and business practice. Highlighting the UN Global Compact (UNGC), the Principles for Responsible Management Education (PRME) and the Sustainability Development Goals (SDGs), it explores conceptual and practical issues, presents case studies and other empirical evidence and offers solutions that will both encourage and assist management educators in the incorporation of sustainability into their courses and research. Written by 34 individuals from 17 countries, the book addresses these topics from a variety of theoretical, disciplinary, geographic and organizational perspectives. The authors demonstrate how management educators, collaborating with business and civic organizations, can be change agents for a better world. Written for educators, scholars and business practitioners, the volume concludes with lessons learned, challenges encountered and implications for responsible management education.

Patricia M. Flynn is Trustee Professor of Economics and Management at Bentley University, USA, where she served as Dean of the McCallum Graduate School of Business for 10 years.

Tay Keong Tan is Director of International Studies and Leadership Studies, and an Associate Professor in the Department of Political Science at Radford University, USA.

Milenko Gudić is Founding Director of Refoment Consulting and Coaching, Belgrade, Serbia, and visiting lecturer at University Donja Gorica, Montenegro.

'The book on integrating sustainability into management education comes timely as the UN Global Compact and Principles for Responsible Management Education (PRME) focus their efforts to advancing the implementation of the Sustainable Development Goals. It provides conceptual reasoning, innovative frameworks, practical evidence and inspirational stories on what business schools could and should do to enable new generations of managers and business leaders to get a better understanding of the very meaning of success in the context of the new role of business in society, sustainable development and responsible leadership. The presented innovative solutions cover all aspects of management education: Programs and contents, educational processes, actors involved, and the institutional and organizational arrangements. They are as diverse as the respective real life practices and contexts are. Yet, they all generate and are consistently interwoven into the main message, which this must-read publication, together with its sister book on integrating sustainability into business and management practice, offers to forward-thinking individuals and future change agents in management education, business, policy making and civic society in general. We all need to *Redefine Success* and, in doing so, we all should work together and go *Beyond the Bottom Line.*'

– **Eric Cornuel**, *Director General and CEO, EFMD*

'The recently adopted Sustainable Development Goals (SDGs) provide a comprehensive and complex framework for global and local multi-stakeholder partnerships to end poverty, protect the planet and ensure prosperity for all. This consecutive volume on integrating sustainability into business and management practices builds on the cross-collaboration of the PRME Working Groups on Anti-Poverty, Anti-Corruption, and Gender Equality, while including valuable inputs from the wider PRME community and beyond. By incorporating a variety of stakeholder perspectives from across the world, the book outlines some of the key voids and opportunities for preparing current and future leaders to understand and deal with pressing global challenges. By providing examples of practical case studies, theories, and innovative approaches, the book makes a strong case for educators, scholars, and practitioners to incorporate sustainability principles and goals into management education programs. In line with the vision of the UN backed Principles for Responsible Management Education (PRME) initiative to realize the SDGs through responsible management education, this book is a must read for individuals who are looking for inspirational examples of sustainability strategies that can be effective across a number academic institutions, businesses, and countries. The book is also a must read for individuals who are not yet clear on the importance of bringing the SDGs to every classroom and every organization.'

– **Jonas Haertle**, *Head, PRME*

'This volume shows how purpose drives innovation in management education. It is a valuable resource for anyone who believes, as I do, that business schools can be a powerful force for sustainable development. The authors are pioneers in the field, and draw on their experiences and research to provide useful frameworks, examples, and insights. But the book is not just for people like us – the believers. It is for any change-minded management educator looking for innovative ways to connect students to practice, engage across disciplines, prepare faculty for curriculum change, and more.'

– **Dan LeClair**, *Executive Vice President and Chief Strategy and Innovation Officer, AACSB*

Redefining
Success

Integrating
Sustainability
into Management
Education

Edited by Patricia M. Flynn, Tay Keong Tan and Milenko Gudić

Routledge
Taylor & Francis Group

LONDON AND NEW YORK

First published 2018
by Routledge
2 Park Square, Milton Park, Abingdon, Oxon OX14 4RN

and by Routledge
711 Third Avenue, New York, NY 10017

Routledge is an imprint of the Taylor & Francis Group, an informa business

British Library Cataloguing-in-Publication Data
A catalogue record for this book is available from the British Library

Library of Congress Cataloging-in-Publication Data
A catalog record for this book has been requested

ISBN: 978-1-78353-548-4 (hbk)
ISBN: 978-1-35126-880-6 (ebk)

Typeset in Utopia and Franklin Gothic
by Florence Production Ltd, Stoodleigh, Devon, UK

MIX
Paper from
responsible sources
FSC
www.fsc.org   FSC® C013604

Printed and bound by CPI Group (UK) Ltd, Croydon, CR0 4YY

Contents

Introduction

Patricia M. Flynn
Bentley University, USA

Tay Keong Tan
Radford University, USA

Milenko Gudić
Refoment Consulting and Coaching, Serbia

Sustainability skills and awareness of responsible management practices are gradually becoming a priority in managerial appointments as business strives to adhere to human rights legislation, environmental standards and labour laws, as well as to promote sustainability goals of the organization. In recent decades, expansion of markets, liberalization of trade, globalization and advancement of technology have greatly extended the reach and impact of businesses globally. Many corporations have been forging new enterprises, creating new products, and entering new markets, resulting in the rise of business as an economic, political, environmental and cultural force that significantly shapes the world in which we live. While some people perceive the ascendancy of business in societies around the world as a positive force, bringing goods and services, technology, jobs and opportunities, others view corporations as the protagonists in exploiting workers, corrupting cultural values, violating human rights, and damaging the natural environment.

Today's business school students are tomorrow's managers, entrepreneurs, business leaders and public policy officials. They will have a critical role in promoting 'the good' in business value creation and restraining 'the bad' in the form of social, ethical and environmental harm. In their day-to-day decisions, they will wield enormous power that can make the world a better place – embracing renewable energy, reducing carbon emissions and keeping the natural ecosystems in balance. They can also serve as social entrepreneurs who will observe labour laws, safeguard human rights and consumer interests, and protect the culture and livelihoods of vulnerable communities. The business practices that so greatly influence our consumption and production patterns today will shape the quality of life for future generations.

This book presents the work of academics, researchers and business practitioners around the world in preparing business students with the knowledge of sustainability practices and ethics related to environmental protection, social inclusion and good governance (ESG). Its central thesis is that for management education to be responsive to the needs of business and society today and to proactively prepare organizations for the future, leaders must redefine business success looking beyond just financial metrics.

This volume also advocates for redefining success in management education to include the teaching of ESG and sustainability concepts that go beyond the "bottom line". It is an edited collection that explores conceptual and practical issues, presents case studies and other evidence, and offers solutions that will assist management educators in addressing sustainability from a variety of theoretical, disciplinary, geographical and organizational perspectives. The book acknowledges the struggles and celebrates the successes of educators striving to advance the practice of responsible leadership and management in pedagogy, in scholarship, and in collaboration with business leaders and managers.

Redefining Success has been framed in the context of the United Nations Global Compact (UNGC) and the Principles of Responsible Management Education (PRME) that serve as norms and voluntary guidelines for global business practices and responsible management education. A few of the chapters also incorporate the UN's more recent Sustainable Development Goals (SDGs) designed "to end poverty, protect the planet and ensure prosperity for all." The UNGC, PRME and SDGs are three powerful forces guiding the shift by companies and business educators towards global sustainability.

More specifically, the UNGC, launched in 2000 under the auspicious of then Secretary General Kofi Annan, is the largest sustainability initiative for corporate leaders in the world today, mobilizing more than 9,000 participating organizations in its global network. The UNGC promulgates 10 principles on business sustainability practices based on the Universal Declaration of Human Rights:

Human Rights

> Principle 1: Businesses should support and respect the protection of internationally proclaimed human rights; and
>
> Principle 2: Make sure that they are not complicit in human-rights abuses.

Labour

> Principle 3: Businesses should uphold the freedom of association and the effective recognition of the right to collective bargaining;
>
> Principle 4: The elimination of all forms of forced and compulsory labour;
>
> Principle 5: The effective abolition of child labour; and
>
> Principle 6: The elimination of discrimination in respect of employment and occupation.

Environment

Principle 7: Businesses should support a precautionary approach to environmental challenges;

Principle 8: Undertake initiatives to promote greater environmental responsibility; and

Principle 9: Encourage the development and diffusion of environmentally friendly technologies.

Anticorruption

Principle 10: Businesses should work against all forms of corruption, including extortion and bribery. Businesses should support and respect the protection of internationally proclaimed human rights and make sure that they are not complicit in human-rights abuses.

Working in tandem with the UNGC principles are the PRME, initiated in 2007 under the auspices of then Secretary General Ban Ki Moon, to encourage business schools and universities worldwide to adopt practices that would advance corporate social responsibility (CSR) and a sustainable global economy. The PRME community, which brings together more than 650 educational institutions in over 85 countries, promotes curricular development and research collaboration. The PRME involve six principles to advance responsible management education and related scholarly activities:

Principle 1 – Purpose: We will develop the capabilities of students to be future generators of sustainable value for business and society at large and to work for an inclusive and sustainable global economy.

Principle 2 – Values: We will incorporate into our academic activities and curricula the values of global social responsibility as portrayed in international initiatives such as the United Nations Global Compact.

Principle 3 – Method: We will create educational frameworks, materials, processes, and environments that enable effective learning experiences for responsible leadership.

Principle 4 – Research: We will engage in conceptual and empirical research that advances our understanding about the role, dynamics, and impact of corporations in the creation of sustainable social, environmental and economic value.

Principle 5 – Partnerships: We will interact with managers of business corporations to extend our knowledge of their challenges in meeting social and environmental responsibilities and to explore jointly effective approaches to meeting these challenges.

Principle 6 – Dialogue: We will facilitate and support dialog and debate among educators, students, business, government, consumers, media, civil society organizations and other interested groups and stakeholders on critical issues related to global social responsibility and sustainability.

As the PRME have evolved, so too, informally, has a 7th principle ("Organizational Practice"), which urges academic institutions to focus on incorporating sustainability into their own policies and operations, including environmental (e.g. buildings, transportation, sourcing and energy use) as well as social programs on campuses (e.g., diversity, health and safety, and training).

Principle 7 – Organizational Practice: We understand that our own organizational practices should serve as examples of the values and attitudes we convey to our students.

More recently in September 2015, 17 SDGs were adopted by the 193 UN member nations in a high-level plenary meeting of the UN General Assembly in New York City. This event firmly placed sustainability in the centre of the world development agenda. The advent of the SDGs, further supports the advocacy roles of the UNGC and the PRME in the development of practices and policies to address the major sustainable development challenges facing our human society. Businesses, in addition to their roles as value creators in the marketplace, have their part to play in reducing poverty and hunger, improving health and education, advancing human rights, protecting the environment, and making cities more liveable and sustainable. And, management education should be preparing current and future leaders to take on these critical roles.

The call for contributions to this book was sounded across the globe to educators, scholars, entrepreneurs, business leaders and public policy makers. It received a welcomed but unexpectedly strong response from potential contributors and collaborating authors, which resulted in development of two books instead of one. The first book published in March 2017, *Beyond the Bottom Line: Integrating Sustainability into Business and Management Practices*, focuses on the application of sustainability principles in business organizations. This sister volume, *Redefining Success: Integrating Sustainability into Management Education*, identifies problems, presents evidence and offers solutions for integrating sustainability into management education programs.

Redefining Success is written for educators, scholars and business practitioners interested in strategies, theories, case studies and innovations related to sustainability and responsible management education. The authors of the chapters are academics, practitioners and activists from a wide range of disciplinary, organizational and global perspectives. The book is written by 34 individuals from 23 institutions in 17 countries from different parts of the world (e.g., Brazil, Canada, France, Germany, Greece, India, Ireland, the Netherlands, Nigeria, the Philippines, Sri Lanka, Romania, Serbia, Singapore, Switzerland, the United Kingdom (UK) and the United States (US)).

The book reflects their scholarship, purposeful writing, and creative expression on a range of sustainability topics including human rights, labour practices, gender equality, environmental concerns and governance. Derek Bok, former President of Harvard University, once quipped: "If you think education is expensive, try ignorance." Similarly, those who consider teaching sustainability as too onerous because it takes considerable effort and expense, should contemplate the alternative. Failing to address sustainability issues in today's management curricula is sending students into a world without the critical competences and ethical perspectives for the responsible practice of their professions. The results could be grave and have unpredictable consequences for business leaders as well as for the many stakeholders who suffer the social, humanitarian, environmental and ethical impacts of business decisions. This is the message in which we strongly believe, and have promulgated throughout this book.

Organization of the book

Redefining Success addresses all major aspects of management education, from educational content and programs, to teaching and learning processes, to research, to the individuals involved and to institutional and organizational practices and policies. It provides inspirational stories on how the principles of sustainability can be integrated into management education across a range of disciplines, organizations and countries.

The book consists of 17 chapters, organized in five sections:

- Frameworks for understanding
- Disciplinary and transdisciplinary perspectives
- Institutional perspectives
- Country and regional perspectives
- Looking ahead

Section 1: Frameworks for understanding

The first section of the book provides frameworks for understanding the issues involved. It starts with an historical overview of the UNGC and PRME principles by Hsu and William O'Keefe (Chapter 1). The chapter highlights the evolving pathways and partnerships associated with these initiatives and their impacts on responsible business practice and management education. Thereafter, new ways of framing these issues are proposed.

In Chapter 2, Anninos demonstrates how management education can be inspired by neuroscientific evidence to develop sensitive but also capable business minds. By understanding the biological underpinnings of brain functioning and processes that are connected to specific behaviours and motivations, management educators can design innovative educational programs and environments that foster deep learning and the cultivation of sustainable development and responsible leadership.

Cicmil, Ecclestone and Colins (Chapter 3) offer a conceptual framework for integrating the sustainability agenda in an educational environment from multiple perspectives (ethical, economic, ecological and epistemological). The "4E" framework encourages the questioning of the epistemic assumptions that tend to dominate contemporary debate on the global ecological crisis and economic growth. Through an experiment based on a participatory approach that acknowledges and respects students and lecturers' differences in values, and cultural and disciplinary backgrounds, the authors seek to instill the UNGC principles in co-creating a responsible community of learners and knowers, ready to influence the way society is developing.

In Chapter 4, Hope introduces an innovative PRME Curriculum Tree as a blueprint for business school curriculum design. The Curriculum Tree integrates learning, teaching, and assessment strategies that engage students of all disciplines with the principles, values, and aspirations of the UNGC, PRME, and SDGs. By promoting holistic understanding and system thinking the framework enables management educators to develop new curricula that more comprehensively address the issues of sustainability and responsible management. It also demonstrates ways of effectively integrating these topics into existing curricular structures.

Section 2: Disciplinary and transdisciplinary perspectives

This section provides perspectives related to the educational curricula in different management education disciplines, such as marketing and accounting. It also tackles the complex issues that go beyond a single discipline.

While advocating for the integration of ethics, CSR and sustainability in marketing education, Bauer (Chapter 5) presents the findings of her empirical analysis of the marketing curricula and textbooks used in UK universities. The study indicates that issues of ethics are more frequently addressed in marketing modules than are those related to CSR and sustainability. As for marketing textbooks, while almost all of them cover ethics, attention to this topic is on average quite small. Moreover, the marketing textbooks rarely address issues of CSR and sustainability.

Gunarathne (Chapter 6) demonstrates how an undergraduate accounting degree program of a state university in Sri Lanka has successfully developed students' competencies in sustainability. The chapter describes course design, delivery and evaluation processes, then addresses challenges encountered and strategies adopted to overcome them. In Chapter 7, Buhmann argues that understanding the implications of human rights for responsible business management requires an understanding of the related legal and managerial issues. This helps in preventing risks of violating human rights associated with management practices and/or business relations. The author also emphasizes the importance of international human and labour rights laws that managers should know about in order to safeguard human rights in their policies and management practices.

Section 3: Institutional perspectives

Section 3 contributes to the understanding of the institutional challenges, opportunities and solutions encountered in efforts to integrate sustainability and responsible practices in management schools in different parts of the world. It starts with a case study incorporating human rights into the curriculum of a business school in Brazil. The integration of responsible management education in an applied science university in Switzerland, follows, along with a comprehensive and transformational approach to ethics and sustainability in a business school in the US.

Chapter 8 by Gomes, Barros and Tonelli presents the specific challenges and solutions related to the integration of human rights into management education in an emerging economy that was addressing large-scale infrastructure projects. The authors delineate how the Getulio Vargas Foundation Business School (FGV) in Brazil, in collaboration with the FGV School of Law, implemented a joint elective course with participatory learning methods for three undergraduate programs.

An institutional experience on the integration of PRME-related research is provided by Schlange in Chapter 9. The chapter describes a process of developing a comprehensive research agenda at the University of Applied Sciences in Switzerland, and provides lessons on the initiation, provision and supervision of diverse sustainability-related activities. Special emphasis is given to the role of student-initiated research. In Chapter 10, Buono discusses a multi-pronged institutional approach to implementing the PRME in various educational activities: The classroom (Principles 2: Values and 3: Method), campus life (Principles 1: Purpose, 2: Values and 7: Institutional), the production of knowledge (Principle 4: Research), and outreach to the business and not-for-profit worlds (Principles 5: Partnerships, and 6: Dialog). The case illustrates how Bentley University in the US has addressed these challenges through the creation of an Alliance for Ethics and Social Responsibility.

Section 4: Country and regional perspectives

Section 4 expands the international and regional perspectives on integrating sustainability into management education. It starts with the experience of a network of catholic universities in the Philippines, each member of which is experimenting in integrating the UNGC and PRME principles. The section also includes assessments of the challenges and opportunities related to the integration of the PRME into business schools in Canada and in Africa.

Santiago in Chapter 11 documents how nine La Salle Christian Brothers' business schools in the Philippines are trying to integrate the principles of the UNGC and PRME into a joint framework to be used by member schools as they redesign their business curricula. In the early stages of implementation the challenge is how to translate the jointly designed framework into the actual curricula and classroom activities of these business schools that are operating in different contexts.

In Chapter 12, Carruthers, Fox and Kakka provide insights into the extent to which the principles of UNGC and PRME are integrated into higher education courses and faculty training in Canadian universities, including both signatories and non-signatories of PRME. The authors expose the barriers and challenges, and also the opportunities for curriculum development and institutional integration around the principles, values and spirit of the UNGC and PRME.

Nwagwu in Chapter 13 discusses the prospects and challenges of integrating sustainability in management education institutions in Africa. Focusing on the PRME principles 3, 4 and 5 (Method, Research and Partnership), the chapter argues that in spite of numerous challenges, the benefits of the implementation of these principles are increasingly evident. The chapter emphasizes the need to work on solutions that are relevant to local conditions, which in this case are characterized by systemic poverty and the prevalence of informal markets.

Section 5: Looking ahead

Section 5 expands upon the collaborative aspects of integrating sustainability into management education. It includes a chapter on partnerships between a management school and its business stakeholders; a global-local partnership of schools and innovators; and a case study in which a business school and a corporation work together in promoting diversity and gender equality. The concluding chapter of this section and of the book raises the question of whether business schools worldwide, as institutions in their own right, can change to better address gender issues within their own organizations.

Based on the Greenhouse Gas Management project on climate action (SDG #13), which won the 2015 Guardian University Award in Business Partnership, Chapter 14 (Molthan-Hill, Winfield, Baddley and Hill) offers a replicable model for PRME principle 5 (Partnerships). Based on the assumption that they can contribute to solving the challenges of sustainability, students at Nottingham Business School in the UK are involved in real-life, work-based projects (PRME principle 3 "Methods"), while at the same time developing their practical skills.

In Chapter 15, Nonet and Petrescu document how the two professors of Management and Marketing successfully integrate into the curricula the pioneering AIM2Flourish global initiative created at Case Western University and supported by the PRME. The AIM2Flourish program connects students with business innovators aligned with the SDGs. It has had inspiring results particularly on the development of a mindset that welcomes innovation for a better world. The role of organizational change is further explored in Chapter 16, where Bevelander and Page highlight the ING Group in the Netherlands and its Orange Code and Diversity Manifesto that played transformative roles in fostering gender equality. A virtuous spiral is delineated with tone at the top and emotional and financial resources instrumental in fostering positive change. The chapter's lessons are relevant for other businesses, and also for management education institutions seeking to implement PRME within their own organizations.

Lastly, in Chapter 17 Hulpke and Lau further build on the gender equality issue, in this case focusing on faculty in business schools. The chapter shows that women are still under-represented in both leadership and faculty positions in management education. The authors demonstrate that the hiring practices in business schools, particularly those that favour candidates with publications in top-tier journals likely contributed to this outcome. The chapter concludes with recommendations for making business schools change agents for gender equality.

Conclusions and looking ahead

The book concludes with a summary of the lessons learned from the chapters, identification of challenges encountered by faculty and institutions in seeking to integrate sustainability principles, and their implications for responsible management education. It emphasizes that helping businesses and other stakeholders to redefine the meaning of success requires business schools to first reframe their own objectives and practices to bring about profound and lasting change towards a more globally sustainable and socially responsible future.

Section 1
Frameworks for understanding

1

Evolving pathways to more effectively align UNGC and PRME in pursuit of the Sustainable Development Goals

Hsu O'Keefe
Pace University, USA

William M. O'Keefe
Pace University, USA

Abstract

In an effort to lead a global transformation, the United Nations Global Compact (UNGC) and Principles for Responsible Management Education (PRME) initiatives are focussing on the pursuit of the sustainable development goals (SDGs) through 2030. Implementation of the SDGs is in concert with pursuit of UNGC's Ten Principles and the embedded social, environment and governance issues. PRME, established and supported by UNGC with six universal principles as guides, works with Higher Education Institutes (HEI)s to better prepare future generations of professionals and leaders who are committed to responsible and sustainable business practices. The purpose of this chapter is to provide an overview of the UNGC and PRME, and their evolving pathways as they adapt and respond to the ever-changing needs of an expanding membership in a dynamic global environment. Highlights of their efforts to explore strategic pathways for enhanced and more inclusive collaborative initiatives focussed on achieving the

SDGs are presented. A wide range of productive UNGC–PRME strategic partnerships have been forged and additional strategic partnering opportunities abound. Key challenges meriting attention are also identified.

United Nations Global Compact (UNGC)

Background

With an initial core group of forty business signatories and representatives of other entities, the United Nations Global Compact (UNGC) was established in the year 2000 as a voluntary initiative fostering the adoption of UN universal sustainability principles and goals by business leaders across the globe (UNGC, n.d.a). In pursuit of this broad mission, the UNGC was conceived as a flexible and dynamic initiative, rather than as a regulatory body responsible for ensuring compliance. To operationalize the general guidance provided by this mission, the UNGC adopted Ten Universal Sustainability Principles focussed on Human Rights, Labor, Environment and Anticorruption as its main compass for directing and coordinating partnering initiatives (UNGC, n.d.b).

In response to the growing awareness of the need to more objectively assess the effectiveness of signatore efforts to embed the principles into their business practices, 5 years into its launch UNGC introduced the Communication on Progress (COP) report requiring signatories to document and share their actions and accomplishments in attaining the principles. Today the UNGC continues to function as the predominant responsible and sustainable leaders' platform where participants can engage in sharing, exchanging, collaborating and communicating their best operational policies and practices in pursuit of the Ten Principles and the evolving UN Development Goals.

UNGC's Evolving Pathways and Ecosystem

The evolution of this network-based entity operating on a multi-centric model (UNGC, n.d.c) is evidenced in Figure 1.1. As membership grew, various business members took the initiative to establish local independent clusters of member networks as self-governing entities. This, in turn, further stimulated business membership growth, creating the need for more formal governance, leading to the establishment of a permanent UNGC headquarters in 2002. These informal local networks demonstrated their ability to help companies better understand what responsible business means within different national, cultural and language contexts and facilitate outreach, learning, policy dialogue, collective action and partnerships (UNGC, n.d.d; UNGC, 2013, August). These results stimulated the formal establishment of Local Networks as part of the UNGC governance framework in 2005 (Whelan, 2010). The Local Networks

Forum soon emerged as the major venue "for Local Networks from around the world to share experiences, review and compare progress, identify best practices and adopt recommendations intended to enhance the effectiveness of Local Networks" (Wynhoven and Stausberg, 2010, p.256).

The year 2004 saw the formal launch of Leaders Summit Triennial events as a high-level business leader platform to lay the ground-work for and endorse strategic initiatives. The 2016 Summit declared the goal for all stakeholders "to achieve the 2030 Sustainability Agenda of the UN" (UNGC, n.d.e). Initiated in 2002, the Global Compact (GC) Advisory Council was replaced by the GC Board in 2006, now chaired by the UN Secretary General (Wynhoven and Stausberg, 2010). To better finance operations, the Foundation for the Global Compact was established in 2006 as a nonprofit organization dedicated to securing funding to meet a range of needs (UNGC, n.d.f). Furthermore, in 2008 a UNGC Trust Fund

FIGURE 1.1 **Evolution of UNGC'S Pathways and Ecosystem**

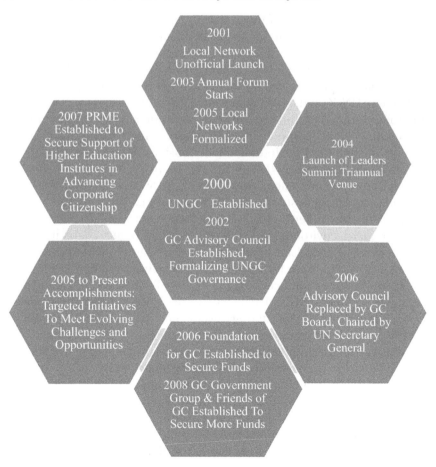

was established together with the Global Compact Government Group and Friends of the Global Compact to manage the UN contributions of governments and their Missions (UNGC, n.d.g).

Selected UNGC accomplishments to date

As of 2005, this evolution in governance structure, formalization of networks and institutionalization of forums stimulated the launch of a series of independent targeted initiatives to meet evolving challenges and opportunities. The strong appeal of the UNGC's Socially Responsible Behaviour concept is evidenced by its growth from 40 to over 9,000 companies and 3,000 non-business signatories today, drawn from 170 nations (UNGC, 2016, November), making this the largest sustainability initiative for businesses in the world. This rapid and broad expansion is also evidence of the UNGC's ability to continuously adapt and reposition itself with innovative and meaningful strategies to cope with the evolving challenges resulting from the constant 'changing global economic realities' (Rasche and Kell, 2010).

A key contributing factor to this success is the enhanced rigor of the now-biannual COP report on company accomplishments in attaining the UNGC Principles and broader Corporate Social Responsibility (CSR) initiatives, launched in 2005. To date, over 28,000 COPs have been posted while 7,678 signatories have been removed for failing to meet this reporting requirement. (UNGC, n.d.h; UNGC, n.d.i; Wynhoven and Stausberg, 2010; Hamid and Johner, 2010). To accommodate the reporting needs of increasingly diverse types of signatores, the UNGC has modified the COP by creating 'Express COPs' for large companies, a simplified version for smaller businesses and a bi-annual Communication on Engagement (COE) for the more limited CSR engagement initiatives of non-business signatores. (UNGC, 2015; UNGC,n.d.j).

In response to the interests of institutional investor participants, the Principles for Responsible Investment (PRI) was launched in 2005 with the commitment to integrate social, environmental and corporate governance issues in financial analyses and financial decision-making processes (Haertle and Miura, 2014). This initiative, in 2012, led to the formation of a partnership with the UNGC, the UN Environment Program Finance Initiative (UNEP FI) and the UN Conference on Trade and Development (UNCTAD) focussed on the creation of the Sustainable Stock Exchanges Initiatives fostering development of a more responsible and sustainable capital market (Sustainable Stock Exchanges Initiative, 2013; UNGC, n.d.k). UNGC academic representatives recognized the education requirements evidenced by such an initiative, launching in 2007 the Principles for Responsible Management Education initiative as described below.

These accomplishments, in 2011, stimulated the formation of the Global Compact LEAD (UNGC LEAD), an exclusive group of corporate sustainability leaders, from major corporations such as Unilever, Nestle, KPMG and Fuji Xerox., drawn "from across all regions and sectors that represent the cutting edge of the UNGC" (UNGC, n.d.l). This group has been the driving force encouraging "close collaboration with investors, business schools and UN agencies, and facilitates proactive engagement with governments, NGOs and other key stakeholders" (UNGC, n.d.m). An example of a significant UNGC LEAD contribution is the 2016 CEO Study, conducted in partnership with Accenture Strategy. A key result shows that 89 per cent of the CEOs "say commitment to sustainability is translating into real impact in their industry" (UNGC and Accenture Strategy, 2016).

Principles for Responsible Management Education (PRME)

Background

PRME Secretariat, together with its Steering Committee, was established in 2007 to encourage and guide those higher education institutions (HEI) that have endorsed the PRME Six Principles (PRME, n.d.a) and are on the path to becoming key change agents and responsible management educators capable of preparing the socially responsible managers needed by businesses (Haertle and Miura, 2014). As the UNGC hosts the PRME Secretariat, this allows "for close coordination and complementarity between PRME and the UNGC . . . PRME's Principles explicitly incorporate UNGC's values, UNGC's support, . . . has allowed it to call itself an 'United Nations supported initiative'. . . . and PRME's still evolving governance structure is modelled after that of the UNGC" (Haertle and Miura, 2014, pp. 14–15).

Evolution of PRME's pathways & ecosystem

PRME also adopted a network-based organization model. Its multicentric governance structure has evolved, creating the desired pathways envisioned by its diverse stakeholders. Key features of the evolution of the PRME ecosystem and pathways are presented in Figure 1.2. PRME can be described as a principle-driven global initiative comprised of interorganizational networks employing a collaborative governance model. Its shared values and purpose guide the actions of network collaborators in support of the UN goals. In addition to the UNGC Office, Steering Committee membership has evolved to comprise the following prominent business school accreditation and regional bodies from across the globe: the Association to Advance Collegiate Schools of Business (AACSB-International), the European Foundation for Management Development (EFMD), the Central and East European Management Development Association (CEEMAN), the Association on MBAs (AMBA), Association of African Business Schools (AABS), Latin America Council of Management Schools (CLADEA),

FIGURE 1.2 **Evolution of PRME'S Pathways and Ecosystem**

Accreditation Council for Business Schools and Programs (ACBSP), the Academy of Business in Society (ABIS) and the Globally Responsible Leadership Initiative (GRLI). It functions as the governance body responsible for providing strategic direction and contributing financial support. In light of PRME's collaborative governance model, an Advisory Committee was formed in 2014 to secure the benefits of informed governance and strategic guidance from a wider range of stakeholders. Its members are drawn from the platforms that PRME has been creating to encourage and enable collaborative learning and practice innovation. (PRME, n.d.b,c,d,e).

Sharing Information on Progress (SIP) is PRME's mandatory biannual reporting system intended to document, share accomplishments and demonstrate commitment to the principles of Responsible Management Education (RME). PRME signatories are delisted if they do not meet this biannual requirement and have the opportunity to rejoin if they meet relisting requirements (PRME, n.d.f; Haertle, 2016, July 8). Concurrent with the 2008 launch of the SIP, PRME Working Groups (WGs) started to form.

Regional Meetings were initiated in 2010 to further disseminate the PRME Principles and expand PRME quantitatively. This led to the formalization of Local and Regional Chapters in 2013 committed to adapt the PRME mission and principles to local needs and expand meaningful corporate citizenship initiatives by regional HEIs. (PRME, n.d.g,h). This success led in 2013 to establishing and in 2016 expanding PRME Champions, a group comprised of selected institutional leaders judged to "have played leading roles in their respective regions" (Haertle and Miura, 2014, p. 12). The Champions work to identify the development programs needed to equip faculty with the knowledge and skills required to conduct RME initiatives in a range of subject categories and regions of the world (PRME, n.d.i)

Selected PRME accomplishments to date

PRME, in alignment with UNGC and other entities, has fostered the evolution of numerous pathways leading to the development of new educational materials, tools and best practices by PRME signatories intended to guide the formation of the future generations of socially responsible leaders. By design, these pathways are intended to be dynamic because PRME's "aim was not to provide definitive answers to . . . questions – far from it. Instead, ... [It expects that their discussions] will encourage further inquiries. . . . which will feed into more collaborative learning and innovation within the PRME community" (Haertle and Miura, 2014, p.16).

The goal of the PRME WGs is to further Sustainable Development Goals (SDGs), thus focusing on collaborative engagements across academic and non-academic institutions. The WGs focus on furthering the understanding of specific issues relevant to advancing PRME implementation. They select one or more principles and associated SDGs, and then develop pathways to integrate the chosen WG topic into curricula. Established WGs that are developing curricula include Poverty, Gender Equality and Anti-Corruption. These pathways frequently involve the development of on-line toolkits (e.g. Anti-Corruption WG), publications (all working groups in their respective issue domains), webinars (e.g. Gender Equality) and research studies such as the Poverty WG 2nd Delphi Survey of members in forty-six countries to identify priority themes (PRME, n.d.j,k,l,m).

Efforts by the WGs to promote PRME and related issues include, for example, the Anti-Poverty WG that organized an All Academy Theme session on *Informal Economy, Poverty and Responsible Management Education* at the Academy of Management 2012 annual meeting and an international experiential learn-ing conference in collaboration with INCAE, on *Leveraging Innovative and Cross-Cultural Learning for Poverty Reduction: Climbing the Economic Ladder –*

Examples from and for Nicaragua, held in Managua in July 2014 (PRME, n.d.m). The Gender Equality WG has developed a 'Global Repository' to help business school faculty integrate gender equality into their courses and research. The Repository, launched at the Rio+20 Forum in 2012, was created by faculty from six countries and currently encompasses fifteen disciplines. Case materials, syllabi, research publications and a wide range of course materials are included in the Repository that is accessible on-line (PRME, n.d.n).

Furthermore, collaborative efforts between PRME WGs and PRME Regional Chapters led to the establishment of PRME Research Conferences on an annual basis, with the first being held in Switzerland in 2014 and the fourth to be held in 2017 in Brazil. The co-organizers of the latter will also include UNDP Brazil and the UNGC Brazil Office. The Anti-Poverty WG organized a business community 'collabatory' in Brazil: the "Foundations for Sustainable Leadership: Responsible Management and Leadership Education" following the Rio+20 Corporate Sustainability Forum (Gudić, 2015). Other examples include two books, the first, *Beyond the Bottom Line: Integrating Sustainability into Business and Management Practices* (Gudić, Tan & Flynn, Eds. 2017), and this volume, *Redefining Success: Integrating Sustainability into Management Education*; both books are the result of collaboration among the Gender Equality, Anti-corruption and Anti-poverty WGs.

PRME Chapters are aligning with UNGC Local Networks and collaborating with PRME Regional Meetings to improve understanding of local challenges and leverage the insights gained into opportunities for advancing SDG implementation. For example, the Brazil Chapter, initiated in 2014, successfully launched an academic institution outreach initiative in the northeastern region of the country intended to further promote understanding of corporate sustainability and responsible management education, stimulating an increase in the number of PRME signatories from 22 in 2013 to 31 in 2015 (PRME Chapter Brazil, 2015; Librizzi *et al.*, 2015).

The initial 22 member PRME Champions Group has successfully completed three game-changing projects in its 2-year pilot phase: Transformational Model for PRME Implementation (Escudero and Csuri, n.d.); Partner with Business Schools to Advance Sustainability (Weybrecht, Csuri and Gerami, 2015); and Faculty Development for Responsible Management Education (Babson College, Copenhagen Business School, IILM Institute for Higher Education, n.d.). Now with eight additional members and working in partnership with the Global Responsible Leadership Initiative (GRLI), the Champions Group will focus its 2016–2017 agenda on organizing sub-groups, which will undertake a range of projects focused on finding pathways that business educators can pursue to advance SDGs, collaborating with UNGC LEAD, in harmony with UNGC strategy deployment (PRME, n.d.i). In addition, guidelines for Regional Chapters and WGs are being developed to further enhance the activities of these PRME entities.

Achieving alignment: Fostering creation of shared UNGC–PRME pathways towards advancing the SDGs

UNGC and PRME are dedicated to encouraging the private sector and academia to embrace their respective principles and associated challenges in a collaborative manner allowing all to successfully advance their chosen SDGs, whose launch in 2015 has greatly expanded the options available to PRME signatories for collaborating with the UNGC, harnessing existing pathways and forming new ones to meet these enhanced challenges (UNGC, n.d.n; UN, n.d.). The 17th SDG, 'Partnership for the Goals', is of particular significance due to the growing recognition that achievement of the SDGs requires the collaborative efforts of all stakeholders.

The June 2016 UNGC Leaders' Summit in New York City offered positive examples of collaborative transformational change pathways that businesses can and are successfully pursuing to fulfil the 2030 SDG Agenda. Business signatories shared descriptions of specific SDGs focused initiatives such as 'Changing Climate, Accelerating Ambitions' (SDG #13) and broader initiatives embracing a wider range of SDGs such as 'The New Era for Business' and 'Financing the SDGs' (UNGC, n.d.o). As the Summit progressed, the rich array of opportunities offered by this multiplicity of SDGs and targets became increasingly obvious. In spite of the broad SDG agenda initially being dismissed as 'worse than useless' due to its breadth, it, in fact, is having a liberating effect that fosters growth of a diverse range of approaches to adopting SDGs (The 169 Commandments, 2015, March 28).

Two hundred students from PRME and non-PRME schools were invited to attend the General Assembly Session on 'Agenda 2030 – The New Era for Responsible Business'. They also participated in the celebration of the efforts and achievements of the new business initiative, Local SDG Pioneers (UNGC, n.d.p), a program intended to showcase examples of innovative approaches businesses can and are taking to create social, economic and environmental benefits for the global community. Energizing and inspiring examples the students were exposed to include a pioneer from India who shared a story related to SDG Goal #3 – 'for safe and healthy birth' and another from Tanzania who shared one about Goal #7, 'for access to clean energy' (UNGC, n.d.q).

Haertle (2016, July 7) emphasized the importance of students' involvement as a way 'to bridge the gap between business practitioners and future leaders'. It is expected that the students returned to their schools enthusiastically sharing with faculty and colleagues what they learned, reinforcing interest in Signatory schools and generating bottom-up demand for involvement at non-Signatory schools. To facilitate involvement, a Student Engagement Platform supporting the SDGs was launched as UNGC–PRME Alignment, September 2016. "This platform consists of two parallel projects that are managed in partnership with

WikiRate and with *AIM2Flourish*. The WikiRate project will facilitate the analysis of information provided in COP reports and present data that will showcase where company and sector improvements can be made. The AIM2Flourish project will categorize activities and data according to each relevant SDG determined through research on innovative business practices that *do good and do well.*" (PRME. 2016, September 19; UN. 2016, September 21).

The UNGC is leveraging the Local Networks as vehicles to facilitate focussed and meaningful application of the SDGs to a wide range of interests and needs across the globe. This extension of the UNGC Principles is fostering adaptation to each location's perception of which SDGs are of greatest relevance and importance in the context of their value system, knowledge and priorities (UNGC, 2016). Their knowledge of how to effectively navigate through the local scenarios and cultures allows them to aggregate value by personalizing ownership of SDG implementation.

This rich localization process is ripe with opportunities for PRME members to contribute research on the localization and adoption process. For example, Miura and Kurusu (2015, p. 320) conducted research among the Japanese UNGC signatories to learn why they joined the UNGC. Their findings state "that companies participate in the UNGC not only proactively, but also reactively; indeed, our analysis hints at the possibility that reactive motives have become more important over time and that such market actors as sustainability index makers and institutional investors are emerging as important external stakeholders that encourage and urge certain companies, especially those aiming at a global market, to join the UNGC". The authors suggest that additional research regarding motives for companies to join the UNGC is needed as "market forces (such as index makers, institutional investors and suppliers) may help increase the quantity of signatories, they may however not contribute to enhancing the quality of the UNGC" (Miura and Kurusu, 2015, p. 327).

UNGC, PRME and Higher Education Sustainability Initiative (HESI) are aligning their work to advance a major topic of the SDGs, Goal #13 on climate change. The partners actively contributed to the 'Caring for Climate Business Forum' at the venue of the Paris Climate Change summit in December 2015. They hosted parallel discussions among attending members on carbon pricing, science-based target setting, responsible climate policy engagement and socially responsible financing of action programs. Members agreed to commit "to implement actions on responsible policy engagement in their company". Such a commitment is historic in that private sector organizations demonstrated "how business can provide credible, transparent and consistent input for effective climate action" (UNGC, n.d.r) while HESI demonstrated how they can contribute to SDG-focused conferences as a means of promoting and providing pathways to incorporate issues such as climate change into their curriculum and research (PRME, 2015, October 14).

PRME and UNGC LEAD are collaborating to identify ways of closing the gaps between business needs and business programs, in addition to sharing ideas about how to "explore opportunities to impact specific sustainability issue area(s) through the implementation of the Global Compact Principles" (Weybrecht, Csuri and Gerami 2015, p.7). LEAD is documenting best practices and developing toolkits for the benefit of other organizations, with current emphasis on supply chain, investor relations and R&D sustainability challenges (UNGC, n.d.s).

Given HEIs multidisciplinary curriculum development challenges, LEAD's initiatives demonstrating practical attempts by businesses to integrate sustainability concepts across core functions are of particular relevance to PRME signatories as models for action. These field-based cross-functional applications of sustainability concepts also offer HEIs multiple management training and academic research opportunities.

PRME signatories can also gain valuable insight into business education and training needs and research ideas, and opportunities by exploring on-line, multi-lingual SDG attainment planning tools, such as the SDG Compass and the SDG Industry Matrix, which the UNGC is developing in partnership with third parties. Perusal of the Compass (UNGC News, 2015, September 26) offers HEIs faculty and students the opportunity to develop a clearer understanding both of how businesses plan and implement SDG attainment projects as well as the implications for their curricula. The SDG Industry Matrix is being created by the UNGC in partnership with the consulting company KPMG (UNGC and KPMG, 2015). The six projects currently under development will contribute data to build a library of industry-specific examples and ideas for value-creating corporate initiatives focused on attainment of a particular SDG.

This Industry Matrix provides academia with valuable case studies and curriculum material for use in the classroom, as well as data for the design of sustainability-focused research within and across the selected industries. The availability of this SDG-anchored matrix can incentivize the creation of RME-focused curricula for traditional business schools as well as for industry-focused higher education entities such as those dedicated to preparing managers and specialists for the Food, Beverage and Consumer Goods Industries and Healthcare and Life Sciences Industries, among others.

Due to their similar structures and parallel activities, evolving UNGC–PRME pathways include exploiting synergy building options through close collaboration between UNGC's various platforms and programmes and PRME's WGs. For example, PRME Gender Equality WG and the Women's Empowerment Principles (WEPs) are focussed on advancing SDG # 5 – Gender Equality.

Other examples of effective UNGC–PRME collaboration include the Anti-Poverty WG and Social Sustainability, Poverty and Health Initiative working to advance SDG #1 Poverty, #2 Zero Hunger and #10 Reduced Inequalities, and PRME and the UNGC Anti-Corruption WGs collaborating to achieve SDG #16 – Peace, Justice and Strong Institutions. Furthermore, the Sustainability Literacy Test – SULITEST, championed by J.C. Carteron and supported by the UN as part of the SDGAction9551, is 'an online multiple choice question assessment' to assess sustainability literacy knowledge for all HEIs and businesses. The goal of this initiative, forged under Partnership for SDGs with various UN institutions, PRME and several PRME Steering Committee members, among others, is to advance SDG# 4 – Quality Education – and #12 – Responsible Consumption and Production (Partnerships for SDGs).

Concluding remarks

The UNGC has worked diligently and creatively to translate its Ten Universal Principles into meaningful social, environmental and governance initiatives that stakeholders are successfully adopting and adapting to local conditions. As the UNGC mission, goals and strategy have evolved over time, its initiatives have fostered in business and business education practices a maturing stakeholder appreciation of the importance of a committed and collaborative pursuit of the SDGs. The growing alignment between the UNGC and PRME will continue to play a central role in the process of enabling the integration of the SDGs into the DNA of a wide spectrum of organizations across the globe. While much has been accomplished, key challenges, particularly those identified below, need to be addressed.

The multi-centric organization model adopted to meet the diverse interests and needs of a wide range of stakeholders fragments the access points of the SDG implementation resources being developed by the UNGC and its strategic partners. This frustrates attempts to learn about and benefit from innovative practices beyond one's immediate linked networks. The establishment of a well-publicized and easy-access central database providing an overview of and links to databases of stakeholder initiatives merits additional attention and the necessary resources.

The lack of secure and adequate sources of funding for PRME continues to limit its development. Unlike its 'sister' organization PRI, and the UNGC, PRME's pool of existing and potential business school signatories are facing economic challenges resulting from a range of industry disruptions. HEIs are unable to fully fund the PRME organization. Additional steps could be taken to secure reliable and committed sources of support beyond the current HEIs' target pool of business schools. Also, the UNGC is well positioned to continue to assist PRME secure additional financial support from foundations as well as local and international government organizations.

The UNGC–PRME launch of the Student Engagement Platform is a positive step towards encouraging student involvement. Note that the PRME Steering Committee is currently comprised largely of prominent business school accreditation and regional bodies. In light of the importance given by both UNGC and PRME to greater student involvement, consideration should be given to devising a way to incorporate student contributions to the governance process, possibly by inviting an appropriate and qualified student group to join the PRME Steering Committee.

Both PRME and the UNGC have experienced significant numbers of non-communicating signatories who have been delisted or left. While efforts have been made to better understand the factors contributing to this behaviour, a comprehensive study is needed to understand the causes and identify the steps that can be taken to secure Signatory commitment and increase membership growth.

Current UNGC–PRME strategic partnerships, such as those with LEADS and the Local Chapters, merit more attention and support. New and innovative ways of partnering need to be explored. For example, the Local SDG Pioneers initiatives offer ample partnering opportunities for the broader PRME signatory community, as do PRME's 'sister' entity PRI and its strategic partners UNEP FI and UNCTAD. It appears that the synergistic potential offered by UNGC strategic partners GC Government Group and Friends of the Global Compact has yet to be fully explored.

In closing, UNGC–PRME strategic partnering opportunities abound. The challenge now is to identify additional promising pathways, harness the needed resources and continue forging new partnerships to successfully advance the SDGs.

References

Babson College, Copenhagen Business School and IILM Institute for Higher Education (n.d.) Faculty development for Responsible Management Education. *PRME*. Retrieved from www.unprme.org/resource-docs/FDReportFinalWeb.pdf

Escudero, M. and Csuri, M. (n.d.). Transformational model for PRME implementation. *PRME*. Retrieved from www.unprme.org/resourcedocs/PRMETransformationalWeb.pdf

Gudić, M. (2015). Poverty, a challenge for management education: The PRME working group journey. *75th International Jubilee Scientific Conference in Economics and Management. Solutions in the 21st*. Svishtov, Bulgaria: Tsenov Academy of Economics

Gudić, M., Tan, T.K. and Flynn, P.M., (Eds.) (2017). *Beyond the Bottom Line: Integrating the UN Global Compact into Business and Management Practices*. Saltaire, UK: Greenleaf Publishing

Haertle, J. (2016, July). PRME July 2016 Newsletter. Retrieved from www.bulletin.unglobal compact.org/t/r-573365E4E087B33A2540EF23F30FEDED

Haertle, J. and Miura, S. (2014, Autumn). Seven years of development: United Nations – Supported Principles for Responsible Management Education. *SAM Advanced Management Journal*, 79 (4), 8–18.

Hamid, U. and Johner, O. (2010). The United Nations Global Compact communication on progress policy: origins, trends and challenges. In A. Rasche and G. Kell (Eds.), *The United Nations Global Compact – Achievements, Trends, Challenges*. 265–280. New York, NY: Cambridge University Press.

Librizzi, F., Parkes, C., Csuri, M. and Haertle, J. (2015). The first report on PRME Chapters. *PRME Chapters*. Retrieved from www.unprme.org/resourcedocs/FirstReportonPRME Chapters2015.pdf

Miura, S. and Kurusu, K. (2015). Why do companies join the United Nations Global Compact? The case of Japanese signatories. In K. Tsutsii and A. Lim (Eds.), *Corporate Social Responsibility in a Globalizing World*, 286–320. United Kingdom, Cambridge, UK: Cambridge University Press.

Partnerships for SDGs. (n.d.). Sustainability Literacy Test (SULITEST) of the Higher Education Sustainability Initiative (HESI). Retrieved from www.sustainabledevelopment.un.org/partnership/?p=9551

Principles for Responsible Management Education (PRME). (n.d.a). *Six Principles.* Retrieved from www.unprme.org/about-prme/the-six-principles.php

PRME. (n.d.b). *PRME governance document.* Retrieved from www.unprme.org/resourcedocs/PRMEAdvisoryCommitteeMembersmandate1January2016to31December2017.pdf

PRME. (n.d.c). *Steering committee.* Retrieved from www.unprme.org/about-prme/steering-committee/index.php

PRME. (n.d.d). *Advisory committee.* Retrieved from www.unprme.org/about-prme/advisory-committee/index.php

PRME. (n.d.e). *Advisory committee members mandate 1 January 2016 to 31 December 2017.* Retrieved from www.unprme.org/resourcedocs/PRMEAdvisoryCommitteeMembers mandate1January2016to31December2017.pdf

PRME. (n.d.f). *Policy on Sharing Information on Progress.* Retrieved from www.unprme.org/sharing- information-on-progress/sip-policy.php 8/17/2016

PRME. (n.d.g). *PRME regional meetings.* Retrieved from www.unprme.org/working-groups/regional-meetings.php

PRME. (n.d.h). *PRME Chapters.* Retrieved from www.unprme.org/working-groups/chapters.php

PRME. (n.d.i). *PRME Champions.* Retrieved from www.unprme.org/working-groups/champions.php

PRME. (n.d.j). *Working Groups.* Retrieved from www.unprme.org/working-groups/working-groups.php

PRME. (n.d.k). *PRME Working Group on Anti-Corruption in Curriculum Change.* Retrieved from www.unprme.org/working-groups/display-working-group.php?wgid=748

PRME. (n.d.l). *PRME Working Group on Gender Equality.* Retrieved from www.unprme.org/working-groups/display-working-group.php?wgid=2715

PRME. (n.d.m). *PRME Working Group on Poverty, A Challenge for Management Education.* Retrieved from www.unprme.org/working-groups/display-working- group.php?wgid=824

PRME. (n.d.n). *Welcome to the Wikispace of the PRME Working Group on Gender Equality.* Retrieved from www.prmegenderequalityworkinggroup.unprme.wikispaces.net/Welcome +to+the+Wikispace and www.prmegenderequalityworkinggroup.unprme.wikispaces.net/Resources+Repository

PRME Chapter Brazil. (2015). *Activity Report.* Retrieved from www.unprme.org/resource-docs/PRMEChapterBrazil2015Report.pdf

PRME. (2015, October 14). *PRME Secretariat issues overview of climate change action activities by PRME signatory Higher Education Institutions.* Retrieved from www.unprme.org/resource-docs/HESIChartFinal.pdf

PRME. (2016, July 8). *Twenty-five schools delisted for failure to comply with Sharing Information on Progress (SIP) reporting requirement.* Retrieved from www.unprme.org/news/index.php?newsid=413#.V7OSX-ApBPY

PRME. (2016, September 19). *New: UN Global Compact and PRME announce student Engagement platform to support the SDGs.* Retrieved from www.unprme.org/news/index.php?newsid=428#.WEGKUGr_pPZ

Rasche, A. and Kell, G. (2010). Introduction: The United Nations Global Compact–retrospect and prospect. In A. Rasche and G. Kell. (Eds.). *The United Nations Global Compact – Achievements, Trends, Challenges.* 1–19. New York, NY: Cambridge University Press

SDG Compass. (n.d.). *Inventory of business tools.* Retrieved from http://sdgcompass.org/business-tools/

Sustainable Stock Exchanges Initiative (SSE). (2013). *About the SSE.* Retrieved from www.sseinitiative.org/about/

The 169 Commandments. (2015, March 28). *The Economist,*14.

UN Global Compact (UNGC). (n.d.a). *About the UN Global Compact.* Retrieved from www.unglobalcompact.org/about

UNGC. (n.d.b). *The Ten Principles of the UN Global Compact.* Retrieved from www.unglobal compact.org/what-is-gc/mission/principles

UNGC. (n.d.c). *A Networked Based Organization.* Retrieved from www.unglobalcompact.org/about/governance

UNGC. (n.d.d). *A Local Lens for Global Change.* Retrieved from www.unglobalcompact.org/engage-locally

UNGC. (n.d.e). *UN Global Compact Leaders Summit 2016.* Retrieved from www.unglobal compact.org/take-action/events/leaders-summit/leaders-summit-programme

UNGC. (n.d.f). *FAQ-Foundation for the Global Compact.* Retrieved from www.globalcompact foundation.org/faq.php

UNGC. (n.d.g). *Our Governance.* Retrieved from www.unglobalcompact.org/about/govern ance.

UNGC. (n.d.h). *Why Report?* Retrieved from www.unglobalcompact.org/participation/report and www.unglobalcompact.org/participation/join/commitment

UNGC. (n.d.i). *Expelled Participants.* Retrieved from www.unglobalcompact.org/participa tion/report/cop/create-and-submit/expelled

UNGC. (n.d.j). *Global Compact Communication on Engagement (COE) in Brief.* Retrieved from www.unglobalcompact.org/participation/report/coe

UNGC. (n.d.k). *Partner with Enlightened Stock Exchanges.* Retrieved from www.unglobalcom pact.org/take-action/action/sustainable-stock-exchange-initiatives

UNGC. (n.d.l). *Advancing Sustainability Leadership through Innovation and Action.* Retrieved from www.unglobalcompact.org/take-action/leadership/gc-lead

UNGC. (n.d.m). *Leaders in Corporate Sustainability.* Retrieved from www.unglobalcompact.org/take-action/leadership/gc-lead/what-is-lead

UNGC. (n.d.n). *17 Goals to Transform the World/How You Can Get Involved.* Retrieved from www.unglobalcompact.org/what-is-gc/our-work/sustainable-development/sdgs/17-global-goals

UNGC. (n.d.o). *UN Global Compact Leaders Summit.* Retrieved from www.unglobalcompact.org/take-action/events/leaders-summit/leaders-summit-programme

UNGC. (n.d.p). *UN Global Compact Leaders Summit 2016 Programme of June 23.* Retrieved from www.unglobalcompact.org/take-action/events/leaders-summit/leaders-summit-programme#june23–0930

UNGC. (n.d.q). *2016 Local Pioneers.* Retrieved from www.unglobalcompact.org/what-is-gc/our-work/sustainable-development/global-goals-local-business/sdgpioneers/2016

UNGC. (n.d.r). *COP 21 – an Unstoppable Momentum.* Retrieved from www.unglobalcompact.org/take-action/action/cop21-business-action

UNGC. (n.d.s). *What Lead Companies Are Doing to Advance the SDGs.* Retrieved from www.unglobalcompact.org/take-action/leadership/gc-lead/lead-sdg

UNGC. (2013, August). *Global Compact Local Networks.* Retrieved from www.unglobalco mpact.org/docs/networks_around_world_doc/LN_Brochure.pdf

UNGC. (2015). *Global Compact Communication on Progress Policy*. Retrieved from www. unglobalcompact.org/library/1851

UNGC News. (2015, September 26). *The SDG Compass Helps Companies Take Action on New UN Goals*. Retrieved from www.unglobalcompact.org/news/2551-09-26-2015

UNGC. (2016). *Making Global Goals Local Business: A New Era for Responsible Business*. Retrieved from www.unglobalcompact.org/library/4321

UNGC. (2016, November). *Our Participants*. Retrieved from www.unglobalcompact.org/ what-is-gc/participants

UNGC, & Accenture Strategy. (2016). *The UN Global Compact–Accenture Strategy CEO Study 2016: Agenda 2030 A Window of Opportunity*. Retrieved from www.accenture.com/us-en/insight-un-global-compact-ceo-study and www.accenture.com/ungcceostudy

UNGC and KPMG. (2015). *SDG Industry Matrix*. Retrieved from www.unglobalcompact.org/ library/3111 and www.kpmg.com/Global/en/IssuesAndInsights/ArticlesPublications/ Documents/corporate-sustainability-v2.pdf

UN Office of the Secretary General's Envoy on Youth (2016, September 21). *UN Global Compact and PRME Announce Student Engagement Platform to Support the SDGs*. Retrieved from www.un.org/youthenvoy/2016/09/un-global-compact-prme-announce-student-engagement-platform-support-sdgs/

UN Sustainable Development Knowledge Platform (n.d.) *Sustainable Development Goals*. Retrieved from www.sustainabledevelopment.un.org/sdgs and www.sustainabledevelop ment.un.org/?menu=1300

Weybrecht, G., Csuri M., & Gerami, P. (2015). Partner with business schools to advance sustainability. *PRME and UNGC LEAD*. Retrieved from www.unprme.org/resource-docs/businessbschoolpartnerships.pdf

Whelan, N. (2010). Building the United Nations Global Compact local network model: History and highlights. In A. Rasche & G. Kell (Eds.). *The United Nations Global Compact – Achievements, Trends, Challenges*. 317–339. New York, NY: Cambridge University Press.

Wynhoven, U. and Stausberg, M. (2010). The United Nations Global Compact's governance framework and integrity measures. In A. Rasche & G. Kell (Eds.). *The United Nations Global Compact – Achievements, Trends, Challenges*. 251–264. New York, NY: Cambridge University Press.

Hsu O'Keefe, PhD, is Adjunct Professor, International Management/Business at Pace University and member of the Faculty Steering Committee for the Center of Global Business Program. She also teaches International Economics/Business to MBA and EMBA students at Fairleigh Dickinson University, New Jersey. Sustainability issues have been in her DNA both academically and professionally. She is an international business management aficionado who strives to enrich her courses by incorporating the critical themes plaguing the world.

hokeefe@pace.edu

William M. O'Keefe, Doctorate in Management, is Adjunct Professor, International Management/Business at Pace University. He instructs corporate business strategy-related courses at the graduate level. His current research focus is on finding sustainable approaches to alleviating the energy poverty challenges facing Sub-Saharan Africa. He has over 40 years of management, research and consulting experience in a range of organizational settings in the Americas and Africa.

wokeefe@pace.edu

2

A responsible business education approach

Insights from neuroscience

Loukas N. Anninos

University of Piraeus, Greece

> Men ought to know that from the brain and from the brain only arise our pleasures, joys, laughter, and jests as well as our sorrows, pains, griefs and tears . . .
>
> (Hippocrates, c. 460–377 BC)

Abstract

During the last few years, efforts have been made towards the conceptualization and realization of a new inspiring model for business education. The advances in the field of neurosciences have contributed in learning more about human behaviour, which is pertinent to the practice of management. This chapter aims to identify how business education can be inspired by neuroscientific evidence so as to build a responsible business education approach aiming to develop sensitive but also capable business minds. Being aware of the biological underpinnings of brain functioning and processes, business educators can gain a more profound knowledge of how the human brain's functions are connected to specific behaviours and motivations, thus being able to design innovative educational programmes that enable deep learning. Neuroscientific suggestions and evidence can be used as a basis on which responsible business education programmes can be developed.

Background and chapter objective

It is an undeniable fact that the endeavours for the conceptualization and realization of a new inspiring approach for business education against the backdrop of corporate misbehaviour incidents have been increasing. Several global initiatives have been undertaken towards that direction, e.g. Principles for Responsible Management Education (PRME), PRME Working Group on Poverty, International Association for Management Development in Dynamic Societies-CEEMAN (PRME, 2016 a, 2016 b; CEEMAN, 2016), and relevant studies have been conducted. These steps aim to develop a new generation of managers characterized by a deeper understanding of the world and their own selves (Anninos, 2014).

The degree of effectiveness of educational systems is determined by the extent they manage to maximize learning at the individual and collective level. In order to achieve their objectives, specific educational policies, practices and behaviours are necessary. The dawn of the so-called 'brain era' offers significant (informative) insights into educators as they strive to continuously improve learning (Blakemore & Frith, 2005; Erlauer, 2003). While there is a proliferation of books, journals, conferences and courses that focus on the benefits of using neuroscientific evidence for education, there are also misbeliefs about the human brain (neuromyths) and unrealistic expectations from the application of neurofindings to education (Hook & Farah, 2013; Fischer, et al., 2007; Organization for Economic Cooperation and Development (OECD), 2007; Goswami, 2006). Some scholars are critical (e.g. Bruer, 1997). Others suggest evaluating the neurobased products and approaches before any attempt for adoption/ implementation based on educational goals and their matching to the purpose of the brain-based approach, research findings, potential limitations and their impact on behaviours (Sylvan & Christodoulou, 2010).

It is *absolutely* necessary for the brain-based approaches of education to be based on scientific evidence (Geake, 2008; Blakemore & Frith, 2005); otherwise, they may actually lead to disappointing results in class and harm the neuroscience–education relationship (Sylvan & Christodoulou, 2010). There is also evidence that educators use neuroscience so as to enhance/strengthen their professionalism, credibility among peers and confidence on the raison d`être of their profession, namely the shaping of their students' brains (Hook & Farah, 2013).

Traditional practices and pedagogies are being reviewed, as educators gain scientific knowledge on the function of the brain and the biology of learning, thus becoming more able to design and deliver educational experiences that literally and conceptually transform the human mind (Erlauer, 2003). Learning how to most effectively learn has become equally important to the learning content (Sprenger, 1999), but it is important to underline that the need for more collaboration among neurosciences and educators is vital (Carew & Magsamen, 2010; Fischer, 2009), so that educators are knowledgeable enough to avoid pitfalls.

The advances in the field of neurosciences have also allowed scholars to learn more about human behaviour, which is pertinent to the practice of management. Significant insights into various human behaviour areas are offered such as change (Whiting *et al.*, 2012), motivation (Mobbs & MacFarland, 2010), learning (Daw & Shohamy, 2008), leadership and social influence (Ringleb, Rock, & Ancona, 2013; Love & Maloney, 2009; Siegel & Pearce, 2009; Ringleb & Rock, 2008), managing emotions (Ringleb & Rock, 2008) and their impact on decision-making (Waldman, Balthazard, & Peterson, 2011; Morse, 2006). Thus, being aware of the biological underpinnings of brain functioning and brain processes, a better understanding of how people are operating and how brain functions are connected to specific behaviours can be achieved (Lee, Butler, & Senior, 2010; Rock & Schwartz, 2007).

While there is still a lot to be learned about the human brain and despite the fact that more research is necessary along with collaboration among neuroscientists and educators in areas of common interest (Varma, McCandliss, & Schwartz, 2008), neuroscientific evidence can be used to inform business educators how to improve educational practices. The purpose of this chapter is therefore to identify how business education can be inspired by neuroscientific evidence so as to build a responsible approach aimed at developing sensitive but also capable business minds.

Neuroscientific insights

Human behaviour can be theorized as a dynamic combination of genetic predispositions and interactions between the individual and its external environment. Certain behavioural patterns are dependent on learning and experience, which means that they are acquired and formed throughout the upbringing and education of individuals (Alahiotis, 2011). Human behaviour is based on motives that are the result of brain regions' interaction and is influenced by emotions and the fulfilment of neuroscientific basic needs, such as the need for attachment, orientation and control, self-esteem, pleasure and pain avoidance (Ghadiri, Habermacher, & Peters, 2012). Through the acquisition of greater insights into brain operation, unproductive behaviours and actions can be prevented. Consequently, learning becomes a critical parameter, if a change in mentality (that would cause further changes in the way people think and act) is desirable, such as in the case of responsible management.

In order to change the behaviour, a change inside the brain (in the organization and operation of neuronal networks that produce a particular behaviour) is necessary, and this is something that is achieved through novel and suitable experiences (Kolb, Gibb, & Robinson, 2003). Learning occurs in the brain, the organ that enables individuals to adapt to their environment (The Royal Society, 2011). It is noted, however, that even if two people have exactly the same experiences, brain diversity (in terms of operation) will produce different changes in each brain (Reimer, 2004).

From a neuroscientific perspective, learning is described as the development of neural networks, i.e. nerve cell networks (Wolfe, 2001). It is estimated that the human brain consists of 86 billion neurons (Herculano-Houzel, 2009) that process and transmit electrochemical signals. Communication between neurons happens at the synapses (the point at which neurons connect) with the help of chemicals called neurotransmitters (e.g. dopamine and oxytocin) that can energize or suppress nerve cells. A stimulus, for example, causes nerve impulses (electric signals) that move across the neuron axon to the synapse. At the synapse, electrical signals are translated to chemical signals (chemicals are released) so as to move to another neuron. Then the signals change to electrical signals. These electrochemical reactions make the second neuron fire and this process can continue, leading to the firing of other neurons. During this phase, dendrites (neuron-branching fibres) tend to connect with each other (dendritic branching). The repetition of the same pattern causes the whole neuron group to fire together, leading to the formation of a neural network (Radin, 2008; Sousa, 2001). Neuron stimulation leads to dendritic growth, which is translated to smoother and quicker communications inside the brain. Every time the brain is stimulated by novel and exciting ways (such as by learning something new), dendritic growth occurs (Jensen, 2005).

Existing neuroscientific studies offer four main insights that are pertinent also to business educators who wish to build a brain compatible learning environment for responsible management (see Exhibit 2.1.)

Using neuroscientific insights for responsible business education

Maxwell (2014) supports that values and ideals are excluded from academic and intellectual endeavours that aim to help us fulfil our aspirations for a prosperous life. This is particularly true for business schools. Giacalone (2004) talks about the lack of higher ideals in business curricula and stresses the need to provide students with aspirational/higher goals along with economic ones, so that unethical business practices are avoided. Personal wealth and share prices are not the only factors that matter; in a world that values such as love, compassion, empathy, forgiveness, peace and hope constitute the foundations for a truly prosperous life. Enlightened societies demand a strong emphasis by universities on human cultivation and connection of science to real-life problems. There is a strong need for a global democratic society of excellent citizens (Dewey & Duff, 2009), who are expert learners with self-awareness, humility and respect, and it is the responsibility of the higher education systems to develop them.

EXHIBIT 2.1 **Basic neuroscientific insights**

Insight	Description
Brain plasticity	The human brain grows and makes new neural connections throughout one's life. This fact contributes to mental growth and impacts directly on learning and change adaptability (Semendeferi & Damasio, 2000; Teffer & Semendeferi, 2012; Kolb, Gibb, & Robinson, 2003; Blakemore & Frith, 2005).
Emotional awareness/ mindfulness	The perception, identification and management of emotions through mindfulness offers to an individual the ability for more conscious thinking and behavior that can further impact decision-making (Love & Maloney, 2009).
Perception of threat and reward	An experience of threat or a reward determines behavior (Rock, 2009), something that has direct implications for leadership, motivation, the design of suitable educational spaces and workplaces, the development of relevant supportive culture and the willingness of people for cooperation. Rewards are related to good, positive feelings stimulated by dopamine. On the contrary, the use of threats is destructive and toxic, as it results in greater consumption of oxygen and glucose from the blood that the brain needs to sustain its mental capabilities (Rock, 2009).
Mirror neurons	The human brain is a social organ which means that social interaction impacts its physiological and neurological reactions (Rock, 2009). Mirroring (the firing of neurons in one's brain simply by observing an action that another person performs, just like the first person was performing the action itself) proves that we are connected to other people and the environment we live in and this has also implications for cultivating empathy and learning by imitation (Ghadiri, Habermacher, & Peters, 2012). Mirror neurons can explain why emotions and behaviors are contagious among people (Cattaneo & Rizzolatti, 2009).

Responsible business practice is interrelated with the ultimate business aim which is excellence (the quest for continuously improved performance). Excellence cannot be restrained strictly to organizational borders, but it relates to the organizational impact on society (i.e. it is not possible for an excellent company to neglect corporate responsibility issues and/or business ethics) (Anninos & Chytiris, 2012). Anninos (2007) describes three hypostases of excellence (man, citizen and scientist/professional) and emphasizes that the existence of these three hypostases in every individual is the necessary (idealized) presupposition for 'true' excellence in organizations and states. In the case of higher education, this is translated to the development of a new mentality (values, attitudes, behaviours and practices) that understands, supports and utilizes the interconnectedness among different disciplines, societies and cultures.

It is evident to business educators, scholars and practitioners that a new teleological (focus on a final revised end) and a deontological (ethical positions based on a set of ethical rules) perspective in business education are needed

(Anninos, 2014). These perspectives are promoted through the United Nations (UN) Global Compact Principles on human rights, environment, labour and anti-corruption. Inspired by the UN Global Compact, the PRME outline the necessity for the transformation of business education based on the intentional develop-ment of an ethical mindset (founded on self-awareness and mindfulness, empathy) to guide decision-making of future managers. Moreover, they are congruent with the idea of excellence (philosophically), which highlights the importance of balance, harmony and co-existence.

Business educators should coordinate their efforts towards crafting suitable learning environments that offer brain stimulation through, for example, emotionally positive learning experiences that use various learning modalities and methodologies. While students may have preferences regarding the way for receiving information (visual, auditory and kinaesthetic), it would be wrong to design teaching strategies based on only one sensory modality. This is because (1) visual, auditory or kinaesthetic stimuli are processed in different inter-acting parts of the human brain (Dekker, 2012); and (2) there is evidence that teaching based on specific learning styles does not lead to better educational results (Coffield *et al.*, 2004). Davachi *et al.* (2010) suggested the A(ttention) G(eneration) E(ngagement) S(pacing) model that aims to promote effective learning.

Implementing the AGES model

The first component of the AGES model is *Attention*. Learners need primarily to focus on what is being taught without distractions (Davachi *et al.*, 2010). To achieve maximum attention, the content needs to be interesting and relevant (students need to understand the value of what they are learning). One way to achieve this is the development and use of business simulations (see Exhibit 2.2). In a business simulation (use of a real business problem/operation for training), for example, students need to learn and understand how to think and assess the impact of their decisions both inside and outside of an organization, as well as how external factors, such as the environment, can be influenced by a company's policy. Connections should be clear among goals, outcomes, knowledge levels (e.g. individual, business and social), fields (e.g. management, finance, environ-ment, politics and anthropology) and reality, requiring students to use higher thinking skills to address multi-faceted business problems.

The content of each course should be presented with various learning tech-niques (e.g. lectures, simulations and case studies) in a climate of healthy competition and learners should also regularly receive feedback through observations, discussions and the formal procedures. It is through these processes that students' brains grow, and achievement is maximized (Erlauer, 2003; Jensen, 1998; Sylwester, 1995), while at the same time, boredom and intro-version are avoided (Radin, 2008; Sousa, 2001). Optimum attention will further ensure better memory encoding.

EXHIBIT 2.2 **Example of business simulation**

Here is an example based on a modification of Narayanan's Strategy Simulation (Harvard Business Publishing) (Narayanan, n.d): An investor is interested in energy companies that present excellent performance regarding sustainability. The goal of the simulation in this case is to enable students to understand the benefits of implementing a strategy for sustainability, address potential difficulties, make decision and evaluate the consequences. It could start with a presentation of sustainability theory, followed by a discussion. Then, the facilitator presents the company to be analyzed and calls for the creation of small teams. Each team (representing the company) would have to decide on a strategy, relevant objectives in every business operation, ways of strategy implementation and evaluation. In certain time intervals the teams also have to decide on those actions that would help the company achieve its strategic objectives. Each decision leads to specific performance results. At the end of the simulation the team that will achieve the highest company performance regarding sustainability will attract the investor.

Regarding attention, it has to be noted that our brain has limited attention capacity; hence, multi-tasking (random attention shifting to and execution of various tasks simultaneously) in classrooms should be avoided as it impacts students' retrieval capacity and limits learning (Davis, *et al.*, 2014; Gherri & Eimer, 2011; Stamoulis, 2011; Arnsten, 1998). Several studies unveil the negative outcomes of multi-tasking for overall academic performance, homework completion (Junco & Cotten, 2011; 2012) and learning outcomes (Fried, 2008; Rosen *et al.*, 2011; Wood *et al.*, 2012). Multi-tasking can be avoided through (a) discussions with students about the negative (learning) outcomes of dividing attention; (b) development of rules for technology use in classes; (c) use of various elements for learning during lectures such as games and videos; and (d) the development of inspiring material.

In addition, as students like choices, educators should organize their courses in such a way that students are able to choose various paths to master the new knowledge. By doing so, stress is minimized and their interest is growing along with their efforts, motivations and engagement (the emotional connection of students to the learning subject that urges them to give their best) which is critical for the activation and use of higher thinking skills (Rock & Tang, 2009). Engaged students have an activated reward brain circuitry and, as a result, they are expected to be more creative and better problem solvers, and have wider perception and increased cognitive resources. On the contrary, when threats are used to engage people, while this can be effective for executing specific projects, it impedes creativity, leads to mental fatigue and burdens health (Boudarene, Legros, & Timsit-Berthier, 2002; Tang & Posner, 2009).

It is worth pointing out the significance of attention not only to the content presented but also to oneself, to ones' thoughts and one's feelings (mindfulness). Being mindful, students learn to gain greater and deeper moment awareness, manage their behaviour, and align their thoughts with ethical beliefs (Love & Maloney, 2009). Through mindfulness irresponsible business decisions can be avoided, as a manager has the time to observe a situation from a distance and slow down potential spontaneous emotional reactions. It is imperative for a leader to have self-awareness, identify and understand his or her feelings and manage possible 'emotional contagion' to other people (through interpersonal dynamics), something which is particularly useful for promoting the enthusiasm for responsible management.

When students are offered opportunities to apply what they have learned, and when they understand, contextualize and apply knowledge in their own way, effective learning occurs (Jensen, 2005; Davis *et al.* 2014). Indeed, the second component of the AGES model, *Generation*, refers to the ability of students to understand, contextualize, retain and apply knowledge in their own presonal ways (Davachi *et al.*, 2010). By acting so, associations are created between the new and the old knowledge, and the easier it becomes to be recalled.

Business schools usually are in a rush to 'produce' graduates who have not been trained enough in reflecting and in the use of knowledge. Reflection is not to be underestimated in business education. John Dewey in his book *How We Think* (1933) supports that it is reflecting on experiences that produce learning. Reflection is considered as a systematic, disciplined and rigorous process of thinking that enables students to link new with old learnings, experiences and ideas; evaluate and combine cognitive and emotional information so as to make meaning; understand how they can apply knowledge in different contexts; and become able to evolve (Rodgers, 2002). It presupposes that individual and social excellence along with relevant attitudes (e.g. life-long learning) is valued and should be achieved in interaction with other people (Costa & Kallick, 2008; Rodgers, 2002). Metacognition, namely a type of reflection focused on one's own cognitive processes engaged in learning, can also help students manage their overall learning strategies (how they approach a learning task, learn and evaluate their learning) (Kaplan *et al.*, 2013; Desautel, 2009). Examples of reflective practices that can be used in responsible business education are shown in Exhibit 2.3.

According to Kovalik and Olsen (1998), *Emotions*, the third component of the AGES model, are the gatekeepers of learning. Whatever new information enters our brain, it is initially processed in its emotional centre and then in its cognitive centre. In addition, memories are tied to emotions (Erlauer, 2003). Emotions in learning determine the things students choose to attend to and the depth of their processing (Byrnes, 2001). Positive emotions can be created by (a) including games, music and storytelling while teaching, (b) enabling students to make connections of the things they learn with their reflections, and (c) providing them guidance and opportunities for metacognition (thinking about thinking) and self-regulation (Schenck, 2003; Given, 2002; Wolfe, 2001; Sousa, 2001; Jensen, 1998). This explains why educators should care to develop positive emotions and link teaching content with enjoyable experiences for their students. This results in

EXHIBIT 2.3 **Examples of reflective practices**

a) **Class Discussions**: Students present their arguments to address responsible management challenges, answer well-designed questions so as to reveal their inner thoughts, re-evaluate class conclusions, share their personal views and learn to listen to their peers' ideas.

b) **Role Plays**: Role plays enable students to get in others' shoes and try to understand their experiences and feelings. Students perform a certain role in searching for a solution to a problem or dealing with a challenge. Through this process they can learn more about their strengths and weaknesses, identify new facets of a problem and assess the possible social, ethical and environmental consequences of their decisions.

c) **Reflective Essays**: Students, for example, describe the value of a responsible management course for them, how capable they feel about themselves regarding responsible management and ideas for improvement.

the production of specific neurotransmitters (such as dopamine) that enable deep learning.

Positive emotions, according to Rock (2008), can also be created by increasing SCARF: People's sense of Status (grades, awards and behaviours), Certainty (regarding behaviour, expectations, performance and quality), Autonomy (choice how to learn, how to show what they have learned), Relatedness (peer to peer, group work) and Fairness (equality) (Martin-Kniep, 2010). The SCARF model (based on the principle of minimizing threat and maximizing reward), however, is not only suitable for positive emotions but also for promoting collaboration and influence on others. Status can be enhanced if a highly ranked manager has managed to persuade his company against adopting an unsafe environmental company policy. Certainty is increased when managers engage in scenario planning and can predict the consequences of various strategies. Autonomy can be enhanced if employees can decide on their training options regarding sustainability. Relatedness can be strengthened if regular meetings (even unofficial) are organized to exchange opinions on anti-corruption initiatives. Fairness is increased when there are certain rules and procedures for protecting human rights regarding employment. It is therefore obvious that the SCARF model provides a vehicle upon which the objectives of the UN Global Compact can be promoted and sought.

The arousal and contagion of positive emotions contributes to neurogrowth (Boyatzis *et al.*, 2010), produces a sense of well-being and contributes to better immune system functioning and emotional and perceptual openness. Negative emotions have been found to reduce creativity and innovation (Subramanian *et al.*, 2009), and it has been suggested that they have an even stronger effect than positive emotions (Baumeister *et al.*, 2001) leading people to cognitive, emotional and perceptual impairment (Dickerson & Kemeny, 2004).

In the case of stressful situations, (e.g. due to strict deadlines, feelings of inferiority or non-caring professors), students' cognitive abilities and reasoning appear to be negatively impacted as cortisol and adrenaline are released, impeding effective decision-making, learning and the generation of creative solutions to complicated problems (Arnsten, 2009; Goleman & Boyatzis, 2008). Stress can also be contagious due to the interpersonal dynamic of mirror neurons, spreading destructive emotions to entire groups/departments. When we observe someone's behaviours, actions and emotions, our mirror neurons reproduce those emotional states and deeds, creating a sense of shared experience. Responsible management behaviours modelled by academic staff and practitioners can have positive effects on students.

Managing emotions is especially crucial at the collective level as it may impact cooperation, conflict resolution, leadership effectiveness, etc. (Brackett & Katulak, 2006). Business educators can, for example, start a class discussion on compassion, by asking students to share personal experiences in which they felt compassionate or not. They then can describe the intensity of their emotions about compassion, what caused them to be compassionate or not, how their feelings influenced specific actions and if there were any consequences of their behaviour. After that, they can start discussing the connection of compassion to managerial and social practices (management theory and practice), and begin identifying the emotions of other people caused by these practices. By participating in class activities that promote reflection on issues such as the above and by facilitating student ownership of relevant projects that promote compassion in management thinking and practice, students can learn to identify, understand and manage their emotions, so that they are better prepared to deal with the challenges of responsible management.

Therefore, the ability of students to learn how to perceive and identify their emotions about themselves and about other people is particularly crucial. If they can succeed, they will be able to make predictions about emotions in potential situations, decide on a suitable approach to deal with a business matter or even guide behaviour. In addition, it is to be noted that empathy is a core issue in responsible management, namely the ability to get into another's shoes and see things from his or her perspective. Biologists, based on mirror neurons operation, agree that people have an innate capacity to empathize (Keen, 2007; Pfeifer & Dapretto, 2009). According to Iacoboni (2008), 20 per cent of brain cells are devoted to mirroring that is the foundation of empathy and morality.

Empathy can be cultivated through *service learning*, namely an experiential and cooperative educational methodology that offers to students the opportunity to participate in projects (in the realm of the not-for-profit world), in which they can apply theory to real-life situations, challenge themselves and reflect on their experiences (Kenworthy-U'ren & Peterson, 2005; Papamarcos,2005; Lester *et al.*, 2005). During service learning (e.g. at churches, retirement home, disabled rehabilitation centres, public schools and non-governmental organizations) students engage as learners, colleagues and service providers to cooperating organizations; learn to understand the feelings of the powerless, poor and afraid; develop moral responsibilities; and evaluate the consequences of their decisions.

Lundy (2007) believes that the enhancement of students' empathy through service learning leads also to an exponential improvement in their academic achievement. It is absolutely crucial that students understand that those who serve in a community might well be their friends or members of their own family. Similarity produces intense feelings of connectivity that translates to intensive empathetic responses (Trout, 2009).

Consequently, by understanding emotions in a business context, students are able to see how the context defines them, something which affects so many parameters of an organization's performance and growth. If, finally, students are able to manage their emotions they will be more able to overcome difficulties, choose where to focus, decide on the feelings they wish to communicate or use their emotions to facilitate cognitive operation and reasoning.

Spacing, the fourth component of the AGES model, refers to the distribution of learning to longer time periods (e.g. between learning sessions and courses) which leads to long-term learning and better performance at future work context in which knowledge must be applied (Carpenter *et al.*, 2012; Davachi *et al.*, 2010; Kornell, 2009). Rohrer & Taylor (2006) have shown, for example, that knowledge retention is facilitated and strengthened by spacing, and this happens because learning, as said earlier, is based on neural connections, a process which is time demanding (Davies *et al.*, 2014). Reflection, for example, (in the case of responsible business education) demands time since students need to be immersed both in the habituation of virtues and the necessary (technical) business knowledge corpus. Students need time so that they learn to reflect, mature and get their brains ready to combine the new with the old knowledge (Spitzer, 2002).

Conclusions

The PRME, with its principles, aims to refine the identity and role of business schools globally by focusing on sustainable growth, with students gaining a deeper understanding of the role of companies in society, the preservation of environment and the awareness of the full complexities of ethical/responsible business practice (Principle1: Purpose). Business curricula are expected to create a new generation of leaders able to combine business logic, humanism and sustainability at the individual, organizational and social levels (Principle 2: Values).

While the aforementioned principles allow for multiple approaches and models of conformance/application from business schools, a question that arises is how their aim (that is founded on specific values such as global social responsibility) can be achieved in the best possible way (Principle 3: Method). The necessity to transform business education based on the intentional development of an ethical mindset (founded on self-awareness and mindfulness, empathy) to guide decision-making of future managers can be addressed through the advances of neurosciences and cautious use of neuroscientific evidence.

Neurosciences can offer knowledge and inspiration on how to improve the learning journey by providing us with insights regarding the relative strength of various brain areas, their interconnectedness (that determines human behaviour) and the development of innovative education approaches. Business educators need to create stress-free and immersive learning environments; facilitate a sense of community among students and scholars; and help students understand and manage their emotions, and set and achieve their goals. At the same time, business educators must act as the people they wish to create, modelling values and responsible management behaviours.

References

Alahiotis, S. (2011). '*Is Behavior Inherited? (in Greek)*'. http://tovima.gr/science/article/?aid= 406746, (accessed 24 January 2016).

Anninos, L. N. (2007), 'The Archetype of Excellence in Universities and TQM', *Journal of Management History*, 13.4:307–21.

Anninos, L. N. (2014) 'From Ignorance, Mental Poverty and Technocratic Knowledge to a New Teleological and Deontological Perspective of Business Education'. In M. Gudić, A. Rosenbloom and C. Parkes (eds.), *Socially Responsive Organizations and the Challenge of Poverty*, Sheffield, UK: Greenleaf Publishing:264–73.

Anninos, L. N. and Chytiris, L. (2012) 'The Sustainable Management Vision for Excellence: Implications for Business Education', *International Journal of Quality and Service Sciences* 4.1:61–75.

Arnsten, A. (1998) 'The Biology of Being Frazzled', *Science, 280*:1711–12.

Armsten, A. (2009) 'Stress Signaling Pathways That Impair Prefrontal Cortex Structure and Function', *Nature Review Neuroscience, 10.6*:410–22.

Baumeister, R., Bratslavsky, E., Finkehauer, C. and Vohs, K. (2001) 'Bad is Stronger Than Good', *Review of General Psychology, 5.4*:323–70.

Blakemore, S. and Frith, U. (2005) 'The Learning Brain: Lessons for Education: A Precis', *Developmental Science, 8.6*:459–71.

Boudarene, M., Legros, J. and Timsit-Berthier, M. (2002) 'Study of the Stress Response: Role of Anxiety, Cortisol and DHEAs', *Encephale, 2*:139–46.

Boyatzis, R., E., Cesaro, R., Passarelli, A. and Khawaja, M. (2010) 'Coaching with Compassion: An fMRI Study of Coaching to the Positive or Negative Emotional Attractor', Presented at the Annual Meeting of the Academy of Management, Montreal, Canada.

Brackett, M. and Katulak, N. (2006) 'Emotional Intelligence in the Classroom: Skill-Based Training for Teachers and Students', in J. Ciarrochi, and J. Mayer (eds.), *Improving Emotional Intelligence: A Practioner's Guide*, New York: Psychology Press/Taylor & Francis:1–27.

Bruer, J. (1997)'Education and the Brain: A Bridge Too Far', *Educational Researcher, 26.8*:4–16.

Byrnes, J. (2001) *Minds, Brains and Learning*, New York: The Guilford Press.

Carew, T. and Magsamen, S. (2010) 'Neuroscience and Education: An Ideal Partnership for Producing Evidence Based Solutions to Guide 21st Century Learning' *Neuron*, 67:685–8.

Carpenter, S., Cepeda, N., Rohrer, O., Kang, S. and Pashler, H. (2012) 'Using Spacing to Enhance Diverse Forms of Learning: Review of Recent Research and Implications for Instruction', *Educational Psychology Review, 24*.3:369–78.

Cattaneo, L. and Rizzolatti, G. (2009) 'The Mirror Neuron System', *Neurobiological Review, 66*.5:557–60.

CEEMAN. (2016). *About Us*. Retrieved from CEEMAN-International Association for Management Development in Dynamic Societies: http://ceeman.org/ (accessed: 24 March 2016).

Coffield, F., Moseley, D., Hall, E. and Ecclestone, K. (2004) *Learning Styles and Pedagogy in Post 16 Learning: A Systematic and Critical Review*, London: Learning and Skills Research Center.

Costa, A.L. and Kallick, B. (2008) *Learning and Leading with Habits of Mind: 16 Essential Characteristics for Success*, Alexandria, VA: Association for Supervision and Curriculum Development.

Davachi, L., Kiefer, T., Rock, D. and Rock, L. (2010) 'Learning that Lasts Through AGES', *Neuroleadership Journal, 3*:53–63.

Davis, J., Balda, M., Rock, D., McGinniss, P. and Davachi, L. (2014) 'The Science of Making Learning Stick: An Update to the AGES Model', *Neuroleadership Journal, 5*:1–15.

Daw, N. and Shohamy, D. (2008) 'The Cognitive Neuroscience of Motivation and Learning', *Social Cognition, 26*.5:593–620.

Dekker, S. (2012) 'Neuromyths in Education: Prevalence and Predictors of Misconception Among Teachers', Frontiers in Psychology, 429 http://ncbi.nlm.nih.gov/pmc/articles/ PMC3475349/ (accessed 12 April 2016).

Desautel, D. (2009) 'Becoming a Thinking Thinker: Metacognition, Self Reflection and Classroom Practice', *Teachers College Record, 111*.8:1997–2020

Dewey, J. (1933) *How We Think*, Buffalo, NY: Prometheus Books (First published in 1910).

Dewey, P. and Duff, S., (2009) 'Reason Before Passion: Faculty Views on Internationalization of Higher Education', *Higher Education, 58*.4:491–504.

Dickerson, S. and Kemeny, M. (2004) 'Acute Stressors and Cortisol Responses: A Theoretical Integration and Synthesis of Laboratory Research', *Psychological Bulletin, 130*.3:355–91.

Erlauer, L. (2003) *The Brain Compatible Classroom*, Alexandria, VA: Association for Supervision and Curriculum Development.

Fischer, K. (2009) 'Building a Scientific Groundwork for Learning and Teaching', *Mind, Brain, and Education, 3*.1:3–16.

Fischer, K., Daniel, D., Immordino-Yang, M., Stern, E., Battro, A. and Koizumi, H. (2007) 'Why Mind, Brain, and Education? Why Now?', *Mind, Brain, and Education, 1*.1:1–2.

Fried, C. (2008) 'In-Class Laptop Use and Its Effects on Student Learning', *Computers & Education, 50*.3:906–14.

Geake, J. (2008) 'Neuromythologies in Education', *Educational Research, 50*.2:123–33.

Ghadiri, A., Habermacher, A. and Peters, T. (2012) *Neuroleadership: A Journey Through the Brain for Business Leaders*, Heidelberg, Germany: Springer.

Gherri, E. and Eimer, M. (2011) 'Active Listening Impairs Visual Perception and Selectivity: An ERP Study of Auditory Dual Task Costs on Visual Attention', *Journal of Cognitive Neuroscience, 23*.4:832–44.

Giacalone, R. A. (2004).' A Transcended Business Education for the 21st Century', *Academy of Management Learning and Education, 3*.4:415–20.

Given, B. (2002) *Teaching to the Brain's Natural Learning Systems*, Alexandia, VA: Association for Supervision and Curriculum Development.

Goleman, D. and Boyatzis, R. (2008) 'Social Intelligence and the Biology of Leadership', *Harvard Business Review, 86*.9:74–81.

Goswami, U. (2006) 'Neuroscience and Education: From Research to Practice?', *Nature Reviews Neuroscience, 7*:2–7.

Herculano-Houzel, S. (2009) 'The Human Brain in Numbers: A Linearly Scaled Up Primary Brain', *Frontiers in Human Neuroscience, 3*:1–11.

Hook, C. and Farah, M. (2013) 'Neuroscience for Educators: What are They Seeking and What They are Finding?', *Neuroethics, 6.2*:331–41.

Iacoboni, M. (2008) Mirroring People: The New Science of How We Connect With Others , New York: Farrar, Straus and Giroux.

Jensen, E. (1998) *Teaching with the Brain in Mind*, Alexandria, VA: Association for Supervision and Curriculum Development.

Jensen, E. (2005) *Teaching with the Brain in Mind*, Alexandria, VA: Association for Supervision and Curriculum Development.

Junco, R. and Cotten, S. R. (2011) 'Perceived Academic Effects of Instant Messaging Use', *Computers and Education, 56.2*:370–8.

Junco, R. and Cotten, S. R. (2012) 'No A 4 U: The Relationship Between Multitasking and Academic Performance', *Computers and Education, 59.2*:505–14.

Kaplan, M., Silver, M., LaVaque-Manty, D. and Meizlish, D. (2013) *Using Reflection and Metacognition to Improve Student Learning: Across the Disciplines, Across the Academy*, Sterling, VA: Stylus Publishing.

Keen, S. (2007) *Empathy and the Novel*, New York: Oxford University Press.

Kenworthy-U'Ren A.L. and Peterson, T. (2005) 'Service Learning and Management Education: Introducing the WE CARE Approach', *Academy of Management Learning and Education, 4.3*:272–7.

Kolb, B., Gibb, R. and Robinson, T. (2003) 'Brain Plasticity and Behavior', *Current Directions in Psychological Science, 12.1*:1–5.

Kornell, N. (2009) 'Optimizing Learning Using Flashcards: Spacing is more Effective than Cramming. *Applied Cognitive Psychology, 23.9*:1297–17.

Kovalik, S. and Olsen, K. (1998) 'How Emotions Run Us, Our Students, and Our Classrooms', *NASSP Bulletin, 82.598*:29–37.

Lee, N., Butler, M. and Senior, C. (2010) 'The Brain in Business: Neuromarketing and Organizational Cognitive Neuroscience', *Der Markt: Journal für Marketing, 49*:129–31.

Lester, S. W., Tomkovich, C., Wells, T., Flunker, L. and Kickul, J. (2005) 'Does Service Learning Add Value? Examining the Perspectives of Multiple Stakeholders', *Academy of Management Learning & Education, 4.3*:278–94.

Love, A. and Maloney, J. (2009) 'Mindfulness as Capacity: At the Threshold of Leadership's Next Wave?', *Neuroleadership Journal, 9*:1–7.

Lundy, B. (2007) 'Service Learning in Life Span Developmental Psychology: Higher Exam Scores and Increased Empathy', *Teaching of Psychology 34.1*:23–7.

Martin-Kniep, G. (2010) 'Neuroscience of Engagement and SCARF: Why they Matter to Schools', *Neuroleadership Journal, 3*:87–96.

Maxwell, N. (2014) *How Universities can Help Creating a Wiser World*, Exeter, UK: Imprint Academic.

Mobbs, D. and MacFarland, W. (2010) 'The Neuroscience of Motivation', *Neuroleadership Journal, 3*:1–10.

Morse, G. (2006) 'Decisions and Desire', *Harvard Business Review, 84*:44–51.

Narayanan, V. G. (n.d) *Strategy Simulation: The Balanced Scorecard.* Harvard Business Publishing https://cb.hbsp.harvard.edu/resources/marketing/docs/M00004_HE_Balance_Scorecard.pdf (accessed 28 April 2016)

Organization for Economic Cooperation and Development. (2007) *Understanding the Brain: The Birth of a Learning Science* (Paris).

Papamarcos, S. D. (2005) 'Giving Traction to Management Theory: Today's Service Learning', *Academy of Management Learning and Education*, 4.3:325–35

Pfeifer, J. and Dapretto, M. (2009) 'Mirror, Mirror in My Mind: Empathy, Interpersonal Competence and the Mirror Neuron System', in J. Decety and W. Ickes (eds.), *The Social Neuroscience of Empathy*, Cambridge, MA: MIT Press:182–98.

PRME. (2016a) *The Six Principles*. Retrieved from PRME-Principles for Responsible Business Education: http://unprme.org/about-prme/the-six-principles.php (accessed: 12 March 2016).

PRME. (2016b) *PRME-Principles for Responsible Business Education*. Retrieved from PRME-Working Groups & Chapters: http://unprme.org/working-groups/display-working-group.php?wgid=824 (accessed 20 March 2016).

Radin, J. (2008) 'Creating Enriched Learning Environments: Lessons from Brain Research'. http://elementalethics.com/files/Radin_2.pdf, (accessed: 12 April 2016).

Reimer, B. (2004) 'New Brain Research on Emotion and Feelings: Dramatic Implications for Music Education', *Arts Education Policy Review*, 106.2:21–7.

Ringleb, A. and Rock, D. (2008) 'The Emerging Field of Neuroleadership', *Neuroleadership Journal*, 8:1–17.

Ringleb, H., Rock, D. and Ancona, C. (2013)'Neuroleadership in 2011 and 2012', *Neuroleadership Journal*, 4:1–35.

Rock, D. (2008) 'SCARF: A Brain Based Model for Collaborating with and Influencing Others. *Neuroleadership Journal*, 1.1:1–9.

Rock, D. (2009) 'Managing With the Brain in Mind', *Business and Strategy*, 56: 1–10.

Rock, D. and Schwartz, J. (2007) *Why Neurosciences Matters to Executives*. Retrieved from Strategy + Business: http://strategy-business.com/article/li00021?gko=60b7d (accessed: 2 October 2015).

Rock, D. and Tang, Y. (2009) 'Neuroscience of Engagement', *Neuroleadership Journal*, 2:1–8.

Rodgers, C. (2002) 'Defining Reflection: Another Look at John Dewey and Reflective Thinking', *Teachers College Record*, 104.4:842–66.

Rohrer, D. and Taylor, K. (2006). 'The Effects of Overlearning and Distributed Practice on the Retention of Mathematics Knowledge', *Applied Cognitive Psychology*, 20:1209–24

Rosen, L. D., Lim, A. F., Carrier, L. M. and Cheever, N. A. (2011) 'An Empirical Examination of the Educational Impact of Text Message-Induced Task Switching in the Classroom: Educational Implications and Strategies to Enhance Learning', *Psicologia Educativa*, 17.2:163–77.

Schenck, J. (2003) *Learning, Teaching and the Brain*, Thermopolis, WY: Knowa.

Semendeferi, K. and Damasio, H. (2000) 'The Brain and Its Main Anatomical Subdivisions in Living Humanoids Using Magnetic Resonance Imaging', *Journal of Human Evolution*, 38.2:317–32.

Siegel, D. and Pearce, M. D. (2009) 'Mindsight at Work: An Inspirational Neurobiology Lens on Leadership', *Neuroleadership Journal*, 2:1–12.

Sousa, D. (2001) *How the Brain Learns*, Thousand Oaks, CA: Corwin Press.

Spitzer, M. (2002) *Lernen: Gehirnforschung und Schule des Lebens*, Berlin: Spektrum Akademischer Verlag).

Sprenger, M. (1999) *Learning and Memory: The Brain in Action*, Alexandria, VA: Association for Supervision and Curriculum Development.

Stamoulis, K. (2011) 'Multitasking in the Classroom'. http://psychologytoday.com/blog/the-new-teen-age/201102/multitasking-in-the-classroom (accessed 12 April 2016).

Subramanian, K., Kounios, J., Parrish, T. and Jung-Beeman, M. (2009) 'Positive Mood and Anxiety Modulate Anterior Cingulate Activity and Cognitive Preparation for Insight', *Journal of Cognitive Neuroscience*, 21:415–32.

Sylvan, L. and Christodoulou, J. (2010) 'Understanding the Role of Neuroscience in Brain Based Products: A Guide for Educators and Consumers', *Mind, Brain and Education*, 4.1:1–7.

Sylwester, R. (1995) *A Celebration of Neurons: An Educator`s Guide to the Human Brain*, Alexandria, VA: Association for Supervision and Curriculum Development.

Tang, Y. and Posner, N. (2009) 'Attention Training and Attention State Training. *Trends in Cognitive Sciences*, 13:222–7.

Teffer, K. and Semendeferi, K. (2012) 'Human Prefrontal Cortex: Evolution, Development and Pathology', *Progress in Brain Research*, 195.1:191–218.

The Royal Society. (2011) *Brain Wave vol. 2- Neuroscience: Implications for Education and Lifelong Learning* (London: Science Policy Center).

Trout, J. D. (2009) *The Empathy Gap: Building Bridges to the Good Life and the Good Society*, New York: Viking Press.

Varma, S., Mc Candliss, B. and Schwartz, D. (2008) 'Scientific and Pragmatic Challenges for Bridging Education and Neurosciences', *Educational Researcher*, 37.3:140–52.

Waldman, D., Balthazard, P. and Peterson, S. (2011) 'Leadership and Neuroscience: Can We Revolutionize the Way that Inspirational Leaders are Identified and Developed?', *Academy of Management Perspectives*, 25.1:60–74.

Whiting, J., Jones, E., Rock, D. and Bendit, X. (2012) 'Lead Change with the Brain in Mind', *Neuroleadership Journal*, 4:1–13.

Wolfe, P. (2001) *Brain Matters*, Alexandria, VA: Association for Supervision and Curriculum Development.

Wood, E., Zivcakova, L., Gentile, P., Archer, K., De Pasquale, D. and Nosko, A. (2012) 'Examining the Impact of Off-Task Multi-Tasking with Technology on Real-Time Classroom Learning', *Computers and Education*, 58.1:365–74.

Loukas N. Anninos, received his PhD in Business Administration from the University of Piraeus. His research portfolio includes publications in peer-reviewed journals, books and presentations in numerous national and international conferences. He teaches Management, Organizational Behaviour and Human Resources Management (undergraduate and postgraduate level) at the University of Piraeus in Greece and serves as a reviewer in journals and conferences.

lnanninos@gmail.com

3

Responsible education in a complex context of sustainable development

Co-creating a pedagogic framework for participatory reflection and action

Svetlana Cicmil
University of the West of England, UK

Richard Ecclestone
University of the West of England, UK

Katie Collins
Wolfson College, Oxford Univerity, UK

Abstract

The central premise of this chapter is to offer a conceptual framework for making sense of the sustainability agenda in an educational environment from multiple perspectives. The focus is on the complex interface between the global ecological crisis and economic growth. Ethical considerations are argued to be necessary in examining the contradictions and risks associated with polarized definitions of problems and with globally entertained solutions. The proposed framework encourages the questioning of epistemic assumptions on the basis of which certain knowledge and truth claims tend to dominate contemporary debate. Its pragmatic use rests on an experiment with a participatory pedagogic approach that respects and acknowledges students' and lecturers' differences in values, and cultural and disciplinary backgrounds. In the spirit of the UN PRME, it is assumed that through their collective experience of participative pedagogy and awareness of the '4Es' – Ethics, Economy, Ecology and Epistemology – facilitated by the framework, the participants can co-create a responsible community of learners and knowers, ready to influence the way society is developing.

Positioning: Sustainability and sustainable development as contested issues

Back in 1992, the World Bank recognised that, 'the achievement of sustained and equitable development remains the greatest challenge facing the human race' (see Gladwin *et al.*, 1995: 900). In 1995, it was argued that transforming 'management theory and practice so that they positively contribute to sustainable development is, in our view, the greatest challenge facing the Academy of Management.' (*ibid.*). Twenty years later, these statements hold true. The United Nations' (UN) seventeen Sustainable Development Goals (SDGs) and Global Compact (GC) reflect the intention to implement universal sustainability principles and encourage an orientation towards 'a principled approach to doing business' (UN Global Compact, 2016).

One responsibility of academic institutions is 'to develop a new generation of business leaders capable of managing the complex challenges faced by business and society in the 21st century' (UN PRME, 2016). But how best to 'teach' sustainable development when the concept is complex, elusive and contested (Cicmil *et al.*, 2015)? It is a point of principle to open to debate the relationship between *development*, defined as the economic growth, and the *sustainability crisis*, characterized by scarcity of non-renewable resources, climate injustice and environmental harm. Sustainable development should be pursued as an ideal, for which the benchmarks are interdependence, connectedness, equity, security and prudence (Gladwin *et al.*, 1995). The aim of the chapter is to contribute to the praxis of responsible management education by proposing a conceptual framework developed to match the complexity of a global sustainability agenda.

Underlying the deliberations exposed in this chapter is a search for meaning in the context of the tension between growth-based development and sustainability, while also recognising that the definitions of sustainability and sustainable development are themselves contested, controversial, elusive and subject to multiple interpretations (Gladwin *et al.*, 1995; Banerjee, 2003; Porritt, 2007; Jackson, 2009; Hutchings, 2010; Curry, 2011; Dow Jones Sustainability Indices, 2016). Sustainability has been described as 'one of the least meaningful and most overused words in the English language' (Owen, 2011:246). Understood as 'functional integrity' of any system, be it social, ecological or economic (Thompson, 2007), it has become a contested term, meaning anything and everything in contemporary ordinary usage, made more ambiguous by models such as the triple bottom line (see also Marshall, 2011; Blowfield, 2013). The focus (linguistic, political and educational) on 'economic' sustainability tends to hijack other interpretations (Marshall, 2011). If economic sustainability remains the priority, what distinguishes sustainability education from the topics that have always been taught: competitiveness, financial performance and profitability, and a narrowly defined notion of development from a dominant standpoint of industrial capitalist growth?

How could someone, as a 'knower' (be it a business leader, lecturer or student), reconcile this tension in his/her mind and then be in a position to make an effective contribution to progress towards a sustainable society? The backdrop is a human society that is already exceeding the environmental carrying capacity of a planet with a finely balanced eco-system and finite resources (Gladwin *et al.*, 1995; Cook, 2004; Rockström *et al.*, 2009; Steffan *et al.*, 2015). The dominant global socio-economic order and the increasing inequalities between citizens, in both developed and developing nations, amplify the tensions between growth and sustainability (Banerjee, 2003; Curry, 2011; Klein, 2014). This chapter takes, as its guide, Thompson's (2007) claim that it is ethically important to recognise and respect the fact that 'there are certain limits in renewal of everything' (p. 381), including society itself, and that the current sustainability crisis evolves around the overuse of resources, endangered biodiversity and uncontrolled greenhouse gas emissions (Rockström *et al.*, 2009). The challenge is that planet Earth has a limited carrying capacity, and planetary boundaries in those categories are already overstepped, representing an existential threat to both humanity and to the other species inhabiting the planet.

Finding a resolution is perhaps the most important issue of our time, and yet highly contested scientifically, politically and ethically (Curry, 2011). Solutions tend to polarise (Blowfield, 2013), with some arguing that free markets, use of resources and technology will deliver prosperity, after which problems such as climate change can be tackled (Nordhaus, 2007; Lomborg, 2010); or that creative design, eco-efficiency and increased resource productivity will deliver prosperity without a negative impact on the environment (Hawken *et al.*, 1999; Braungart and McDonough, 2009; McDonough and Braungart, 2013). Others see growth-based prosperity as the enemy, advocating mobilisation of grassroots movements and a reversal of the privatisation of the public sphere (Klein, 2014). A middle ground incorporates a reformed capitalist model that recognises the value of natural, social and human capital (Porritt, 2007). 'Sustaincentrism', introduced by Gladwin *et al.*, (1995), focuses on the greater balance within the elements of the economy–ecology–ethics triad, and 'offers a vision of development which is both people-centered (concentrating on improvement in the human condition) and conservation-based (maintaining the variety and integrity of nonhuman nature)' (p. 894). Therefore, the challenge for educators, particularly organisation and management scholars, is to re-examine their approach to organisational existence, and to illuminate often neglected aspects like the organic, biotic and intersubjective moral dimensions. The PRME principles, particularly 1 (Purpose), 3 (Method) and 4 (Research), encourage this kind of holistic and inclusive thinking in management education.

The '4Es' Framework – A conceptual proposition

What would it mean to reconceive the scholarly domain of organisation and management studies as 'one of organisation-in-full community, both social and ecological. . . as if sustainability matters' (Gladwin *et al.*, 1995)? What kind of pedagogic framework could accommodate the complexities of the sustainability vision and the need to reconceive the onto-epistemological foundations of management education? Moreover, how could it be used as a dialogical tool to encourage and facilitate a dialogue between varied, possibly opposing, but equally valid voices and points of view (in line with PRME Principle 6 – Dialogue). These deliberations inspired the Chapter's authors to, collaboratively with their students, develop the '4Es' framework (Figure 3.1) as a construct to facilitate a critical evaluation of the global sustainability agenda viewed through the four lenses of Epistemology, Ecology, Ethics and Economy. Critically examining the disparate definitions of the crisis and proposed solutions against all four elements surfaces the risks surrounding them and allows for deeper and more transparent consideration of, e.g., what is risky? Who is at risk? What else is at risk?

FIGURE 3.1 **The '4Es' Framework**

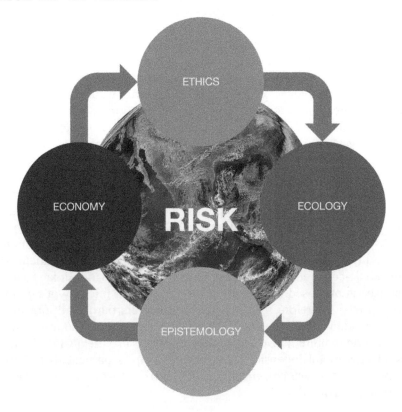

Ultimately, it is about accountability and responsibility in the appraisal of problems and suggested solutions to the sustainability crisis, in a global context where diverse communities are exposed to the same existential vulnerabilities (resource and food shortages, pollution and climate change, security and safety).

The '4Es' framework foregrounds risk and ethics as always implicated in framing sustainability/sustainable development problems and their solutions at a global level and encourages the dialogue with a polyphony of voices: from purely scientific and analytical to those that embrace complexity. Risk is always pragmatically connected with the choices made and moral responsibility taken for resulting actions in an imperfect, indeterminate, globalised world of inter-connected and interdependent strangers (Hutchings, 2010), because in such a world

- unpredictability is always present;

- cause–effect relationships between hazard and impact are often un-known in advance, which limits the predictive power of risk assessment models;

- it is very easy to misunderstand what is at stake in ethical conflicts because no one can control all of the consequences of his/her actions, however well intended.

As the next section explains, the main quality of this framework, as a dialogical tool, is in facilitating a space for contemplation and learning in which partici-pants are free to express their humanity in healthy and mutually respectful relationships with others, and to question dominant values, discourses and agendas in relation to any of the elements in the framework, as follows:

Ethics – concerning the questions of values (how should we live our lives?) and problems which have emerged out of the global interconnection and interdependence of the world's population in the contemporary social order (e.g. poverty, ecological harm, rights of women and children);

Ecology – concerning biodiversity, natural resources, and healthy envi-ronment (e.g. clean air, water and soil) as elements of the ultimate life-supporting system for most species on earth; understanding the rela-tionship between eco-sustainability and social-cultural sustainability;

Economy – concerning the contemporary drive towards increased capitalist production and economic growth; understanding the relationship between corporate sustainability and social responsibility;

Epistemology – concerning the epistemic assumptions on the basis of which certain knowledge and truth claims tend to dominate contem-porary debates about the sustainability crisis and define the level of credibility of a knower/speaker; understanding the link between epis-temic variety, ethics and aesthetics.

The '4Es' Framework as a dialogic tool: Getting into the mood for critical participatory pedagogy

'Ultimately, nature is what enables us to do anything, including assess truth [. . .] For the same reason [. . .] to 'know', or 'assess' or 'consider' is not possible without participating in a relationship with what is being known, assessed or considered.' (Curry, 2011:271)

The '4Es' framework emerged over time in the process of the authors' experimenting with a critical pedagogic approach grounded in participatory praxis (Freire, 1970; Fals Borda, 2001; Reason and Bradbury, 2008; Evans, 2010; Collins, 2016) to deliver courses related to sustainable development. In practice, this means involving students as equal partners, as far as possible, in the co-creation of both knowledge during the module and a learning strategy at large (Cicmil *et al.*, 2015) and encouraging them to be critical enquirers who learn through action and reflection, 'creating' curriculum in the process. The principles of participation are transparent at the outset and open to students' comments in a cyclical, hermeneutic enquiry. Students, visiting practitioners and lecturers are encouraged to reflect together on their own deeply held assumptions about human beings and human reason and how they shape and influence their views about particular ethical questions arising from the discussions.

At its core, participation in knowledge creation (both pedagogy and research) is about transformation, about making change for the better. Freire (1970) understood that before people could engage in transformative action they had to become aware of their current circumstances. This awareness could not be achieved in a traditional paternalistic, or 'banking' mode of education (which, he argued, was designed to perpetuate the status quo, treating the people as objects and sustaining their oppression by the powerful elite), but through a participative process with fellow citizens within their community. The raising of consciousness enables the student to engage his/her critical faculties, reflect on situations, question the existing order and conceive the possibility of a better world. This, in turn, could lead to action for social change and more equitable development. Shaull (1970), in his introduction to Freire's *Pedagogy of the Oppressed*, argues that parallels exist between the objectification of the peasants in 1950s' Brazil and the education of students in the technological society of the Western world to conform to the logic of the current system. Therefore, a participatory pedagogy after Freire can be seen to be relevant in today's context of education for sustainable development, where the ability to critically question the dominant socio-economic order is a necessary prerequisite for transformative change. Collins (2016) acknowledges the key influence of Freire and points to this radical heritage as reminding us of what participatory work is supposed to be, i.e. looking critically at the dynamics of power, enabling participants to express themselves and create their own knowledge, all in the context of creating social change.

In the authors' experience, university students on sustainability-related modules epitomise the diversity of the global society (backgrounds, ages and nationalities). Equally diverse are their expectations, anxieties and values. Some are searching for a 'recipe' or best practice for implementing organisational sustainability; others harbour deep concern for the health of the planet, twinned with a sense of powerlessness amid the spectrum of views about business and society, as discussed in the previous sections. The classes typically contain a mixture of nationalities and languages, and students are regularly asked to find an adequate word, in their own language, for 'sustainability'. This quote captures one among the responses:

> In our international class, we have been asked to translate the term sustainability in our own native languages. The class is quiet as we ponder on this – the silence is overwhelming. Then, someone translates the word to mean 'never give up' in his language. . .then, someone says 'longevity, long-term orientation', nurturing and caring with patience, from below' . . . I felt a mix of emotions of where my true identity lay. I found myself getting very angry about the global situation.

This student quote illustrates how limiting the imaginative powers of the English word 'sustainability' can be, and also reveals the cultural, psychosocial and ethical ambiguities that can be silenced by a Western-centric, English-language-based education for sustainability. Facilitated by the '4Es', collective deliberations upon anxieties and concerns give primacy to the importance of culture, imagination, narrative and spirituality, and are in the spirit of PRME Principle 2 (Values) and Principle 6 (Dialogue). Regarding language that is used to discuss 'critical issues related to global social responsibility and sustainability' (PRME, 2016), there is a tendency for the vocabulary of economics to dominate, crowding out other valid perspectives, such as the innate value of the non-human natural world. A student stated: 'My concern is that the language of marketing and pricing can be used to support a particular ideology or dogma, to the detriment of the value of nature.' Take, for example, SDG 15, Life on Land, 'Protect, restore and promote sustainable use of terrestrial ecosystems, sustainably manage forests, combat desertification, and halt and reverse land degradation and halt biodiversity loss' (UN, 2015). While the goal and the related targets (UN Sustainable Development Knowledge Platform, 2016) of protecting and restoring balanced ecosystems is laudable, on further critical examination the promotion of sustainable *use* in the statement implies that ecosystems remain a resource for humans to exploit, legitimising interpretations that would privilege the continuation of business as usual (exploitation of natural resources). No target (again, a term with economic connotations) embodies the intrinsic value of nature. There is no emphasis on the web of life, the dependence of both human and non-human species on a functioning ecosystem, and all the scarce natural resources, essential for their survival and sustainability (Curry, 2011; Thiele, 2013).

The language concern flows into an epistemic one. If the language of today's dominant socio-economic order suppresses the languages of nature and different cultures, then knowledge created through the prism of the globalised Western-centric economic model potentially suppresses knowledge derived from other diverse sources, allowing them to languish in the background at a time when alternative epistemologies could potentially offer healthier solutions to modern-day global problems. In the process of co-creating the '4Es' framework, one student put it, 'What is knowledge? With the media giving voice to everything, it leads to too much superficiality and insufficient substance.' Another student observed, 'We are losing our cultural identity and adopting someone else's. Just look at the [global] chain culture.' This student was remarking on the homo-genising effects of global brands and western values and the consequent displacement of local identity and indigenous cultures. The '4Es' framework and participatory approach adopted in class not only encourage a critical evaluation of such contradictions in the use of language but also highlight the challenges and contradictions posed by the UN Global Compact's Ten Principles and seventeen SDGs at the intersection between different perspectives, while remaining transparent and relevant, that is, true to the complex realities of the unpredictable and diverse life we share on the 'globalised' Earth.

The perceived reality of some current business behaviours is another source of debate, one that illuminates the incompatibility of vision, values and inter-ests between the capitalist imperative of unlimited growth and ecological sustainability, including environmental justice. The catastrophic forest fires that occurred in Indonesia in autumn 2015 provide a topical example. Rainforest clearance for conversion to palm oil, pulp and paper plantations 'reduced millions of hectares of vibrant, living tropical rainforest and peatland to smoking ash – and with it, some of the last habitat of Indonesian orangutans' (Rahmawati, 2016). Two of the largest multinational corporations, PepsiCo and Johnson & Johnson, both participants in the UN Global Compact, are allegedly making insufficient headway in ensuring that no deforestation is involved in their palm oil supply chains (Rahmawati, 2016). This calls into question their commitment to Principles 7 and 8: 'businesses should support a precautionary approach to environmental challenges' and, 'undertake initiatives to promote greater environmental responsibility' (United Nations Global Compact, 2016). In this case, business entities with the greatest influence appear to be under-performing on their public commitments. This example highlights the criticality of SDG 8, the promotion of sustainable and inclusive economic growth, as it implies a radical change in the criteria for evaluating business success.

Practical implications and concluding remarks

The elusiveness and contradictions surrounding the ideal of sustainable develop-ment can give rise to both emotional and intellectual challenges for students.

Some indicated that they 'felt a tension because trade-offs appear to be necessary when striving for sustainability'; another said, 'I felt overwhelmed. The subject matter caused me a lot of emotional strain.' Facilitated by a participatory 'reflective process that brings to consciousness knowledge one may have acted on but not fully realized or elaborated, making possible future, purposeful action' (Lyons, 2002: 96), the '4Es' framework encourages students to develop a personal stance based on their learning and then to be 'coherently persuasive' (Gladwin *et al.*, 1995:882) in communicating it. Used as a dialogical tool, the '4Es' enable the following:

- inclusion and debate of multiple 'truths', epistemologies and ways of knowing (PRME Principle 4 – Research) towards a spirit of dialogue and action that creates new understandings of 'responsibility' and new possibilities for development (PRME Principle 6 – Dialogue);

- engagement of educators, practitioners from profit and non-profit sectors, and students from a variety of disciplinary backgrounds, with a potential to strengthen 'partnering' relationships among colleagues across the university and beyond (PRME Principle 5 – Partnership);

- assuagment of anxiety (at both individual and group level) in a multi-cultural, international learning environment by prioritising and developing sensitivity to difference and giving time for thinking and reflection; and

- development of a sense of fairness, emancipation and practical wisdom (theory–practice relationship).

As an implementation guide, Table 3.1 summarizes the key pedagogic practices that have worked for the chapter authors.

The '4Es' conceptual framework can also help managers comprehensively and pragmatically address risks and responsibilities concerning these complex and changing issues in policy and practice, acting in an economically sound, environmentally friendly and socially responsible way. One of the authors was a course participant and part of the participatory 4E-informed pedagogic experiment, and also a sustainability practitioner in a local community. This was his reflective account at the time, which illustrates the practical impact of this experience:

> I came to the course overwhelmed with anxiety about whether there really is a way of dealing with the issues around sustainability in practice; I felt powerless to influence events towards a less ecologically destructive path. Also a lack of confidence in countering the dominant economic arguments that seemed to be routinely presented by the majority of people I was talking to. I was not necessarily looking for a blueprint or recipe for success, but a safe space for contemplation of the issues that I felt had moral and ethical dimensions. I found the '4Es' framework a valuable tool to understand this conflict of ideas and perspectives and it gave me the confidence

to approach the subject with a considered stance. Concurrently I had responsibility for a community project that I had initiated. Over the life of this project I discovered that my learning and my actions became inseparable. The 4E-based dialogical tool provided me with the confidence to lobby my Member of Parliament, to approach bodies for grant funding, negotiate with the Local Authority and promote the project to the wider community, secure in the knowledge that I had considered issues from all four perspectives and weighed up risks and trade-offs appropriately. I found that by marrying the 4Es, as a way of framing my thinking about the issues associated with the project, with an understanding about my own role as an initiator, community organiser and researcher, I was able both to guide the project to a successful conclusion and derive meaningful learning both for myself and the community concerned. Later, I returned to the classroom as a contributor to the module in the spirit of this participatory approach. I noticed that this approach can be problematic and confusing for those participants in the learning process who expect ready-made academic answers to sustainability related problems. For example, those looking for tools and techniques for concrete action would find a dialogue-based examination of the controversies within the sustainability debate unsettling. This for me raises a wider issue of the extent to which the contemporary academic curriculum encourages sufficient ethical scrutiny of this and other complex global phenomena. Perhaps, the '4Es' framework could have a more general application within other areas of the curriculum?

TABLE 3.1 **Pedagogic practices in the spirit of the '4Es' Framework**

Element	Concrete practical examples and tools
Teaching team	Multidisciplinary team of active researchers; syllabus is research-informed exposing a number of different, sometimes irreconcilable, views on: sustainable development (including legal, anthropological, sociological, political-economy), sustainability itself (e.g. strong/weak), corporate social responsibility (e.g. normative/critical), and organisational leadership (e.g. complexity/spirituality); the critical examination of the suggested solutions (techno-scientific, market-based, socio-political) and contemplation and theorizing (including ethics, phenomenology, hermeneutics).
Out-of-classroom activities	In addition to conventional classroom activities, outings and walks, site visits and conversations with employees and management: (social enterprises, businesses, national parks) exercises encouraging reflexivity and paying attention to language; visual means (drawings, art, poetry and film) have been included..
Practitioner guest from speakers	Sustainability champions and decision makers with various levels of seniority and various sectors of industry; consultants and activists.
Modes of student participation	Curriculum co-creation (direct teaching inputs by participating students with relevant practical experience; suggestions for syllabus change); inter-cohort collaboration (different stages of study including alumni); cross-disciplinary learning (e.g. MBA and MSc in Sustainable Development studying together), final year research dissertations involving pedagogic research.

Looking ahead

The chapter provides reflections on a participatory pedagogic practice (Table 3.1), that was created and simultaneously informed by the '4Es' framework (Figure 3.1) to provide an inspirational space accommodating epistemological, ethical and conceptual plurality and flexibility in the learning process that always involves multiple and diverse knowers with their individual anxieties, values, agendas and existential vulnerabilities. The resulting shared understanding bonds the participants, irrespective of their backgrounds and nationalities, and provides an informal support network built on mutual trust. Perhaps, through their collective experience of this participative style of pedagogy, they have co-created a responsible community of learners and knowers, who can go on to be influencers towards a more sustainable future. They could be the countervailing voices arguably so desperately needed to critically evaluate the risks inherent in the way most modern societies are 'developing'. Students' reflections indicate that this approach to education for sustainability co-creates communities of virtue, engaged in continuous conversations, advocacy and social activism.

The evolving understanding of the interconnectedness between economy, ecology, epistemic judgement and global ethics dovetails with PRME Principle 3 (Method): 'we will create educational frameworks, materials, processes and environments that enable effective learning experiences for responsible leadership'. The proposed '4Es' framework indicates that the debate about the sustainability crisis simultaneously reflects these four interconnected concerns against which choices, progress and risks in a global context could be evaluated. It provides the means for structuring such evaluations and simultaneously allows for the consideration of the ideal of sustainable development that the seventeen SDGs and Ten UNGC Principles endeavour to capture. As such, this dialogical tool is suggested to have both theoretical and practical applications for learners, equipping them with the capabilities to be 'future generators of sustainable value for business and society at large and to work for an inclusive and sustainable global economy' (PRME Principle 1 – Purpose).

References

Banerjee, S. (2003) 'Who Sustains Whose Development? Sustainable Development and the Reinvention of Nature' *Organization Studies, 24*,1: 142–80.

Blowfield, M. (2013) *Business and Sustainability.* Oxford: Oxford University Press.

Braungart, M. and McDonough, W. (2009) *Cradle to Cradle: Remaking the Way we Make Things.* London: Vintage.

Cicmil, S. (2014) 'Sustainable Organisation: Vision into Practice – Module Handbook'. *MSc Sustainable Development in Practice,* https://my.uwe.ac.uk (Accessed: 22 February 2016).

Cicmil, S., Collins, K. and Ecclestone, R. (2015) 'Responsible Education for Sustainable Development: Creating a Pedagogic Approach which Reflects the Complexity of the Vision', *2nd Annual Conference UK & Ireland Chapter of UN PRME, 'From Millennium*

Development, to Sustainable Development Goals – A Vision for Responsible Management Post-2015'. Glasgow Caledonian University *http://eprints.uwe.ac.uk/28542/* (Accessed: 29–30 June 2015).

Collins, K. (2016) 'Participation in Behaviour Change: Technique or Tyranny?' in Spotswood, F. (ed.), (2016) *Beyond Behaviour Change: Key Issues, Interdisciplinary Approaches and Future Directions.* Bristol, UK: Policy Press.

Cook, D. (2004) *The Natural Step: Towards a Sustainable Society.* Totnes, UK: Green Books for the Schumacher Society

Curry, P. (2011) *Ecological Ethics,* 2nd edn. Cambridge, UK: Polity Press.

Dow Jones Sustainability Indices (2016) 'Sustainability Indices', http://sustainability-indices.com/sustainability-assessment/corporate-sustainability.jsp (Accessed: 23 February 2016).

Evans, T. (2010) 'Critical Social Theory and Sustainability Education at the College Level: Why it's Critical to be Critical', *Journal of Sustainability Education.* 1 (May).

Fals Borda, O. (2001/2006) 'Participatory (action) Research in Social Theory: Origins and Challenges' in Reason, P., and Bradbury, H. (eds). *Handbook of Action Research: Participative Inquiry and Practice.* London: SAGE, pp. 27–37.

Freire, P. (1970) *Pedagogy of the Oppressed.* (Trans. Ramos, M.) New York: Continuum.

Gladwin, T., Kennelly, J., Krause, T.-S. (1995) 'Shifting Paradigms for Sustainable Development: Implications for Management Theory and Research', *Academy of Management Review 20.*4: 874–907.

Hawken, P., Lovins, L.B. and Lovins, L.H. (1999) *Natural Capitalism: Creating the Next Industrial Revolution.* London: Little, Brown & Company.

Hutchings, K. (2010) *Global Ethics – An Introduction.* Cambridge, UK: Polity Press.

Jackson, T. (2009) Prosperity without Growth? The Transition to a Stable Economy. *Sustainable Development Commission.* www.sd-commission.org.uk/data/files/publications/prosperity_without_growth_report.pdf. (Accessed: 22 February 2016).

Klein, N. (2014) *This Changes Everything: Capitalism vs The Climate.* London: Allen Lane.

Lomborg, B. (2010) *Smart Solutions to Climate Change: Comparing Costs and Benefits.* Cambridge, UK: Cambridge University Press.

Lyons, N. (2002) 'The Personal Self in a Public Story: The Portfolio Presentation Narrative.' in: Lyons, N. and Kubler LaBoskey (eds), *Narrative Inquiry in Practice: Advancing the Knowledge of Teaching.* New York: Teachers College Press. pp. 87–100.

Marshall, J. (2011) 'En-gendering notions of leadership for sustainability' *Gender, Work and Organization 18.*3: 263–81.

McDonough, W. and Braungart, M. (2013) *The Upcycle: Beyond Sustainability – Designing for Abundance.* New York: North Point Press.

Nordhaus, W. (2007) *The Challenge of Global Warming: Economic Models and Environmental Policy.* Newhaven, CT: Yale University.

Owen, P. (2011) *The Conundrum: How Scientific Innovation, Increased Efficiency, and Good Intentions Can Make our Energy and Climate Problems Worse.* New York: Riverhead Books.

Porritt, J. (2007) *Capitalism: As if the World Matters.* London: Earthscan.

Principles for Responsible Management Education (2016) 'Overview', www.unprme.org/about-prme/index.php (Accessed: 1 March 2016).

Rahmawati, A. (2016) 'Palm oil: who's still trashing forests?' *Greenpeace* [blog]. (3 March) www.greenpeace.org.uk/blog/forests/palm-oil-whos-still-trashing-forests-20160303 (Accessed: 11 March 2016).

Reason, P. and Bradbury, H. (2008) *The SAGE Handbook Of Action Research: Participative Inquiry And Practice.* 2nd edn. London: SAGE.

Rockström, J., Steffen, W., Noone, K., Persson, A., Chapin, F.S.I., Lambin, E., Lenton, T.M., Scheffer, M., Folke, C., Schellnhuber, H.J., Nykvist, B., de Wit, C.A., Hughes, T., van der

Leeuw, S., Rodhe, H., Sörlin, S., Snyder, P.K., Costanza, R., Svedin, U., Falkenmark, M., Karlberg, L., Corell, R.W., Fabry, V.J., Hansen, J., Walker, B., Liverman, D., Richardson, K., Crutzen, P. and Foley, J. (2009) 'Planetary Boundaries: Exploring the Safe Operating Space for Humanity', *Ecology & Society 14*, 2: 32.

Shaull, R. (1970) 'Foreword' in Freire, P. *Pedagogy of the oppressed*. (Trans. Ramos, M.) New York: Continuum.

Steffen, W., Richardson, K., Rockström, J., Cornell, S., Fetzer, I., Bennett, E., Biggs, R., Carpenter, S., de Vries, W., de Wit, C., Folke, C., Gerten, D., Heinke, J., Mace, G., Persson, L., Ramanathan, V., Reyers, B. and Sorlin, S. (2015) 'Planetary Boundaries: Guiding Human Development on a Changing Planet'. *Science. 347*, 6223: 1259855-1–10.

Thiele, L. (2013) *Sustainability*. Cambridge, UK: Polity Press.

Thompson, P. (2007) 'Norton's Sustainability: Some Comments on Risk and Sustainability', *Journal of Agricultural an Environmental Ethics 20*: 375–86.

United Nations (2015) *Transforming our World: The 2030 Agenda for Sustainable Development* [online]. General Assembly Resolution 70/1. Available from: www.un.org/ga/search/view_doc.asp?symbol=A/RES/70/1&Lang=E (Accessed: 23 February 2016).

United Nations Global Compact (2016) [online]. Available from: https://unglobalcompact.org/what-is-gc (Accessed: 23 February 2016).

United Nations PRME (2016) [online]. Available from: www.unprme.org/index.php.

Unite Nations Sustainable Development Knowledge Platform (2016) [online] Available from: https://sustainabledevelopment.un.org/sdg15 (Accessed: 22 June 2017)

Svetlana Cicmil, Director of Doctoral Research, Faculty of Business and Law, University of the West of England. A civil engineer by training, Svetlana had worked in the construction industry before taking up an academic career as a researcher and management educator internationally. Her research focuses on the critical study of project-based work and management as economic, social and political phenomena and on the pursuit of advanced understandings of sustainability, complexity and risks in organisations and global operations.

Svetlana.Cicmil@uwe.ac.uk

Richard Ecclestone, student on the MSc Sustainable Development in Practice programme, Faculty of Environment and Technology, University of the West of England. Prior to returning to university, Richard had careers as an army officer and a police officer before running his own consultancy business providing services in the fields of business continuity, emergency planning and security. He is an active contributor to his local community, including being a school governor.

Richard2.Ecclestone@live.uwe.ac.uk

Katie Collins, Visiting Research Fellow, Wolfson College, Oxford University. Katie's research is multidisciplinary, and coalesces around the ways in which the stories of marginalised and stigmatised groups are received and then written by social researchers. She works with creative and arts-based methods of enquiry like autoethnography, creative non-fiction and poetic transcription, critical ethnography and participatory action research, exploring the intersection of identity, inequality, and policy.

Katherine.Collins@wolfson.ox.ac.uk

4

The PRME Curriculum Tree
A framework for responsible management education in undergraduate business degree programmes

Alex Hope
Northumbria University, UK

Abstract

This chapter introduces the PRME Curriculum Tree, a conceptual framework, which seeks to provide a blueprint for business school curriculum design that integrates learning, teaching and assessment strategies that engage students of all disciplines with the Principles of Responsible Management Education, the UN Global Compact and the Sustainable Development Goals. The framework is built on the premise that sustainability and responsible management topics can function to build a bridge across disciplines and integrate the business curriculum as a whole by promoting holistic understanding and systemic thinking. The key to the framework is that it seeks to integrate and complement existing curricular structures that have evolved within business schools over many years. As such, business school academics can use the framework to inform the development of curriculum and approaches to teaching that promote responsible management education.

Background

Events such as the credit and banking crisis alongside global corporate social responsibility (CSR) and sustainability concerns have led to questions as to the legitimacy and purpose of business in society. Many are now calling for a new approach, one that eschews the profit-oriented exploitative business practices of the past for a new model of 'responsible management'. Indeed, many business organizations are already moving beyond social and environmental compliance and fundamentally rethinking the role their business should play in light of broader societal changes (Barkemeyer *et al.*, 2011). In addition to this, business leaders themselves are increasingly aware of the need to embrace the principles of sustainable development (Elkington, 1997; Porter & Kramer, 2006). There is then a recognition that far from a niche area of business, sustainability and sustainable development are considered global megatrends in the 21st Century, which results in profound implications for corporate interactions with society and the natural environment (KPMG, 2012). Despite the evolution of knowledge on responsible management, there is still an important question of how sustainable development is operationalised in a business context.

The acknowledgement, and increased awareness of sustainability and sustainable development from corporations and business support organizations, raises the question as to whether current management education is adequate to equip and develop future leaders with the requisite skills to meet these new demands (Carroll & Buchholtz, 2014; Colby *et al.*, 2011; Datar, Garvin, & Cullen, 2011; Weybrecht, 2010). Many business leaders are suggesting that business graduates lack knowledge in the area of sustainable business and responsible management (de Sousa Jabbour, Sarkis, & Govindan, 2013; Peoples, 2009).

At the same time, evidence suggests that there is a growing demand from business students for a more globalised curriculum and focus on CSR initiatives within management programmes (Haski-Leventhal, 2012; Leveson & Joiner, 2014). While there are a growing number of publications discussing these issues (Cornuel & Hommel, 2012; Morsing & Rovira, 2011; Muff *et al.*, 2013), the core of academic business teaching activities remains largely immune to the challenge of addressing broad societal concerns (Hommel, Painter-Morland, & Wang, 2013).

Some business schools are undertaking programmes to realign their curriculum, research and engagement activities around the core concept of responsible management and thus increase the range and depth of such topics. However, despite increasing interest in responsible management education (RME) driven by initiatives such as the UN Principles for Responsible Management Education (PRME) and the United Nations (UN) Global Compact, deep and holistic integration of such issues into undergraduate business school curricula remains rare. While there is emerging research and increased information on how business schools are seeking to integrate, combine and synthesize certain elements of responsible management into business education (Kelley & Nahser, 2014), there is little research that seeks to develop more holistic, programme level, whole curriculum-based approaches (Christensen *et al.*, 2007; Doh & Tashman, 2012).

The PRME Curriculum Tree is a conceptual framework, which sets out a blueprint for business school curriculum design that integrates learning, teaching and assessment strategies engaging students of all disciplines with the PRME and responsible management agenda. In this respect, it speaks to PRME principle 1 'Purpose' by developing the capabilities of students to be future generators of sustainable value for business and society at large and to work for an inclusive and sustainable global economy. The framework is built on the premise that sustainability and responsible management topics can build bridges across disciplines and integrate the business curriculum as a whole by promoting holistic understanding and systemic thinking addressing the criticism that most business school's curricula only address responsible management issues in isolation (Smith & Alexander, 2013). The framework seeks to operationalise and embed the six principles of PRME (purpose, values, methods, research, partnerships and dialogue) and ten UN Global Compact principles articulated under the themes of human rights, labour, environment and anti-corruption into undergraduate business curricula. The key to the framework is that it seeks to integrate and complement existing curricular structures that have evolved within business schools over many years. The analogy of the tree is useful, and it provides multiple metaphors for explaining the relationships between business and society, while allowing for the articulation of core concepts and addressing discipline specific issues.

The PRME Curriculum Tree

The framework is broken down into four main levels that represent elements of the tree: roots, trunk, branches and leaves. The *roots* of the PRME Curriculum Tree represent grounding, impact, history and connectivity. The role of business in society can be articulated and critiqued along with the dominant shareholder value perspective held by many students arriving in a business school. They are exposed to a range of different perspectives and encouraged to think critically about the relationship between business and society (Principle 1 'Purpose'). The prevailing context is *why* business exists, as well as *why* the challenges that society faces are relevant to business and the role of business not only in creating, but also solving these problems. Here PRME principle 2 'Values' is demonstrated by incorporating values of global social responsibility into curricula.

The *trunk* represents core concepts, theory, strength and dependability. Here, the principles and norms of business can be examined and critiqued. The focus is on *what* business does; how it operates; and the functional hard and soft skills that managers and leaders require day to day. Students are challenged to articulate *what* responsible management looks like across a range of business and management job roles, functions and departments. For example, *what* is the role of the Human Resources' (HR) Department of an organization from a responsible management perspective? Here principles' 5 'Partnership' and 6 'Dialogue' of

PRME can be demonstrated through schools' interaction with managers of businesses and other stakeholders to articulate real world challenges to students.

The *branches* of the tree allow for range and breadth, the exploration of multiple pathways, and discipline specific issues. Here the focus is on *how* do, and *how* should, business disciplines and functions deal with responsible management; for example, how are material sustainability risks identified, examined and addressed in business strategy or operations. Students are challenged to design strategic responses to a range of sustainability and societal challenges. Here PRME principle 4 'Research' can be used to convey contemporary approaches to meeting sustainability challenges.

Finally, the *leaves* of the tree represent innovation, new opportunities and future developments. Here the focus is on *where* are the opportunities for business and *where* should business be positioned in relation to the society in the future. Students can be challenged to imagine new business models for sustainable development, responsible innovation pathways and social business, which integrate with the UN's seventeen Sustainable Development Goals (SDGs). Figure 4.1 depicts the PRME Curriculum Tree visually, and the following sections describe the approach of each stage in more detail.

FIGURE 4.1 **The PRME Curriculum Tree**

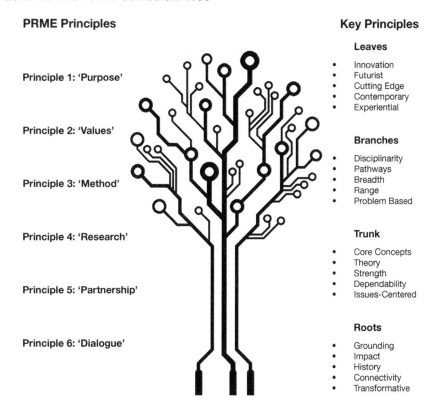

PRME Principles

Principle 1: 'Purpose'

Principle 2: 'Values'

Principle 3: 'Method'

Principle 4: 'Research'

Principle 5: 'Partnership'

Principle 6: 'Dialogue'

Key Principles

Leaves
- Innovation
- Futurist
- Cutting Edge
- Contemporary
- Experiential

Branches
- Disciplinarity
- Pathways
- Breadth
- Range
- Problem Based

Trunk
- Core Concepts
- Theory
- Strength
- Dependability
- Issues-Centered

Roots
- Grounding
- Impact
- History
- Connectivity
- Transformative

Roots of the Curriculum Tree

The roots of the PRME curriculum would be taught during the first year of undergraduate studies. Many schools use this first year to introduce students to the key elements of business and communicate core competencies. However, introduction to management courses can prove problematic for business school faculty, students and curriculum designers, who are eager to include as broad a range of topics as possible. In many business programmes, Principles of Management or Introduction to Organizational Behaviour and Business Strategy courses are the only management classes that students complete in their undergraduate programme (Christopher, Laasch, & Roberts, 2016).

Introductory courses, however, are an essential component of RME, as in many cases, they represent the first impression for students as to what business and management are and what they should be. They have been described as the foundation stones upon which undergraduate business education is built (Thompson, Purdy, & Fandt, 1997). In this respect, they play a central role in creating a vision as to what 'good' managerial behaviour is. Furthermore, research suggests that an introductory Business and Society course can significantly accelerate and improve the rate of moral development of some students (Boyd, 1981; Glenn, 1992). Despite this, not all business schools include such a course in the first year of their business and management programmes (Hope, n.d.).

With this is mind, there are a number of key theoretical perspectives that introductory courses need to communicate to aspiring business and management practitioners. First, management education needs to go beyond communicating the functional components of business and management and encourage students to embed reflections on sustainability, responsibility and ethics (Rasche & Gilbert, 2015). The focus should be on why business exists; what is its role in society; how does it interface with the wider world; and what are the main environmental issues that business leaders face. Here students can be introduced to the ten principles of the UN Global Compact which are grouped under the themes of 'human rights', 'labour', 'environment' and 'anti-corruption'.

Courses can be designed to help students open up their understanding of the relationships between business and society through a focus on responsibility. Again, many business and management programmes introduce the concept of ethical behaviour through business ethics courses much later in the curriculum (Hope, n.d.). Encouraging students to explore such questions and exposing them to a broad range of views and opinions as to the purpose and nature of business would help to break from the dominant paradigm that many business students believe holds true, i.e., this business is all about profit maximisation. Business and management practice do have underlying principles that tend to stay relatively constant and thus serve as foundations, or roots, to academic theory.

The roots of responsible management can be articulated in a number of ways and at different levels. First, the main issues encountered by business from ethical, responsibility and sustainability perspectives are debated. Next, students can be introduced to the specific drivers of a company's responsible management activities, both internal and external, and how these change overtime and relate to strategy. Finally, the inhibitors, criticisms and challenges encountered in responsible management can be introduced and provide context before students explore how these impact on specific business areas and functions.

Trunk of the Curriculum Tree

The trunk of the PRME Curriculum Tree should be taught primarily in the second year of study. Students should now have the sufficient grounding in the nature of business, but also the necessary critical view of business and management which enables them to bring a more open and free thinking perspective to their studies. This allows students to build upon the underlying principles of business articulated during the 'roots' stage of the Curriculum Tree while at the same time empowering them to debate, challenge and, where needed, refine and revise them. The focus at this stage is on the core functions and competencies of those functional business areas.

The core functional areas are those that are crucial to every business regardless of its size or speciality. These areas include human resources, finance and accounting, marketing, customer service, distribution and purchasing, administration and IT support. The focus here is on what business does across the range of business and management functions and what this means for responsible business and management. While CSR practices are taught in many, if not most, business and management programmes and embraced by many corporations, the specific contributions of professions such as HR, operations management, accounting and strategic management professionals have often been overlooked (Gond *et al.*, 2011).

It is also at this stage that the roles of these core competencies are articulated and debated in relation to the principles of responsible management. Core competencies are the main strengths or the strategic advantages that business upholds. They represent the combination of pooled knowledge and technical capabilities that enable a business to become competitive (Prahalad & Hamel, 1990). Traditional core competences are not only communicated to students but also debated and critiqued in recognition of the view that responsible management necessitates competences distinct from those traditionally required (Laasch & Moosmayer, 2015). While some core competences may be specific to a given discipline or functional area, it is likely that there are many which are generic and universally relevant.

Often, business schools create specific courses under titles such as 'sustainability', 'business ethics' or 'corporate social responsibility'; however, there is an opportunity here to embed the key principles of ethics, responsibility and sustainability into existing courses while reminding students of the ways in which different functional areas of business interact. Once students have a deep theoretical and practical understanding of the functional areas of business organizations, there is a chance to specialise and develop a complete understanding of what responsible management means from a disciplinary perspective. This understanding is facilitated in the next stage of the framework.

Branches of the Curriculum Tree

Building on the trunk of the learning tree, the *branches* allow for range and breadth, the exploration of multiple pathways, and discipline specific issues. They also allow for a more explicit and hands-on approach to learning. This process would begin during the second year of study and be consolidated in the final year. Here the focus may be on how can and how should business disciplines and functions deal with responsible management issues; for example, how are material sustainability risks identified, examined and addressed in business strategies or operations? How do responsible HR issues differ from traditional perspectives of HR? How can marketing departments effectively communicate social and environmental business performance and develop responsible marketing strategies? During this stage in the PRME curriculum, students are challenged to design strategic responses to a range of sustainability and societal challenges and adopt a more hands-on, experiential approach to learning.

One example may be the move towards sustainable supply chain management as over the last few decades there has been growing pressure on business to give further attention to environmental and resource implications of the products and services that they offer (Kleindorfer, Singhal, & Wassenhove, 2005). This has led to a corresponding need for the revision of the operations' management curriculum in business schools and professional training courses to include sustainable operations' management and business development among other responsible management topics (Gunasekaran & Ngai, 2012). Similarly, strategic management also has a part to play in the responsible management of organizations. Many companies lack a strategic approach to CSR and tend to follow unsystematic procedures resulting in reduced operational efficiency (Hahn, 2012). Sustainable and responsible strategic management involves a set of processes and strategies such as strategy formation, strategic analysis and strategy implementation that are economically, socially and environmentally focussed (Stead & Stead, 2013).

At this stage, there is a danger that students will form a silo mentality as many discipline-specific courses and the teaching materials that accompany them tend to focus on discipline specific issues (Dyllick, 2015). Furthermore, many ethics, responsibility and sustainability textbooks tend to take a rather generic focus. Some more recent business and management textbooks, however, are attempting to articulate what responsible business and management look like from a functional perspective; for example, Laasch & Conway's *Principles of Responsible Management* (2014) offers a view of responsible management from a practice and functional area perspective while integrating the different disciplines into a holistic fashion. The branches of the Curriculum Tree allow students to specialise in a specific area and gain a more in-depth understanding of ethics, responsibility and sustainability within and across business functions. The next step is to allow students to explore contemporary issues and co-envision the future of business from a responsibility perspective.

Leaves of the Curriculum Tree

The way in which we do business is changing rapidly, and this represents a challenge for future managers and leaders in understanding the behaviours and competences required to create a fairer society and more responsible business practices. Here, it is important to introduce students to contemporary issues in business and management, to current innovations, new opportunities and future prospects. The focus is on *where* are the opportunities for business and *where* will business sit in relation to society in the future. With these solid foundations in place, business schools and curriculum designers can explore new topics and introduce students to many innovations in responsible business. This is important as it has been recognised that the fields of corporate responsibility, CSR and sustainability are not static, but rather evolving constantly driven mainly by businesses seeking to meet the changing needs of the market and society (Department for Business Innovation and Skills, 2014). Students can be challenged to imagine new business models for sustainable development, responsible innovation pathways and social business.

Such innovations may include the shift away from a 'linear' production and consumption model towards a 'circular' one based on the re-use, sharing of, and re-manufacture of resources, and waste reduction or energy recovery techniques. Another area is the development of responsible business models, ones that turn to a service-based model of provision which enables customers to cut the cost of ownership that can arise from depreciation, operation and maintenance of capital assets. For example, new consumer models such as car clubs or peer-to-peer leasing enable customers to extract value from under-utilised assets (The Economist Intelligence Unit, 2013). These topics could be offered in elective courses that students could choose based on their interest or field of specialisation. The leaves analogy serves to demonstrate the unpredictability of business and management practice and enable curriculum designers to introduce students to novel perspectives leading to an understanding of the need to cope with uncertainty and change.

The Role of Pedagogy

When considering any curriculum development activities such as the PRME Curriculum Tree, thought must be given to the role of pedagogy in delivering learning and teaching content. Here PRME principle 3 'Method' is considered through the creation of educational frameworks, materials, processes and environments, which enables effective learning experiences for responsible leadership. It has been suggested that there are three critical levers for change in RME: transformative learning, issue-centred or problem-based learning and reflective practice and experiential learning (Baden & Parkes, 2013; Muff, 2013).

Transformative learning seeks to expand limited or problematic terms of reference into perspectives that provoke exploration into more future-orientated, holistic and responsible solutions (Erhard, Jensen, & Granger, 2013). For example, many undergraduate students begin introductory management courses with some experiential understanding of management as a practice (Wright & Gilmore, 2012). They may have been previously involved in paid employment or will have interacted with organizations in some way as consumers, students or participants in a group of some kind. Because of these experiences, many students approach management as a common-sense practice, something that people just 'do' (Whetten, 2007). In truth, management is a practice informed by theory, and as Wright and Gilmore (2012) suggest, the realisation of this can prove transformative for first year undergraduate students.

Issue-centred or problem-based learning requires a transdisciplinary, holistic, systems-orientated approach to problems, and this is orientated around issues rather than subjects. Here it is the interconnectivity of social, economic and environmental problems that are stressed in order to develop students' abilities to lead on complex decision-making processes typical of ethical, responsible and sustainability issues (Muff, 2013). Such problems and issues are clearly articulated and addressed by the UN Global Compact principles and the SDGs giving further weight to the argument for their integration into business and management education. Reflective practice and experiential learning provide students with practical, experiential learning accompanied by guided reflection which enables them to learn from their experiences (Dyllick, 2015). As such, it is important to recognise the role of different pedagogical approaches in enabling students to gain a balanced understanding of social, economic and environmental challenges.

Alongside these principles, the way by which students' learning and under-standing are assessed is an important consideration. An institution's assessment practices are a reflection of its values and its assessment practices should further the aims and purposes of the higher education institution (Astin, 2012). It follows that a business school committed to RME should practice responsible assess-ment and evaluation practices and that responsible management knowledge, skills and competencies are assessed alongside more traditional business learning and built into formal learning outcomes. Responsible management can be treated like every other learning outcome in that it is the responsibility of the business school itself to ensure as many students as possible meet the outcome (Vendemia & Kos, 2013). Building on the notion of transformative, issue-centred and reflective practice-focussed learning, where possible, assessments should provide students with the opportunity to demonstrate their knowledge in a practical, holistic and innovative manner, such as producing strategy or consult-ancy reports focussing on real-world problems.

Opportunities and challenges

Many opportunities and challenges are encountered when attempting to redesign undergraduate business curricula to incorporate principles of RME. The PRME Curriculum Tree has been conceived as a vehicle to exploit these opportunities while overcoming the challenges. One opportunity that the incorporation of RME closes the gap that some business academics and practitioners have suggested exists in what business students are taught and what they experience when they begin work in industry (David, David & David, 2011). Alongside this is the criticism that traditional business and management curricula revolve almost exclusively around established principles (Binks, 2016).

The PRME Curriculum Tree, with roots, trunk, branches and leaves, ensures that core principles are taught to establish the theoretical grounding necessary for academic study while allowing for specialisation, flexibility and innovation in the latter stages. Opportunities also arise from the introduction of pedagogical techniques that are more disposed to the teaching of ethics, responsibility and sustainability topics. The use of transformative, issue- or problem-based learning can bring opportunities for students to work with social entrepreneurs and responsible business professionals through experiential learning programmes, which can provide students with inspirational role models and positive social learning opportunities (Baden & Parkes, 2013). From a societal perspective, business and management schools can play a transformational role by educating (present and future) decision-makers, leaders and entrepreneurs in ethics, responsibility and sustainability (Lozano *et al.*, 2013).

The challenges that arise when seeking to re-orientate business and management education around the principles of responsible management are both practical and ideological. Space in the business school curriculum is already limited and creating more space for responsible management topics and subjects can be problematic (Reynolds & Dang, 2015). The PRME Curriculum Tree does not necessarily require the inclusion of new topics or subjects into business school programmes, rather it is attempting to provide a framework though which to incorporate key principles into existing courses. In this respect, it is more of a philosophy than an agenda. Many business schools also face the challenge of not having sufficient expertise in the areas of ethics, responsibly and sustainability issues. It is here that the PRME Curriculum Tree can assist in providing a framework that faculty can use as a starting point to begin embedding responsible management within their programmes and courses.

Conclusions

It is becoming increasingly clear that there is a need to re-orientate mainstream business education to incorporate the principles of responsible management and to better reflect societal trends as well as changing industry priorities. While many business schools are seeking to embed ethics, responsibility and sustainability into their undergraduate curricula, many still have a long way to go. One of the barriers to the integration of the PRME principles across management programmes is the lack of a common framework though which to do so. The result is that each institution adopts its own approach to the problem which takes time and resources that are often scarce and makes it difficult for the academy at large to ensure that best practices are followed and replicated across the sector. The PRME Curriculum Tree has been designed to articulate an integrated framework for developing RME in business schools and other higher education institutions. It is not meant to be prescriptive in terms of what should or should not be included in business and management curricula, but rather to provide some core principles that may be considered at different stages of study. In doing so, it can be used as a vehicle to encourage debate among management educators and curriculum designers. It can also provide a framework for helping faculty across disciplines coordinate, strategize and plan for effective integration of RME into the business and management curricula.

While focussing primarily here on undergraduate education, the overall philosophy of the Curriculum Tree is also highly relevant and applicable for other segments of management education such as postgraduate, executive development and doctoral studies. In addition to this, the Tree metaphor provides a useful platform and tool for enhancing external dialogue and partnerships between schools and businesses and other stakeholders on the new role of business in society, sustainable development, responsible management and the advancement of the SDGs.

References

Astin, A. W. (2012). *Assessment for excellence: The philosophy and practice of assessment and evaluation in higher education.* Rowman & Littlefield: Lanham, MD.

Baden, D. and Parkes, C. (2013). Experiential learning: Inspiring the business leaders of tomorrow. *Journal of Management Development, 32*(3), 295–308.

Barkemeyer, R., Holt, D., Preuss, L. and Tsang, S. (2011). What happened to the "Development" in sustainable development? Business guidelines two decades after Brundtland. *Sustainable Development, 22*(1), 15–32.

Binks, M. (2016). Towards an integrated curriculum. *EFMD Blog.* Available at: www.efmd.org/accreditation-main/equis/2012-01-10-10-56-23/view/1019-towards-an-integrated-curriculum-two

Boyd, D. P. (1981). Improving ethical awareness through the Business and Society course. *Business & Society, 20*(2), 27–31.

Carroll, A. B. and Buchholtz, A. (2014). *Business and society: Ethics, sustainability, and stakeholder management.* Cengage Learning: Stamford, CT.

Christensen, L. J., Peirce, E., Hartman, L. P., Hoffman, W. M. and Carrier, J. (2007). Ethics, CSR, and sustainability education in the Financial Times Top 50 Global Business Schools: Baseline data and future research directions. *Journal of Business Ethics, 73*(4), 347–368.

Christopher, E., Laasch, O. and Roberts, J. (2016). New approaches to introduction to management courses. *Journal of Management Education, 40*(2), 223–225.

Colby, A., Ehrlich, T., Sullivan, W. M. and Dolle, J. R. (2011). *Rethinking undergraduate business education: Liberal learning for the profession.* Jossey-Bass: Stanford, CA.Cornuel, E. and Hommel, U. (2012). Business schools as a positive force for fostering societal change. *Business and Professional Ethics Journal, 31*(2), 289–312.

Datar, S. M., Garvin, D. A. and Cullen, P. G. (2011). Rethinking the MBA: Business education at a crossroads. *Journal of Management Development, 30*(5), 451–462.

David, F. R., David, M. E. and David, F. R. (2011). What are business schools doing for business today? *Business Horizons, 54*(1), 51–62.

Department for Business Innovation and Skills. (2014). *Good for business & society: Government response to call for views on corporate responsibility.* (3 April) Corporate Governance, UK.

de Sousa Jabbour, A. B. L., Sarkis, J. and Govindan, K. (2013). Understanding the process of greening of Brazilian business schools. *Journal of Cleaner Production, 61,* 25–35.

Doh, J. P. and Tashman, P. (2012). Half a world away: The integration and assimilation of corporate social responsibility, sustainability, and sustainable development in business school curricula. *Corporate Social Responsibility and Environmental Management, 21*(3), 131–142.

Dyllick, T. L. (2015). Responsible management education for a sustainable world. *Journal of Management Development, 34*(1), 16–33.

The Economist Intelligence Unit. (2013), *Supply on demand: adapting to change in consumption and delivery models* (pp. 1–25) The Economist: London.

Elkington, J. (1997). *Cannibals with forks: The triple bottom line of 21st century business.* Capstone.

Erhard, W., Jensen, M. C. and Granger, K. L. (2013). Creating leaders: An ontological/phenomenological model. In Snook, S., Norhina, N. and Khurana, R. *The handbook for teaching: Knowing, doing and being.* SAGE: Thousand Oaks, CA.

Glenn, J. R., Jr. (1992). Can a business and society course affect the ethical judgment of future managers? *Journal of Business Ethics, 11*(3), 217–223.

Gond, J.-P., Igalens, J., Swaen, V. and Akremi, El, A. (2011). The human resources contribution to responsible leadership: An exploration of the CSR–HR Interface. *Journal of Business Ethics, 98*(S1), 115–132.

Gunasekaran, A. and Ngai, E. W. T. (2012). The future of operations management: An outlook and analysis. *International Journal of Production Economics, 135*(2), 687–701.

Hahn, R. (2012). ISO 26000 and the standardization of strategic management processes for sustainability and corporate social responsibility. *Business Strategy and the Environment, 22*(7), 442–455.

Haski-Leventhal, D. (2012). Corporate responsibility and responsible management education in the eyes of MBA Students. *New York: United Nations PRME.* Available at: www.unprme.org/resource-docs/PRMEMBAStudentStudy.pdf (Accessed June 2016).

Hommel, U., Painter-Morland, M. and Wang, J. (2013). Gradualism prevails and perception outbids substance. In *EFMD insights into sustainability and social responsibility* (1st edn), pp. 119–122. European Foundation for Management Development in association with GSE Research.

Hope, A. *Beyond business ethics: Sustainability and responsible management in business school undergraduate programme curricula.* Manuscript in preparation.

Kelley, S. and Nahser, R. (2014). Developing sustainable strategies: Foundations, method, and pedagogy. *Journal of Business Ethics, 123*(4), 631–644.

Kleindorfer, P. R., Singhal, K. and Wassenhove, L. N. (2005). Sustainable operations management. *Production and Operations Management, 14*(4), 482–492.

KPMG. (2012). Expect the unexpected: Building business value in a changing world. Policy paper (19 June) KPMG International.

Laasch, O. and Conaway, R. (2014). *Principles of responsible management: Glocal sustainability, responsibility, and ethics.* Cengage Learning: Stamford, CT.

Laasch, O. and Moosmayer, D. (2015). Competences for responsible management education: A structured 3literature review. *CRME Working Papers 1*(2).

Leveson, L. and Joiner, T. A. (2014). Exploring corporate social responsibility values of millennial job-seeking students. *Education + Training, 56*(1), 21–34.

Lozano, R., Lozano, F. J., Mulder, K., Huisingh, D. and Waas, T. (2013). Advancing higher education for sustainable development: international insights and critical reflections. *Journal of Cleaner Production, 48*, 3–9.

Morsing, M. and Rovira, A. S. (2011). *Business schools and their contribution to society.* SAGE: London.

Muff, K. (2013). Developing globally responsible leaders in business schools. *Journal of Management Development, 32*(5), 487–507.

Muff, K., Dyllick, T. L., Drewell, M., North, J., Shrivastava, P. and Haertle, J. (2013). *Management education for the world.* Edward Elgar Publishing: Cheltenham, UK.

Peoples, R. (2009). Preparing today for a sustainable future. *Journal of Management Education, 33*(3), 376–383.

Porter, M. E., & Kramer, M. R. (2006). Strategy and society: The link between competitive advantage and corporate social responsibility. *Harvard Business Review, 84*(12), 78–92, 163.

Prahalad, C. K. and Hamel, G. (1990). Organization of transnational corporations. *Harvard Business Review*, 79–91.

Rasche, A. and Gilbert, D. U. (2015). Decoupling responsible management education why business schools may not walk their talk. *Journal of Management Inquiry, 24*(3), 239–252.

Reynolds, S. J. and Dang, C. T. (2015). Are the "customers" of business ethics courses satisfied? An examination of one source of business ethics education legitimacy. *Business & Society*, 1–28.

Smith, K. T. and Alexander, J. J. (2013). Which CSR-related headings do fortune 500 companies use on their websites? *Business Communication Quarterly, 76*(2), 155–171.

Stead, W. E. and Stead, J. G. (2013). *Sustainable strategic management.* Greenleaf Press: Oxon, UK.

Thompson, T. A., Purdy, J. M. and Fandt, P. M. (1997). Building a strong foundation: Using a computer simulation in an introductory management course. *Journal of Management Education, 21*(3), 418–434.

Vendemia, W. G. and Kos, A. J. (2013). Impact of undergraduate business curriculum on ethical judgment. *Business Education Innovation Journal, 5*(2), 95–101.

Weybrecht, G. (2010). *The sustainable MBA: A business guide to sustainability.* John Wiley & Sons: Chichester, UK.

Whetten, D. A. (2007). Principles of effective course design: What I wish I had known about learning-centered teaching 30 years ago. *Journal of Management Education, 31*(3), 339–357.

Wright, A. L. and Gilmore, A. (2012). Threshold concepts and conceptions: Student learning in introductory management courses. *Journal of Management Education, 36*(5), 614–635.

Dr Alex Hope, is Senior Lecturer in Business Ethics at Newcastle Business School, Northumbria University. He undertakes teaching, research and consultancy on responsible business, sustainable development, CSR, energy policy and business ethics. He is co-convener of the Responsible Business research group and leads the school's Responsible Management Education project.

alex.hope@northumbria.ac.uk

Section 2

Disciplinary and transdisciplinary perspectives

5

Ethics, CSR and sustainability in marketing education

A review of curricula and textbooks

Theresa Bauer

SRH Fernhochschule, Germany

Abstract

Ethics, corporate social responsibility (CSR) and sustainability have become important, yet challenging tasks for marketers. An integration of these issues in marketing education is needed. This chapter examines the integration of ethics, CSR and sustainability in marketing education empirically. The curricula of universities in the UK are analysed to determine whether marketing courses contain coverage of ethics, CSR and/or sustainability. The results indicate a great variety regarding the extent to which universities integrate the three topics into marketing modules. Ethics tends to be more present than CSR and sustainability; the latter two are only incorporated into a marginal number of the examined marketing modules. The study also addresses whether current marketing textbooks include sections on ethics, CSR and/or sustainability. This step reveals almost all textbooks cover ethics; yet the number of pages dedicated to this topic is on average very small. CSR and sustainability are taken into account even less by these textbook authors.

Introduction

Ethical issues, corporate social responsibility (CSR) and sustainability have become important, yet difficult issues for marketers. Because of negative examples such as faulty products, misleading prices or offensive advertising, marketing is often considered rather unethical. For example, in a recent survey, only 13 per cent of consumers agreed when asked if marketing benefits society (Parekh, 2012). The increased consumer awareness about ethics, CSR and sustainability offers challenges, but also opportunities for the marketer, such as in the form of cause-related marketing.[1] Besides, CSR and sustainability communication have become vital for many companies that use specific communication channels such as CSR reports and websites and/or communicate their CSR activities via advertising or product packaging (Du, Bhattacharya, & Sen, 2010). Research has dealt with marketing ethics (see, e.g. Brenkert, 2008; Chonko, 1995; Eagle & Dahl, 2015; Laczniak & Murphy, 1985; Murphy, 2005), links between CSR and marketing (Hill & Langan, 2014; Maignan & Ferrell, 2004) as well as sustainable marketing (Emery, 2012; Martin & Schouten, 2013).

At the same time, scholars and practitioners have begun calling for a marketing education that incorporates ethics, CSR and sustainability (see, e.g. Bridges & Wilhelm, 2008; Nill, 2015, p. 12). The Principles for Responsible Management Education (PRME) provide an engagement structure for higher education institutions to advance social responsibility through the incorporation of universal values into curricula and research, including various disciplines such as marketing. However, while the Management discipline has played a leading role regarding the introduction of these topics into business programs, other disciplines have been found deficient (Nicholson & DeMoss, 2009). A few studies on ethics, CSR and sustainability in marketing curricula have yielded mixed results (Nicholls *et al.*, 2013; Rundle-Thiele & Wymer, 2010; Weber, 2013). Also, there is little knowledge about the adequacy of textbooks to teach these topics in marketing programs. A 2005 study found limited, sporadic coverage of sustainability in marketing textbooks (DeMoss & Nicholson, 2005).

The purpose of this chapter is to investigate to what extent ethics, CSR and sustainability are currently included in the education of future marketing professionals by focusing on two aspects: (1) to what degree are ethics, CSR and sustainability integrated within marketing curricula in the UK? and (2) are textbooks available that sufficiently cover these topics?

The chapter is structured as follows: it starts with a brief review of the literature, including definitions of business ethics, CSR and sustainability as well as an overview of research findings on the integration of these topics in business education and textbooks. Next, the chapter provides the methodology and results of (i) the curricula review and (ii) the textbook review conducted by the author. The chapter concludes with implications for incorporating content of ethics, CSR and sustainability in marketing education and links the findings to the PRME initiative.

Responsible business education

Business ethics, CSR and sustainability have become vital issues for many companies. The three are related, yet distinct concepts. Business ethics refers to "the study of business situations, activities, and decisions where issues of right and wrong are addressed" (Crane & Matten, 2010, p. 5). Following Carroll (1979; 1991), ethics is one aspect of CSR in addition to other elements: his CSR model conceptualizes four types of responsibilities for the firm including economic, legal, ethical and discretionary/philanthropic responsibility. Sustainability was initially discussed as an environmental concept, but has been gradually extended to include socio-economic issues (Steurer *et al.*, 2005). It implies meeting "the needs of the present without compromising the ability of future generations to meet their own needs" (World Council for Economic Development/WCED, 1987).

In light of the increasingly recognized importance to ensure responsible business practice, a move towards more responsible business education has started in recent years. One important step in this development was the launch of the PRME initiative in 2007. PRME aims at transforming management education and research by promoting the incorporation of universal values into curricula and research. PRME, currently, has 636 signatories globally, among which 65 institutions were located in the UK in 2016.

Several studies have attempted to determine the extent to which topics such as ethics, CSR and sustainability play a role in business education. Business schools in the USA are often considered the pioneers in integrating social responsibility issues into curricula (Campbell, 2007, p. 958). This finding is not surprising, as U.S. companies were the first ones to introduce formal CSR programmes, whereas European companies have tended to make more use of codified norms, rules and legal regulation (Matten & Moon, 2008). However, the UK has longer and stronger manifestations of formal CSR programmes than many other European countries (Matten & Moon, 2008, p. 419). In the UK, signs of growing provision of business ethics teaching were noted more than 10 years ago (Cowton & Cummins, 2003). Europe as a whole seems to be moving towards explicit CSR, i.e. formal CSR programmes are spreading. Accordingly, European business schools increasingly provide some sort of ethics, CSR and sustainability education (Matten & Moon, 2004; Moon & Orlitzky, 2011).

Several studies have looked at the extent to which the curricula in various business sub-disciplines deal with ethics, CSR and sustainability. Evans *et al.* (2006) proposed that marketing faculty would be more likely than faculty in other business disciplines to promote ethics in curricula, as marketing has psychological principles at its foundation. Yet, evidence for this assumption has been mixed. Rasche *et al.* (2013) found that business schools doubled the number of ethics-related courses in different disciplines between 2005 and 2009. However, the analysis concluded that integration of ethics varied considerably. Marketing, in particular, was found not to expose students extensively to ethical issues. In 2010, Rundle-Thiele & Wymer concluded that only 27 per cent of universities in Australia required students to take a dedicated (standalone) ethics, CSR and/or sustainability course; only 8 per cent of universities offered a dedicated core marketing course on ethical or social responsibility. Weber (2013) focused research on twenty-seven business schools mainly in the USA and some other countries worldwide and detected a significant increase in the number of courses focusing on ethics, social and sustainability issues offered by marketing departments between 2005 (with a total of 90 graduate marketing courses dealing with these issues) and 2009 (140 such courses). In a study of the integration of ethics, CSR and sustainability in all business school disciplines in U.S. business schools, Nicholls *et al.* (2013) found that ethics was incorporated into more than 50 per cent of the undergraduate and graduate marketing courses; CSR was incorporated in about one-third of these courses; and sustainability in more than 40 per cent of the courses.

There is little knowledge about the adequacy of textbooks to teach these topics in marketing programmes, but sustainability has been found to lack sufficient coverage in marketing textbooks. DeMoss & Nicholson (2005) content-analysed twenty-one introductory marketing textbooks and found that coverage of sustainable practices ranged from less than 1 per cent to almost 6 per cent. On average, the authors devoted space on 2.7 per cent of their pages to topics related to, or assignments for, environmentally sustainable marketing practices.

Marketing curricula

As a first step, this empirical study considered the curricula of universities in the UK to determine to what extent marketing modules contain coverage of ethics, CSR and/or sustainability.[2] The use of a web-based analysis (instead of questionnaires and interviews) has previously been found appropriate to research sustainability-related curricula of business schools (Wu *et al.*, 2010) and hence has been chosen for this study.

With regard to sample selection, all UK universities are offering Business and Management Studies where selected.[3] This resulted in a sample of 117 institutions. Among these, 30 universities did not list any modules/module descriptions online and hence were excluded from the analysis. The websites of the remaining 84 institutions were scrutinized for all marketing-related modules offered to students enrolled for undergraduate or graduate programmes. Specifically, all modules were selected that were offered in Academic Year 2015/2016 and contained the keyword "marketing" in the title. The module descriptions (as listed in the module catalogues) were then searched for the following keywords: (1) 'CSR'/'corporate social responsibility'/'social responsibility', (2)'ethics'/'ethical'; and (3) 'sustainability'/'sustainable marketing'. The study also aimed at detecting modules specifically dedicated to 'responsible marketing', e.g. marketing ethics, sustainable marketing. Stand-alone ethics/CSR/sustainability classes that do not specifically focus on marketing issues were not included, as the goal was to investigate to what extent marketing and its relation to ethics, CSR and sustainability are present in the courses.

Overall, 1,300 marketing modules were analysed. Among these, 250 (17.5 per cent) mentioned ethics in the module description; 100 (8.3 per cent) listed content on CSR; and 82 (5.4 per cent) on sustainability. The breadth of coverage varies widely among the universities. The percentage of marketing modules per university ranged from 0 to100 for ethics and CSR content; and between 0 and 64.7 for sustainability content. While the majority of institutions had one or several marketing modules that offered ethics, CSR and/or sustainability-related content, there is still a large number (twenty-one) of universities that do not include any of those topics in marketing modules. In contrast, eighteen universities offered one or two marketing modules that were dedicated specifically to ethics, CSR and/or sustainability. Overall, twenty-three modules were identified that used titles such as 'Marketing Ethics', 'Marketing and Society' or 'Sustainability and Marketing Practicum'.

Some universities have introduced specialized degree programs that combine marketing with a focus on ethics, CSR and/or sustainability. Most notably, specialized Master programs are offered by the Salford Business School (Social Business and Sustainable Marketing) as well as Heriot-Watt (International Marketing Management with Sustainability).

Textbooks

Next, the study investigated to what extent current marketing textbooks include discussion of ethics, CSR and/or sustainability.

Twenty marketing text books published in 2010, or later were identified using the 'Advanced Books Search' available on www.amazon.co.uk. All book titles that contained 'marketing textbook' were searched. The resulting list (as of 9 December 2015) was then scrutinized by the author for the first twenty titles that could be clearly identified as: (i) a printed textbook, and (ii) a general marketing introduction. The selected textbooks were then searched for CSR, ethics and sustainability content: Indexes and Tables of Contents (i.e., chapters and subchapters) were searched for keywords relating to 'CSR'/'corporate social responsibility'/'social responsibility', 'ethics'/'marketing ethics and sustainability'/'sustainable marketing'. The number of pages dedicated to these topics was also noted.

Ethics again received the most attention of the authors (see Table 5.1.) All except one of the textbooks listed ethics in the Index; the number of pages dedicated to this topic ranges between 0 and 47. Sustainability was mentioned in the Index of sixteen textbooks, with a page range of 0–28, while fifteen of the textbooks listed content on CSR in the Index, with a page range of 0–47. On average, 17.3 (3.1 per cent) pages were dedicated to ethics per textbook. Comparable data for CSR are 10.6 (1.8 per cent) pages, and for sustainability 6.7 (1.2 per cent).

TABLE 5.1 Coverage of CSR, ethics and sustainability in marketing textbooks

Author(s)	Title	Publisher, Edition (Date)	Total Pages	CSR listed in Index? (no. of pages)	% pages covering CSR	Ethics listed in Index? (no. of pages)	% pages covering ethics	Sustainability listed in Index? (no. of pages)	% pages covering sustainability	CSR listed in Table of Contents?	Ethics listed in Table of Contents?	Sustainability listed in Table of Contents?
G. Armstrong; P. Kotler	Marketing an Introduction	Pearson Education; 3e (2015)	620	18	2.9	46	7.4	15	2.4	yes; chapter	yes; chapter	yes; chapter
P. Baines; C. Fill	Marketing	Oxford University Press; 3e (2014)	737	4	0.5	31	4.2	7	1.0	yes; subchapter	yes; chapter	yes; chapter
P. Baines; C. Fill; K. Page	Essentials of Marketing	Oxford University Press (2013)	440	0	0.0	2	0.5	3	0.7	no	yes; subchapter	no
J. Blythe	Essentials of Marketing	Pearson; 5e (2012)	360	0	0.0	2	0.6	28	7.8	no	yes; subchapter	yes; chapter
D.W. Cravens; N.F. Piercy	Strategic Marketing	McGraw-Hill Higher Education; 10e (2012)	653	2	0.3	34	5.2	0	0.0	yes; chapter	yes; chapter	no
S. Dibb; L. Simkin	Marketing Essentials	Cengage Learning; 2e (2013)	512	0	0.0	2	0.4	0	0.0	no	yes; subchapter	no
N. Ellis; J. Fitchett; M. Higgins; G. Jack; M. Lim; M. Saren; M. Tadajewski	Marketing: A Critical Textbook	Sage Publications (2010)	256	0	0.0	10	3.9	0	0.0	no	yes; chapter	no

Author	Title	Publisher	Pages	N	%	N	%	N	%	Col A	Col B	Col C
J. Fahy; D. Jobber	Foundations of Marketing	McGraw-Hill Higher Education; 5e (2015)	359	3	0.8	4	1.1	0	0.0	no	no	no
O.C. Ferrell; S. Dibb; L. Simkin; W.M. Pride	Marketing Concepts & Strategies	Cengage Learning; 6e (2012)	320	14	4.4	27	8.4	4	1.3	yes; subchapter	yes; subchapter	yes; subchapter
D. Jobber	Principles and Practice of Marketing	McGraw-Hill Education 7e (2013)	885	30	3.4	35	4.0	4	0.5	yes; chapter	yes; chapter	yes; chapter
R.A. Kerin; S.W. Hartley; W. Rudelius	Marketing: The Core	McGraw-Hill Higher Education; 12e (2014)	784	9	1.2	8	1.0	3	0.4	yes; chapter	yes; chapter	yes; chapter
P. Kotler; G. Armstrong	Principles of Marketing	Pearson; 16e (2015)	731	41	5.6	40	5.5	28	3.8	yes; chapter	yes; chapter	yes; chapter
P. Kotler; K. Keller	A Framework for Marketing Management	Pearson; 6e (2015)	352	5	1.4	1	0.3	1	0.3	yes; chapter	yes; chapter	yes; subchapter
P. Kotler; K.L. Keller	Marketing Management	15th Global ed (2015)	832	7	0.8	5	0.6	3	0.4	yes; subchapter	no	yes; subchapter
C. W. Lamb, J. F. Hair, C. McDaniel	Marketing	South Western; 9e (2015)	432	15	3.5	16	3.7	4	0.9	yes; chapter	yes; chapter	yes; chapter
M.P. Levens	Marketing: Defined, Explained, Applied	Pearson; 2e (2013)	352	11	3.1	8	2.3	10	2.8	no	no	no
R. Masterson; D. Pickton	Marketing: An Introduction	Sage Publications; 3e (2014)	608	4	0.7	0	0.0	0	0.0	no	no	no
B. Sharp; K. Anderson; D. Bennett; S. Bogomolova	Marketing: Theory, Evidence, Practice	Oxford University Press; 1e (2013)	656	47	7.2	47	7.2	14	2.1	yes; chapter	yes; chapter	yes; subchapter
M.R. Solomon; G.W. Marshall; E.W. Stuart	Marketing: Real People, Real Choices	Pearson; 8e (2015)	576	0	0.0	16	2.8	8	1.4	no	no	yes; chapter
O.C. Walker; J. Mullins	Marketing Strategy: A Decision-Focused Approach	McGraw-Hill Higher Education; 8e (2013)	384	1	0.3	11	2.9	2	0.5	no	yes; subchapter	yes; subchapter
Average			542.5	10.6	1.8%	17.3	3.1%	6.7	1.2%			

Table 5.1 also indicates whether these topics appear in the Table of Contents: fifteen textbooks listed ethics (ten in a chapter title and five in a subchapter title); eleven textbooks listed CSR (eight in a chapter title and three in a subchapter title); and eight textbooks listed sustainability (five in a chapter title and three in a subchapter title).

Coverage of subtopics

The specific topics related to CSR, ethics and sustainability issues discussed in the textbooks were than analysed. The framework developed was based on Schlegelmilch & Öberseder's (2009) assessment of the importance of specific topics in the marketing ethics debate. After conducting a comprehensive literature review, these authors identified eighteen issues relevant to marketing ethics. After slight adaptations,[4] the following topic list was appropriate for the textbook analysis:

1 CSR, ethics and sustainability issues related to product [PD]: e.g. product safety

2 CSR, ethics and sustainability issues related to price [PR]: e.g. price fairness

3 CSR, ethics and sustainability issues related to distribution/place [PL]: e.g. gifts and bribes in supplier relations

4 CSR, ethics and sustainability issues related to promotion [PM]: e.g., advertising ethics

5 CSR, ethics and sustainability issues related to sales [SA]: e.g. ethical conflicts of salespeople

6 Marketing ethics and ethical decision making [DM]: e.g. ethical values and ethical behaviour of managers and marketers

7 Norms and codes [NC]: e.g. marketing and CSR policies

8 CSR, ethics and sustainability issues related to consumers [CO]: e.g. consumerism

9 CSR, ethics and sustainability issues related to vulnerable consumers [VC]: e.g. ethical aspects of marketing to children

10 CSR, ethics and sustainability in the context of international/cross-cultural marketing [ITL]: e.g. unethical conduct of multinational corporations

11 CSR, ethics and sustainability issues related to marketing research [MR]: e.g. privacy issues

12 CSR, ethics and sustainability related to social/societal marketing [SM]: e.g. definition of social/societal marketing

13 Green and sustainable marketing [GM]: e.g. meaning of green marketing

14 CSR, ethics and sustainability issues related to law [LA]: e.g. relationship between law and ethics

15 CSR, ethics and sustainability issues related to internet [ITN]: e.g. web privacy

16 CSR, ethics and sustainability issues related to religion [RE]: impact of religion and religious values on marketing ethics.

Each textbook was reviewed using this framework. When any relevant content was identified in the Index or in the Table of Contents, the relevant pages were reviewed. The texts were then rated under each topic item using the following scale: 0 (the respective topic was not addressed), + (the respective topic was mentioned, but covered with one paragraph or less), ++ (the respective topic was covered in detail, i.e. with several paragraphs or pages).

Table 5.2 exhibits the results of this content analysis. Overall, there was great variety regarding the appearance of different subtopics in textbooks. "Marketing ethics and ethical decision-making" as well as "Green marketing" were covered in relative detail by thirteen textbooks. For example, Jobber (2013) explains the meaning of ethics and marketing ethics in length and describes ethical issues in marketing; Baines & Fill (2014) define marketing ethics, describe the role of ethics in marketing decision-making and explain how ethical breaches occur in marketing programmes and activities. To cite an example for the coverage of green marketing, Sharp *et al.* (2013) introduce the concept of sustainable marketing as one stage within the concept of green marketing and introduce the green marketing grid. "CSR, ethics and sustainability issues related to marketing research" were covered in relative detail by eleven textbooks, whereas the focus tended to be on ethics. For example, Masterson & Pickton (2014) underline the importance of ethics in marketing research and discuss guidelines. "CSR, ethics and sustainability issues related to price" and "CSR, ethics and sustainability issues related to promotion" can also be considered important subtopics, as eleven textbooks provided more than one paragraph on each.

In contrast, little attention was given to several of the subtopics. For example, no textbook covered "CSR, ethics and sustainability issues related to religion" in much detail, although four textbooks did mention the topic. While nine textbooks made reference to "Ethical issues related to law", only one covered it in detail. Three of the textbooks covered "CSR, ethics and sustainability issues related to sales" in detail; two others did mention the topic.

Conclusion

This study of marketing curricula and textbooks at the university level focuses on ethics, CSR and sustainability, in response to increasing calls for incorpor-

TABLE 5.2 Coverage of specific CSR, ethics and sustainability content in marketing textbooks

Author(s)	PD	PR	PL	PM	SA	DM	NC	CO	VC	ITL	MR	SM	GM	LA	ITN	RE
Armstrong; Kotler	++	++	0	++	++	++	++	++	++	0	++	++	++	+	++	+
Baines; Fill	++	++	++	++	0	++	+	+	++	++	++	++	++	+	++	+
Baines; Fill; Page	+	0	0	+	0	+	+	0	0	+	++	0	++	0	0	0
Blythe	+	+	+	+	+	++	+	++	0	+	0	++	0	0	0	0
Cravens; Piercy	+	++	++	0	+	++	++	++	++	+	++	0	+	0	+	0
Dibb; L. Simkin	0	0	0	0	0	0	+	++	0	0	++	0	+	0	0	0
Ellis et al.	0	0	0	++	0	++	0	++	++	++	++	0	0	0	++	0
Fahy; D. Jobber	+	++	+	++	0	+	++	+	0	0	+	0	+	0	0	0
Ferrell et al.	+	+	+	+	0	++	++	++	++	0	++	++	++	0	0	0
Jobber	++	++	++	++	++	++	0	++	+	++	++	++	++	++	++	0
Kerin et al.	+	++	+	+	0	++	+	+	0	0	+	0	++	0	++	0
Kotler; Armstrong ("Principles")	++	++	++	++	++	++	++	++	++	+	++	++	++	+	++	+
Kotler; Keller ("Framework")	0	0	+	+	0	+	0	0	+	0	0	++	++	+	0	0
Kotler; Keller	++	0	0	++	0	++	0	0	++	0	0	++	++	+	0	0
Lamb et al.	0	+	++	0	0	++	++	+	0	++	0	0	++	+	0	0
Levens	0	+	0	0	0	+	+	++	0	0	0	+	++	+	0	0
Masterson; Pickton	+	++	+	++	0	0	0	+	+	0	++	+	+	0	0	0
Sharp et al.	++	++	++	++	0	++	+	+	++	+	0	0	++	+	0	+
Solomon et al.	++	++	++	++	0	++	++	+	+	+	+	+	++	0	+	0
Walker; Mullins	+	0	0	0	0	++	+	+	++	0	++	0	+	+	++	0
# of texts with ++	7	10	8	10	3	13	6	9	8	4	11	8	13	1	7	0
# of texts with +	8	4	6	5	2	5	8	8	5	6	3	3	5	9	2	4
# of texts with 0	5	6	6	5	15	2	6	3	7	10	6	9	2	10	11	16

ating these topics into marketing education. Marketing faculty should provide students with awareness of the importance of the diverse social, ethical and environmental issues related to marketing and the social responsibilities of those in the marketing profession, as well as guidelines for responsible conduct. The analysis shows that some universities have recognized this need and integrated ethics, CSR and sustainability into their marketing modules. Many others, however, still have not taken steps to teach these topics to marketing students. Of the three topics, ethics was most present in the module descriptions; CSR and sustainability are much less likely to be addressed in marketing modules. This result is consistent with previous studies in the USA that concluded that ethics had the greatest level of integration into the curriculum relative to CSR or sustainability (Nicholls *et al.*, 2013). Similar findings can be drawn from the textbook analysis presented. The selected marketing textbooks cover ethics more frequently than either CSR or sustainability. One of the twenty textbooks in the study did not mention ethics in its Index. However, the number of pages dedicated to ethics is still marginal, considering the average percentage of pages covering ethics is just over 3 per cent. Overall, while ethics is present to some extent in marketing curricula and textbooks, there is clearly room for improvement. This applies even more to CSR and sustainability.

These findings have profound implications for PRME and the UN Global Compact, as they indicate something about the factors and conditions enabling the integration of ethics, CSR and sustainability into curricula and business practices. By agreeing to the six principles of PRME, signatories promise among others to incorporate into "academic activities and curricula the values of global social responsibility as portrayed in international initiatives such as the United Nations Global Compact" (Principle 2) and to "create educational frameworks, materials, processes and environments that enable effective learning experiences for responsible leadership" (Principle 3). This research shows that both member and non-member institutions need to continue to strive for a broader incorporation of the values of global social responsibility into the marketing discipline. This refers to ethics, even though the marketing discipline had started to deal with marketing ethics already in the 1960s (Schlegelmilch & Öberseder, 2009, p. 3). This is equally true for the comparatively new topics on CSR and sustainability. A marketing education that incorporates all three topics is in the best interest of institutions, students and companies, especially at times when ethical lapses and scandals can present catastrophic reputation risks to corporations and derail the best marketing campaigns.

This study contributes to a better understanding of the state of ethics, CSR and sustainability education offered to marketing students. Future studies are needed to gain knowledge about the integration of these topics in marketing curricula, not only in the UK, but also in other countries. Moreover, the study provided a review of English language textbooks available for marketing students; yet further studies are needed to gain knowledge about the integration of these topics in textbooks in other languages.

Notes

1   Cause-related marketing is "characterized by an offer from the firm to contribute a specified amount to a designated cause when customers engage in revenue-providing exchanges that satisfy organization and individual objectives" (Varadarajan & Menon, 1988, p. 60).
2   The UK term "module" has the same meaning as the U.S. term "course".
3   As listed on www.thecompleteuniversityguide.co.uk/league-tables/rankings?s=Business %20%26%20Management%20Studies (accessed on 9 Dec 2015)
4   The topics "ethical issues related to marketing education" and "literature reviews" were excluded for this analysis, as they are not considered relevant for coverage in marketing textbooks.

References

Brenkert, G. G. (2008). *Marketing ethics*: Blackwell Publishing, Malden, MA.

Bridges, C. M. and Wilhelm, W. B. (2008). Going Beyond Green: The "Why and How" of Integrating Sustainability into the Marketing Curriculum. *Journal of Marketing Education, 30*(1), 33–46.

Campbell, J. L. (2007). Why Would Corporations Behave in Socially Responsible Ways? An Institutional Theory of Corporate Social Responsibility. *Academy of Management Review, 32*, 949–967.

Carroll, A. B. (1979). A Three-dimensional Conceptual Model of Corporate Social Performance. *Academy of Management Review, 4*, 497–505.

Carroll, A. B. (1991). The Pyramid of Corporate Social Responsibility: Toward the Moral Management of Organizational Stakeholders. *Business Horizons, 34*(4), 39–48.

Chonko, L. B. (1995). *Ethical decision making in marketing*: SAGE Publications, Thousand Oaks, CA.

Cowton, C. J. and Cummins, J (2003). Teaching Business Ethics in UK Higher Education: Progress and Prospects. *Teaching Business Ethics, 7*(1), 37–54.

Crane, A. and Matten, D. (2010). *Business ethics* (3rd edn): Oxford University Press, Oxford.

DeMoss, M. and Nicholson, C. Y. (2005). The Greening of Marketing: An Analysis of Introductory Textbooks. *Journal of Education for Business, 80*(6), 338–346.

Du, S., Bhattacharya, C. B. and Sen, S. (2010). Maximizing Business Returns to Corporate Social Responsibility (CSR): The Role of CSR Communication. *International Journal of Management Reviews, 12*(1), 8–19.

Eagle, L. and Dahl, S. (2015). *Marketing ethics & society*: SAGE Publications, London.

Emery, B. (2012). *Sustainable marketing*: Pearson, Harlow, UK.

Evans, J. M., Treviño, L. K. and Weaver, G. R. (2006). Who's in the Ethics Driver's Seat? Factors Influencing Ethics in the MBA Curriculum. *Academy of Management Learning & Education, 5*(3), 278–293.

Hill, R. P. and Langan, R. (2014). *Handbook of research on marketing and corporate social responsibility*: Edward Elgar Publishing, Cheltenham, UK.

Laczniak, E. R. and Murphy, P. E. (1985). *Marketing ethics: Guidelines for managers*: Lexington Books, Lexington, MA.

Maignan, I. and Ferrell, O. C. (2004). Corporate Social Responsibility and Marketing: An Integrative Framework. *Journal of the Academy of Marketing Science, 32*(1), 3–19.

Martin, D. and Schouten, J. (2013). *Sustainable Marketing*: Pearson, Harlow, UK.

Matten, D. and Moon, J. (2004). Corporate Social Responsibility Education in Europe. *Journal of Business Ethics, 54*(4), 323–337.

Matten, D. and Moon, J. (2008). 'Implicit' and 'explicit' CSR: A conceptual framework for understanding CSR in Europe. *Academy of Management Review, 33*(2), 404–424.

Moon, J. and Orlitzky, M. (2011). Corporate social responsibility and sustainability education: A trans-Atlantic comparison. *Journal of Management & Organization, 17*(05), 583–603.

Murphy, P. E. (2005). *Ethical marketing*: Pearson Prentice Hall, Upper Saddle River, NJ.

Nicholls, J., Hair, J. F., Ragland, C. B. and Schimmel, K. E. (2013). Ethics, Corporate Social Responsibility, and Sustainability Education in AACSB Undergraduate and Graduate Marketing Curricula: A Benchmark Study. *Journal of Marketing Education, 35*(2), 129–140.

Nicholson, C. Y. and DeMoss, M. (2009). Teaching Ethics and Social Responsibility: An Evaluation of Undergraduate Business Education at the Discipline Level. *Journal of Education for Business, 84*(4), 213–218.

Nill, A. (2015). *Handbook on ethics and marketing*: Edward Elgar Publishing, Cheltenham, UK.

Parekh, R. (2012). *Marketers rate below politicians, Bankers on respectability scale*. AdvertisingAge (24 October). Available at: http://adage.com/article/news/marketers-rate-politicians-bankers-respectability/237937/.

Rasche, A., Gilbert, D. U. and Schedel, I. (2013). Cross-Disciplinary Ethics Education in MBA Programs: Rhetoric or Reality? *Academy of Management Learning & Education, 12*(1), 71–85.

Rundle-Thiele, S. R. and Wymer, W. (2010). Stand-Alone Ethics, Social Responsibility, and Sustainability Course Requirements: A Snapshot from Australia and New Zealand. *Journal of Marketing Education, 32*(1), 5–12.

Schlegelmilch, B. B. and Öberseder, M. (2009). Half a Century of Marketing Ethics: Shifting Perspectives and Emerging Trends. *Journal of Business Ethics, 93*(1), 1–19.

Steurer, R., Langer, M. E., Konrad, A. and Martinuzzi, A. (2005). Corporations Stakeholders and Sustainable Development I: A Theoretical Exploration of Business-Society Relations. *Journal of Business Ethics, 61*, 263–281.

Varadarajan, P. R. and Menon, A. (1988). Cause-Related Marketing: A Coalignment of Marketing Strategy and Corporate Philanthropy. *Journal of Marketing, 52*(3), 58–74.

World Council for Economic Development/WCED (1987). *Our Common Future*: Oxford University Press, Oxford.

Weber, J. (2013). Advances in Graduate Marketing Curriculum: Paying Attention to Ethical, Social, and Sustainability Issues. *Journal of Marketing Education, 35*(2), 85–94.

Wu, Y.-C. J., Huang, S., Kuo, L. and Wu, W.-H. (2010). Management Education for Sustainability: A Web-Based Content Analysis. *Academy of Management Learning & Education, 9*(3), 520–531.

Theresa Bauer is a Professor of international management and marketing at SRH Fernhochschule (Germany). She has work experience as a lecturer at Raffles University Iskandar (Malaysia) and as a public relations manager in various European companies and institutions. She received her PhD from Humboldt-University Berlin (Germany). Her current research focuses on CSR, Responsible Lobbying and CSR Communication.

thkbauer@gmail.com

6

Developing graduate competence in sustainability management

The case of an accountancy programme in Sri Lanka

A. D. Nuwan Gunarathne

University of Sri Jayewardenepura, Sri Lanka

Griffith University, Australia

Abstract

Because of the lack of past experience and the limited number of management-oriented sustainability education programmes, universities and business schools now face a challenge to incorporate sustainability into their curricula to satisfy the growing demand of business communities and various other stakeholders for such programmes. This chapter demonstrates how an undergraduate accounting degree programme of a state university in Sri Lanka has successfully developed students' competencies in sustainability. Though this university is not a signatory to the Principles for Responsible Management Education (PRME), the approach used in this course is well aligned with its principles. The chapter describes how the state university introduced a novel course on sustainability accounting to develop students' sustainability competencies under three main themes: course design, delivery and evaluation. The chapter also discusses the challenges encountered and the strategies adopted to overcome them.

Background

Calls for corporations to be more responsible in areas such as human rights, labour, environment and anti-corruption as pronounced in the United Nations Global Compact's (UNGC's) Ten Principles (UNGC 2014) create pressure to change corporate decision-making and behaviour. This situation has generated a growing demand for professionals with expertise in sustainability management. Having understood the emerging expectations related to sustainability (Godemann *et al.* 2014), an increasing number of management education institutions around the world have shown a keen interest in catering to this new demand (Mader *et al.* 2013; Hesselbarth and Schaltegger 2014) while developing the capabilities of students to become future generators or facilitators of sustainable values. Yet, universities and business schools are faced with the challenge of incorporating sustainability into their curricula due to a limited number of management-oriented sustainability education studies being available (Hesselbarth and Schaltegger 2014). The vital question that arises is how management education should change to satisfy the growing demand for sustainability among business communities and various other stakeholders. What has been written on how business schools around the world have embraced sustainability education in their curricula, particularly in MBA programmes (Godemann *et al.* 2014), is mostly confined to developed countries. Little is known on how universities in developing countries have taken steps to develop postgraduate- and undergraduate-level competencies in sustainability. Given this context, the purpose of this chapter is to demonstrate how an undergraduate accounting course of a state university in Sri Lanka successfully develops the students' competencies in sustainability by closely following the Principles for Responsible Management Education (PRME). Though this university is not a signatory to the PRME, the approach used is well-aligned with the PRME's principles and ethos. This chapter examines how sustainability could be integrated into the curricula, particularly in management education, in the developing countries, even without the participation or commitment of the institutions as signatories of the PRME. The chapter presents the approaches taken in curriculum development, delivery and evaluation; it also addresses the challenges encountered and possible strategies to overcome them.

Decision setting

Sri Lanka is an Indian Ocean island nation in South Asia, a subcontinent that is home to about 20 per cent of the world's population (UN Environment Program (UNEP) and Development Alternatives 2008; South Asia Co-operative Environment Program (SACEP) 2014). Sri Lanka's strategic location near major Indian Ocean sea lanes (CIA World Fact Book 2016) led to its development as a maritime hub for thousands of years. Its written history dating back more than 2,500 years provides "a text book example of many modern dilemmas, including the dilemma of striking a balance between development and the environment" (Weeramantry 2002:10). The country had a stable and thriving economy in Asia when it gained independence from the British in 1948 (de Silva 2014). However, its economic development and social progress were largely hindered by nearly three decades of civil war. After the war in 2009, Sri Lanka has achieved noteworthy economic development (Central Bank of Sri Lanka 2014), and it is now considered one of the best places to travel to in the world (CN Traveler 2015[1]).

Sri Lanka has a vibrant accounting profession dating back to its colonial period making the island a hidden gem for accounting and finance outsourcing services (A. T. Kearney 2012). The island nation, whose accounting professionals are rated among one of the highest per capita in the world, is a global source for accountants across the globe including, for example, regions such as Australia, the Middle East and Africa (Senaratne and Gunarathne 2016). Sri Lanka's accounting profession, in both professional and academic streams, has received plaudits from the World Bank, among others (World Bank 2015).

Sri Lanka has fifteen state universities, all of them being government funded. Dating back to 1991, the accounting degree offered by the Department of Accounting of the University of Sri Jayewardenepura (SJP), which is the largest university in the country, was the first academic accounting degree offered in the country (Senaratne and Gunarathne 2016). It is a 4-year honours degree programme for students who have obtained the highest marks in their General Certificate of Examination (GCE) Advanced Level examination. These students usually become professional accountants soon after their graduation.

Development of graduates' competencies in sustainability

The Department of Accounting of the SJP introduced the new course on Sustainability Accounting in 2012.[2] Since then, this course that reflects many of the PRME Principles has been offered annually as an elective in the fourth year of the undergraduate degree programme. On average, fifteen students have opted for this course in each semester. The approach taken in this course is presented under three main themes: course design, delivery and evaluation.

Course design

In recent years, the accounting profession has been changing in keeping with the complexity of problems encountered by the profession, such as corporate sustainability issues faced by business (Tingey-Holyoak and Burritt 2012). Following a similar trend, the main imperative for designing the course came from recent developments in the accounting profession, including demand from stakeholders, feedback from companies and the author's personal interest. The introduction of such a non-conventional accounting course was not without challenges. The main challenge came internally from faculty members, who questioned the need for a course of this nature. Fortunately, the author was able to convince the faculty and the leadership of the Department of Accounting of the emerging need for the sustainability skills of the future accountants. As the former head of the Accounting Department once expressed:

> "We introduced sustainability reporting some time back in our curriculum. But we realized the need for and the importance of introducing the organizational systems and processes that would lead to sustainability reporting. That is why we supported an introduction of such a novel course though it was really new for us."

The purpose of the course is to introduce students to a pragmatic approach to sustainability accounting while developing their understanding of the complexity of the issues of corporate sustainability as highlighted by Tingey-Holyoak and Burritt (2012). In line with the UNGC Ten Principles, the course was designed with the objective of providing students with a sound conceptual understanding of the triple-bottom-line concepts in the economic, environmental and social perspectives. The course aims to equip the students with the new talents demanded as the future generators of sustainable value (Mader *et al.* 2013; Hesselbarth and Schaltegger 2014). This aspect is also highlighted in PRME Principle 1 (Purpose). It also teaches practical application of these concepts, while developing the students' professional competence in terms of knowledge, skills, attitudes and values (as outlined in PRME Principle 2, "Values") (See Table 6.1).

In developing the course, the author used his years of experience in engaging the industry in projects relating to corporate sustainability. The contents of the course have been updated regularly in line with the changing demands of the corporate sector. For example, in recent years, there has been diffusion of corporate reporting mechanisms such as integrated reporting both in Sri Lanka and other countries (Gunarathne and Senaratne, 2017). Hence, a greater amount of content on integrated reporting (as described in International Integrated Reporting Council (IIRC) 2017) was recently incorporated into the course.

Course delivery

To achieve the purpose of the course, several innovative modes have been adopted in the course delivery. Though the main mode of delivery for this course is through lectures, it was made interactive to allow the students to reflect on and discuss the concepts they have learnt. After the basic concepts/principles are explained, the students are required to engage in group-based discussions. In order to facilitate such deliberations, several cases were developed and practical examples are used. A social media group on Facebook was created

TABLE 6.1 **Themes of the sustainability accounting course**

Area	Coverage
New developments in accounting towards sustainability	Sustainable development, the triple-bottom-line movement, corporate sustainability management, managing the business case for sustainability, need for sustainability accounting
Environmental Management Accounting (EMA)	Scope, applications, drivers, benefits and roadblocks, environmental costs, EMA tools and techniques (energy and materials accounting, capital budgeting analysis, accounting for ecological, carbon and water foot-printing, life-cycle analysis/assessment (ISO 14040 series), environmental audit, material flow cost accounting (ISO 14051), accounting for waste, and accounting for biodiversity)
Accounting for the social dimension of sustainability	Social accounting and sustainability management accounting, social audit, social return on investment
Integration of the three pillars of sustainability	Sustainability Balanced Scorecard (SBSC), addressing the economic bottom line, role of an accountant
Frameworks available for reporting and managing sustainability	ISO 14000, 19011, 22000, 26000, 50001 Standards, sustainability reporting based on Global Reporting Initiative Guidelines and sustainability assurance, integrated reporting (IR)
Sustainability accounting theory	Importance of theoretical frameworks, contingency theory, institutional theory, stakeholder theory, legitimacy theory
Sustainability accounting: a Sri Lankan perspective in the global setting	Global perspectives of sustainability management and accounting, Sri Lankan status

for the subject and students were invited to join. This was used as a platform for sharing interesting news items, videos, images and articles on a regular basis as a means of improving student interaction outside the classroom. The students found this approach interesting, and they, too, started sharing valuable materials and posts which reflected their learning of the theoretical perspectives. During and outside the lectures, the students are encouraged to engage in group discussions on the practical issues they encounter in their daily lives. These discussions, while enhancing their competencies, are focused on improving their reflective learning experiences. All of these approaches contributed to providing effective learning experiences for the students, as outlined in PRME Principle 3, 'Method'.

To provide practical exposure, the students participate in a field visit after gaining sufficient knowledge of the subject. They are asked to research the practices in these organizations while critically analyzing the gaps between theory and practice. This empirical research approach enhances the students understanding of the role, dynamics and impact of corporations in sustainable development as highlighted in PRME Principle 4 'Research'.

After each lecture, the students were taught to switch off the lights, computers and air conditioners as they were no longer needed. This emphasizes the contribution that can be made on an individual level to sustainable development. They were advised to submit their assignments printed on both sides of the paper and not to take unnecessary printouts of reading materials. Also, the existing unsustainable practices in the university, visited organizations and the students' personal lives were discussed at length to deliberate on the possible avenues for improvements. Most of these initiatives stressed need to align the practices of the university with its commitment to sustainability (Godemann *et al.*, 2014), as outlined in the PRME Principle 7 'Institutional practices'.

Course evaluation

The traditional end-semester evaluation method that the universities in Sri Lanka were mostly using posed some challenges in assessing the students' professional competence development in sustainability (which included their knowledge, skills, attitudes and values). New approaches to course evaluation within the academic framework of the university had to be adopted. One such approach was the requirement to develop a mini research-based case study on a real-life organization following the case study design approach of Yin (2009). In addition to the field visits, this exercise also encouraged students to undertake independent research to enhance their understanding, in accordance with PRME Principle 4 'Research'. The students were responsible to select an organization that offered them sufficient accessible information for their study. In some instances, the instructor directed the students for specific organizations that he had contacts with, when they were unable to find an organization on their own. A formal letter was issued by the University to all these organizations requesting their support for the students' assignment. The students selected organizations in diverse industries and sectors, including banking and finance, apparel, plantations, engineering, manufacturing, printing and hotels. Most of these organizations were large, publicly listed companies with noteworthy sustainability practices. In these research studies, the students examined areas such as:

- Energy management practices (including the optimum use of alternative types of energies) and accounting for energy
- Waste management practices (in the spheres of solid waste and waste water treatment) and accounting for these waste streams
- Biodiversity management practices and accounting for biodiversity (in the spheres of flora, fauna and habitat)
- Raw material management practices, efficient resource utilization and material flow cost accounting

As part of the continuous assessment requirements, in the case study development assignment the students had to work with professionals who have diverse disciplinary backgrounds, including engineers, biologists, safety officers, environmental managers, purchasing managers and architects. This approach enabled the breaking of silos and provided an understanding of the language of other professions before the students embark on a professional career in accounting. This approach was adopted in an attempt to bring in interdisciplinarity to sustainability accounting and management education, as highlighted by Schaltegger *et al.* (2013) and Lamberton (2005), while developing graduate competences. With a view towards ensuring student commitment to the projects, 25 per cent of the course grade was allocated to the assignments that included submission of a report and making a presentation.

The objective was also to develop soft skills in the students, which are highly relevant for change agents regarding sustainability (Hesselbarth and Schaltegger 2014). Since this assignment was a group exercise, the students fostered their skills in networking, team work, leadership and communication through their experiences of working in groups. Moreover, the students were required to present the final report to the organization they visited as an additional requirement. The organizations were incentivized to support the students in carrying out their assignment since the students' report and presentations provided them many recommendations to improve the accounting and sustainability management practices. In this way, the students were provided with an effective learning experience (PRME Principle 3 'Method'). Many of these organizations also provided accommodation during field visits, and sponsored the publication of research materials. This enabled the instructor to not have to rely on the University for funding the additional activities required of students in the course.

This approach, while fostering partnerships with industry, enabled the students to extend their understanding of the challenges faced by business organizations and apply their theoretical knowledge in jointly exploring effective solutions (PRME Principle 5, 'Partnerships'). It also benefited the business organizations as well. A Sustainability Officer of a large apparel maker mentioned:

> "The project carried out by the students was really useful for us since it showed us some new areas in which we could improve our sustainability performance. Especially their approach to fabric waste quantification (by using material flow cost accounting) was an eye opener for us, and we had never thought in that direction before. Due to their accounting background, these students highlighted us the monetary value of the waste."

Moreover, this approach facilitated and supported dialogue and debate among various stakeholders such as academics, students, business organizations and other stakeholders (PRME Principle 6, 'Dialogue'). A compilation of students' case studies was also published in 2014 as a special issue in the *Journal of Accounting Panorama*, the research-based student journal of the Department.[3]

Concluding remarks and future outlook

So far the course has been offered for 4 years and more than sixty students have enrolled. As a means of improving the students' experience, anonymous mid-term and end-semester feedback was obtained. The feedback suggests that in addition to enhancing the students' knowledge and skills, the course also influenced their attitudes and values in inculcating behavioural changes.[4] One student expressed how his behaviour was changed as a result of this course.

> "After following this course, I just happened to change myself. Now I understand the gravity of the environmental problems which we simply have ignored in our daily activities. For example, after having lunch, I used several tissues to wipe my hand, but now I know my excessive consumption could lead to cutting down of trees somewhere in the world."

While explaining the motivations of selecting this course another student said;

> "I have learned enough accounting. I wanted to learn something different. That is why I selected this course. In fact, this course really changed the way we think, act and behave. "

Employers have started considering these graduates as valuable professionals possessing knowledge and skills in sustainability. A student who was recently recruited as a 'Stakeholder Interactions Executive' by one of the largest conglomerates in the country had mailed the author stating;

> "Recently I applied to a position called 'Executive-Stakeholder Interactions' at [Company 'X']. After a couple of interviews and a round of presentations I was offered the job and I'll be starting from next month . . . In the interview first they needed to make sure that I'm really ok with a job role like this other than a conventional reporting job [a traditional accounting job]. And they were quite hesitant at first to recruit an accountant for this, but convincing them was made possible when I started talking about the Sustainability Accounting subject we studied . . . Even the impromptu presentation I had to do was not really a challenge thanks to the so many presentations we made in the lectures."

A Sustainability Manager of a large hotel group expressed the following view to highlight the role that accountants could play in sustainability:

> "It is absolutely vital for the future accountants to possess sustainability knowledge and skills since they play a critical role in organizations. Due

> to the organization-wide knowledge, accountants can play really a value adding role in sustainability. They can highlight the economic, environmental and social importance of sustainability projects by using their analytical skills."

An engineer who is in charge of sustainability of a manufacturing organization had a similar view:

> "In many organizations, finance teams become the major barrier for sustainability initiatives. They need to realize that the sustainability projects do not yield paybacks similar to that of other projects, simply because there are so many parameters which we can't quantify still. So when we look at the rate at which the world is changing, I think there is a need for finance professionals to learn the importance of sustainability, equally as a means of organizational prosperity or survival."

At a time when professional accounting bodies and other accounting degree programmes do not cater to the growing demand for sustainability skills in the country, the course has successfully gained status as a programme that develops graduates' competence in the field of sustainability. The design, delivery and evaluation methods adopted in the course provided examples of how universities in developing countries, even if they are not PRME signatories, can take innovative measures well-aligned with PRME principles to overcome constraints such as the lack of government funding for higher education, as outlined Albrecht and Ziderman (1992).

Offering courses of this nature is not without challenges. One main challenge is the lack of a clear career progression for accounting graduates outside the mainstream accounting profession, despite their additional skills in sustainable development. It is only recently that the corporate sector in Sri Lanka started to establish systems, separate positions and business units dedicated to sustainability. Accountants or other management professionals have not yet seen a career ladder in these fields (Hesselbarth and Schaltegger 2014). This could discourage accounting or management professionals from embarking on a career track in these novel fields. Perhaps, with the growing interest of the business sector in sustainability, this issue may only be a temporary drawback.

Another key challenge is the lack of support from the higher authorities in education systems in Sri Lanka. This might also be the case in other developing countries. It is still hard to convince the country's educational authorities of the need to become a signatory to PRME (or at least follow the ethos of PRME) and improve the organizational systems and processes. This is mainly owing to the fact that there are severe constraints such as lack of funding and infrastructure facilities, as well as other urgent priorities and inefficient bureaucratic systems. Thus, the initiatives of this nature could encourage the national authorities to help universities and schools to meet these challenges and adopt PRME, if not formally, the at least through its spirit.

When introducing the course, there was no other similar accounting or management course offered in the country. Hence, benchmarking this course was not feasible. However, over the years it has been offered, the course has been reviewed and updated to keep abreast with the latest developments in the field of sustainability accounting to create new patterns of behaviour among the future finance professionals.

Notes

1 Condé Nast Traveler, a famous luxury and lifestyle travel magazine, ranks Sri Lanka as the second best place to travel in 2016 (refer to CN Traveler for more details).
2 The author is the course designer and the subsequent instructor.
3 This special issue can be accessed online: http://journals.sjp.ac.lk/index.php/joap.
4 In order to assess the changes in students' attitudes and values the instructor uses post-completion interviews and behaviour observations. The instructor plans to introduce a more formal and structured approach in the future.

References

Albrecht, D. and Ziderman, A. (1992) *Financing Universities in Developing Countries*, Washington: The World Bank, Education and Employment Division, Population and Human Resources Department.

A. T. Kearney. (2012) *Competitive Benchmarking: Sri Lanka Knowledge Services*, Korea: A. T. Kearney.

Central Bank of Sri Lanka (CBSL) (2014) *Annual Report*, Colombo, Sri Lanka: CBSL.

CIA World Factbook. (2016) 'South Asia: Sri Lanka', https://cia.gov/library/publications/the-world-factbook/wfbExt/region_sas.html (accessed 04 March 2016).

CN Traveler. (2015) '16 Best Places to Visit in 2016' www.cntraveler.com/galleries/2015-12-29/the-top-16-places-to-go-in-2016/1 (accessed 30 October 2016).

De Silva, K. M. (2014) *A History of Sri Lanka*, Colombo, Sri Lanka: Vijitha Yapa.

Godemann, J., Haertle, J., Herzig, C. and Moon, J. (2014) 'United Nations Supported Principles for Responsible Management Education: Purpose, Progress and Prospects', *Journal of Cleaner Production*, 62: 16–23.

Gunarathne, N. and Senaratne, S. (2017) 'Diffusion of Integrated Reporting in an Emerging South Asian (SAARC) Nation', *Managerial Auditing Journal*, 32 (4/5): 524-548

Hesselbarth, C. and Schaltegger, S. (2014) 'Educating Change Agents for Sustainability-Learnings From the First Sustainability Management Master of Business Administration', *Journal of Cleaner Production*, 62: 24–36.

International Integrated Reporting Council (IIRC). (2013) 'The International <IR> Framework', http://integratedreporting.org/wp-content/uploads/2013/12/13-12-08-THE-INTERNATIONAL-IR-FRAMEWORK-2-1.pdf (accessed 10 April 2016).

Lamberton, G. (2005) 'Sustainability Accounting – A Brief History and Conceptual Framework'. *Accounting Forum*, 29 (1): 7–26.

Mader, C., Scott G. and Razak D. A. (2013) 'Effective Change Management, Governance and Policy for Sustainability Transformation in Higher Education', *Sustainability Accounting, Management and Policy Journal*, 4 (3): 264–284.

Schaltegger, S., Beckmann, M. and Hansen, E. G. (2013) 'Transdisciplinarity in Corporate Sustainability: Mapping the Field', *Business Strategy and the Environment*, 22 (4): 219–229.

Senaratne, S. and Gunarathne, N. (2016) 'Excellence in Management Education: Perspectives from a global hub of accountants in Asia', in Baporikar, N. (ed.), *Management Education for Global Leadership*, USA: IGI Global, pp. 158–180.

South Asia Co-operative Environment Program (SACEP), (2014), *Post 2015 South Asia Development Agenda*, Colombo, Sri Lanka: SACEP.

Tingey-Holyoak, L. and Burritt, R. (2012) 'The Trans-disciplinary Nature of Accounting: A Pathway Towards the Sustainable Future of the Profession', in: Evans, E., Burritt R. and Guthrie, J. (eds), *Emerging Pathways for the Next Generation of Accountants*, Australia: The Institute of Chartered Accountants in Australia, pp. 93–103.

United Nations Environment Program and Development Alternatives. (2008) *South Asia Environment Outlook 2009*, Bangkok: United Nations Environment Program, Kathamndu: South Asian Association for Regional Cooperation and New Delhi: Development Alternatives.

United Nations Global Compact (UNGC). (2014) *Guide to Corporate Sustainability Shaping-A Sustainable Future*, New York: UNGC.

Weeramantry, C. G. (2002) '*Sustainable Development: An Ancient Concept Recently Revived*', Johannesburg, South Africa: Global Judges Symposium on Sustainable Development and the Role of Law. www.unep.org/delc/Portals/119/publications/Speeches/Weeramantry.pdf (accessed 8 December 2015).

World Bank. (2015) *Report on the Observance of Standards and Codes, Accounting and Auditing- Sri Lanka*, Washington: World Bank.

Yin, R. (2009) *Case Study Research: Design and Methods*, Thousand Oaks, CA: Sage.

A.D. Nuwan Gunarathne is a doctoral candidate at the Griffith University, Australia and a Senior Lecturer at the University of Sri Jayewardenepura, Sri Lanka. He is an associate member of the Chartered Institute of Management Accountants, UK, and Institute of Certified Management Accountants, Sri Lanka. He holds a bachelor's and a master's degree in Business Administration from the University of Sri Jayewardenepura.

nuwan@sjp.ac.lk, nuwan.gunarathne@griffithuni.edu.au

7

Business and human rights
Connecting the managerial and legal aspects

Karin Buhmann
Copenhagen Business School, Denmark

Abstract

Translating the implications of human rights for responsible business management requires an understanding of what human rights are and how to identify human rights risks or potential violations in management practices or with business relations. Human rights are integral to the United Nations Global Compact (UNGC): all ten of its principles either directly or indirectly address human rights. The UN Guiding Principles (UNGPs) on Business and Human Rights complement the UNGC by providing further details on the implications of human rights to business, and on how businesses should act to avoid infringing on these rights. This chapter explains how the UNGPs and the UNGC can help translate human rights concepts into managerial processes. Particular emphasis is given to context and international human and labour rights law that managers should know about in order to incorporate human rights in their policies and management practices.

What are human rights, and why do they matter to business?

Human rights issues arise in a number of managerial contexts that do not carry a human rights label. For example, human rights issues may occur in relation to procurement, finance, supply-chain management, stakeholder engagement and consultation, risk management, human resource management, communication and non-financial reporting. This makes it pertinent for managers exercising a broad range of tasks to have human rights knowledge.

Identifying business-related human rights issues can be likened to a process of 'translating' human rights concepts into managerial processes in order to understand their implications and manage them appropriately. Human rights knowledge helps managers identify whether business practices may affect human rights, assess how to respond to avoid infringing on human rights and consider whether expert advice should be sought.

An increasing convergence of human rights principles for business in transnational business governance instruments, including the UN Global Compact (UNGC), the ISO 26000 Social Responsibility Guidance Standards and Organization of Economic Cooperation and Development's (OECD) Guidelines for Multinational Enterprises, means that key international human rights instruments issued by the UN and the International Labour Organisation (ILO) now form a core body of normative guidance for business with regard to human rights.

Human rights are integral to the UNGC: the UNGC Principle 1 states that businesses should support and respect the protection of internationally proclaimed human rights. Principle 2 states that businesses should ensure that they are not complicit in human rights abuses. These two principles refer to the Universal Declaration on Human Rights (UDHR, United Nations, 1948), which constitutes the UN's first and comprehensive list of human rights. Between them, Principles 1 and 2 emphasize that a responsible manager must consider the human rights impacts that result from the company for whom the manager works, as well as those that result from the company's business relations with other companies or with governmental institutions.

UNGC Principles 3–6 refer to core labour rights, which are also human rights as explained below. Environmental Principles 7–9 aim at reducing environmental damage that may cause harm to, for example, health or land that people cultivate or on which they live. These impacts may have significant human rights implications. Aiming to prevent corruption, Principle 10 contributes to reducing practices that result in injustice and that are typically averse to human rights implementation.

From a moral perspective, human rights derive from the inherent dignity of the human person. This fundamental idea underpins the international regime on human rights which has evolved since the UN was established in 1945 with the protection and promotion of human rights as a core objective. Adopted in 1948 as one of the first steps in implementing this objective, the UDHR lists the rights to freedom from slavery and torture, freedom of movement, and freedom of peaceful assembly and association. It also lists the rights to equal pay for equal work, to just and favourable remuneration, to rest and leisure, to form and join trade unions, and to a standard of living adequate for the health and well-being of oneself and one's family, including food, clothing, housing, medical care and necessary social services. The UDHR also identifies the rights to education, to marry, to own property and not to be arbitrarily deprived of that property, and to take part, directly or through representatives, in the exercise of government and the conduct of public affairs (which basically entails public decision-making relating to one's life). The UDHR establishes that these rights should be enjoyed without discrimination based on gender, religion, political or other opinion, national or social origin, race, colour, language, property, birth or other status.

The rights in the UDHR were later elaborated on by two international treaties, the International Covenant on Economic, Social and Cultural Rights (ICESCR, United Nations, 1966a) and the International Covenant on Civil and Political Rights (ICCPR, United Nations, 1966b). The ICESCR and ICCPR address states, but can provide valuable guidance for firms. Together, the UDHR, the ICESCR and the ICCPR are referred to as the *International Bill of Rights.*

The ILO's *'Declaration on Fundamental Principles and Rights at Work'* lists freedom from discrimination, the right to collective bargaining, freedom of association (including to form and belong to a trade union), the elimination of child labour, and the abolition of slavery, involuntary and forced labour. These *core labour rights,* and ensuing obligations of states and employers and rights of employees are described in detail in eight treaties considered to be *ILO fundamental conventions.*

As core labour rights are mentioned in the International Bill of Rights, the labour issue principles of the UNGC are also considered human rights. This illustrates the fact that human rights themselves and the international human rights instruments that set out the standards are both broad and deep, and intricately intertwined. For example, the human right of everyone to the enjoyment of just and favourable conditions of work, which is prescribed in ICESCR Article 7, covers working standards in a broad sense and also specific issues, such as fair wages and equal remuneration, occupational health and safety, and reasonable limitation of working hours that are set out in greater detail in ILO instruments.

Adopted in 2011, the UN Guiding Principles (UNGPs) on Business and Human Rights do not set out new human rights but explain the human rights implications for businesses of already existing rights (United Nations, 2011). The UNGPs refer to the International Bill of Rights and ILO's core labour rights as the minimum baseline that companies should respect. The UNGPs provide detailed guidance for implementation of the UN's *'Protect, Respect and Remedy'* Framework (UN Framework, United Nations, 2008), which was adopted in 2008. Both were developed through broad multi-stakeholder processes involving business, civil society and experts.

Pillar One (the State Duty to Protect) implies that *governments must protect individuals and communities against human rights abuse caused by firms.* Governments already have such obligations under international law, for example, to develop appropriate national legislation and enforce it, but their measures can be ineffective. *Pillar Two* (the Corporate Responsibility to Respect, sometimes referred to as the CR2R) sets out the dual responsibility of firms to *comply with the law in their countries of operation, and to ascertain that they also live up to international human rights law.*

Such international law often informs social expectations and the 'social licence to operate' (United Nations, 2008, para. 54). The corporate responsibility to respect human rights applies to any type of business, regardless of size or sector. The UNGPs establish that a human rights policy adopted by top management, along with the exercise of a risk-based due diligence process to identify, prevent and manage the adverse human rights impacts of a company's actions, are key elements in the corporate responsibility to respect human rights (UNGPs Nos. 16 and 17–21). Contrary to the financial and legal liability due diligence processes that are typically used by firms to identify and assess risks *to* the firm, risk-based due diligence enunciated by the UNGPs aims to protect society from harm caused by the firm.

Of course, if done well, it may also, in turn, protect the firm against risks, such as reputational or economic, associated with human rights violations. *Pillar Three* (Access to Remedy) covers the *joint responsibility of states and firms to provide remedy where human rights are perceived to have been abused by a firm.* Human rights abuse may occur even when a firm has made sincere efforts to identify, prevent and mitigate violations. Companies should provide remedy at the operational level through culturally and socially appropriate redress mechanisms.

The UNGPs and their predecessor, the UN *'Protect, Respect and Remedy'* Framework are sometimes referred to as the 'Ruggie Principles' and 'Ruggie Framework' after Professor John Ruggie, a political scientist, Harvard Professor and a former UN Assistant Secretary General, who was charged with developing them. As both were developed for the UN, they are correctly referred to as the UN Guiding Principles and UN Framework.

Illustrating the complexity of human rights for management: Three cases

The complexity and diversity of situations in which human rights relate to business practices and a company's responsibility for human rights impacts of its business relations (the value chain) are illustrated by three cases described in the following paragraphs.

The first case concerns an agricultural small/medium-sized enterprise in Denmark that employed migrant workers for seasonal work. The owner was alleged to have retained employees' passports as security for advance salary payments. Retaining an employee's passport can restrict movement and travel and lead to conditions that may amount to slavery or forced labour, which are gross human rights violations. An employer's holding ID documents can prevent employees from leaving the company if the employer refuses to return their passports. Ultimately, employees are held against their will under conditions that can be associated with slavery or forced labour in violation of the ICCPR (Article 8: "no one shall be required to perform forced or compulsory labour"; Article 12: "everyone lawfully within the territory of a State shall, within that have the right to move freely and freedom to choose his residence") and ILO's core labour right to freedom from slavery or forced labour.

Managers may ask employees to bring a copy of their passport, or they may obtain the consent of the employee to take a photocopy or scan of the employee's ID (Danish NCP, 2014), but they must respect the rights of employees to have possession of the documents needed for them to travel and move within a country. The case shows the importance for managers to understand the practical human rights implications of generalized human rights including 'freedom from forced labour' in a business context. Most managers have no intention of causing human rights abuse, such as slavery or forced labour, when asking employees for personal information or obtaining security for an advance on payment. Knowledge of the human rights set out in the International Bill of Rights and core labour standards helps the manager identify such problems and alternative options for action.

The second case concerns a cargo airline operating out of several places in Africa. In a case handled by the United Kingdom complaints body (National Contact Point) under OECD's Guidelines for Multinational Enterprise, an NGO alleged that the airline was involved in transporting coltan (a rare earth mineral used in electronics) from the eastern Democratic Republic of Congo (DRC), an area identified with extremely weak governance and severe human rights violations perpetrated by rebel groups. The airline held that it acted as freighters on a contractual basis and was not aware that the coltan transported originated in a conflict area.

The connection between rare earth minerals and severe human rights abuse committed by rebel groups in the DRC was widely debated at the time. International reports from the UN and other information documented a close connection between the coltan industry and DRC rebel groups involved in human rights abuse. On this basis, the airline should have been aware of the risk that the coltan originated from DRC, and consequently the risk that transporting the mineral might benefit the rebel groups and therefore contribute to enabling their human rights abuse due (UK NCP, 2008). The case shows the importance of a company conducting a risk-based due diligence process to ensure that it does not contribute to human rights harm through its business relations. The case, therefore, also relates to both the UNGC Principle 1 and Principle 2.

The third case involves a company based in the Global North, which entered into a large contract to deliver wind turbines for a large wind farm in Mexico with support from a governmental Export Credit Agency in its home country. The project was to be located in Oaxaca, an area that is home to several indigenous peoples and ancient cultures (Ramirez, 2013). In its interactions with the local authorities involved in making decisions on the use of land and with the local people in the affected area, the company neglected to engage adequately with the local communities about their concerns. Nor did it take their concerns on the potential impact of the project on their culture into account in a manner that was felt to be adequate by the local communities.

The local communities felt that they had not been adequately involved in decisions that had critical impacts on their lives. These concerns relate to the rights to enjoy one's culture (UDHR Article 27, ICESCR Article 15), and to take part in the conduct of public affairs (UDHR Article 21, ICCPR Article 25). Through its inadequate stakeholder engagement, the company neglected to carry out adequate due diligence to identify human rights violations related to indigenous groups' culture. The result was a series of severe delays and public outrage, eventually forcing the company into a costly withdrawal of its business operations in Oaxaca.

Moreover, the Export Credit Agency had neglected to make sufficient demands on the company for it to respect human rights and to monitor the human rights impact of its activities. The case shows the importance of stakeholder consultation in order to enable potentially affected individuals and groups to have a say; of involving stakeholders in a company's due diligence to identify human rights impacts of a business endeavour and, of a company's appreciation of local customs and culture, especially those that pertain to minorities and indigenous groups. Stakeholder involvement is relevant to the human rights to participate in decision-making as part of the conduct of public affairs. It is also relevant to learn about concerns with what from the human rights perspective amounts to the enjoyment of community culture, such as practices related to areas of religious significance to local indigenous groups. Moreover, indigenous groups have special rights to be consulted, according to ILO Convention 169.

Business and human rights: Relation to CSR

The detailed normative background based on the International Bill of Rights and ILO core labour standards sets the field of Business and Human Rights apart from much of the guidance or practices on general Corporate Social Responsibility (CSR), which remains much less specific in terms of normative guidance and which allows firms greater discretion in choosing norms to follow. The field also differs from CSR in that human rights theory recognizes a clear role of governments to protect human rights against abuse caused by business through law, policy and other relevant means.

This role includes what the UNGPs refer to as smart regulation that mixes *hard* law (mandatory requirements) and *soft* law (guidance). Smart regulation may comprise incentives, reporting and disclosure in order to promote proactive self-regulation within firms and reduce their adverse human rights impacts.

In recognition of the difference between general CSR and the particularities of the Business and Human Rights field, the latter is increasingly referred to as BHR.

At the same time, the normative guidance and recognition of the duality between the roles of business and those of governments is influencing the practice of CSR by corporations around the world. For example, the OECD Guidelines for Multinational Enterprises adopted the UNGP's risk-based due diligence approach and expanded it from human rights to also cover, i.a. the environment, labour rights and consumer concerns. ISO 26000 also applies the UNGP's risk-based due diligence approach (Buhmann, 2015).

The idea that business organizations have responsibility for their human rights impacts also remains an important part of CSR, and therefore, for organizations committed to the UNGC.

While human rights are multi-disciplinary in terms of theory (Buhmann and Wettstein, 2017), the practical application of human rights is highly guided by legal standards set in international law. Knowledge of relevant human rights standards and finding additional elaboration and expert guidance becomes easier for the business manager who has a basic knowledge of human rights law. Such knowledge is typically not required for CSR management to the same extent. The next section explains how this knowledge can be taught.

Teaching BHR in the classroom

Studies leading to the UNGPs showed that human rights impacts may cause firms considerable reputational damage and economic losses, but the incidents and human rights issues are often hidden among more general information (Ruggie, 2013). The three cases noted earlier in this chapter testify to the difficulties that firms have in conceptualizing and therefore dealing adequately with the human rights risks that are caused by themselves or their business partners.

To identify specific risks and business responsibilities for human rights, a first step is to recognize that human rights are not only moral or social expectations but also backed by specific standards of conduct. For example, if questioned, many company managers would commit to human rights as a matter of morals, and many would state that they do not and would not subject their employees to slavery-like conditions or forced labour. Yet the aforementioned passport-retention case shows that practices that are not uncommon, for example, when managers wish to obtain security for an advance on payment, may cause the company to inadvertently put employees' human rights at risk. The transportation case shows that the human rights impacts of business partners, such as those who deliver goods to be transported, are equally important to the service industries as the productive industries. The wind-turbine case highlights the importance of respecting indigenous groups' culture and shows that human rights, such as the right to be included in decision-making that may affect one's life, are not only relevant for political processes but also for a business in its relations with local communities potentially affected by its projects.

The connection between a firm's actions and its human rights impacts may appear lofty from the moral perspective. However, when we look at international human rights law and seek to understand the interest that a specific human rights provision aims at protecting, it becomes possible to identify adverse impacts and to substantiate the problem with reference to a specific human right that prescribes a standard of conduct.

The International Bill of Rights, including the UDHR, and the ILO's core conventions were originally not addressed to firms but to states. Application to business contexts typically requires a 'translation' into practical business contexts. This translation is equally important in teaching human rights in a management context.

The fundamental human and labour law texts, noted in the preceding paragraph are relatively brief. Reading them helps obtain an appreciation of the range of issues that human rights cover and stimulates the student's or manager's reflection on contexts in which business activities might impact specific human rights. Taking a bottom-up approach is often useful; rather than thinking about forced labour or slavery as specific practices that we often associate with particular political regimes, think about what business practices may result in employees working under conditions where they are not free to leave (*the passport case* noted above). Rather than thinking of contractual relations with up- or downstream business relations as legal obligations to perform or as guarantees of economic income, think about the practical connection that they create to the impacts which may be caused by the business partner (*the transportation case*). Think of stakeholder engagement not just as a way to identify business potential but as related to the human right to participation in decision-making and an element in risk-based due diligence (the *wind-turbine case*).

A key message of the UNGPs is that while firms may do much good that may also contribute to fulfilling human rights – including since 2015 through implementation of the Sustainable Development Goals (SDGs) – firms should also do no harm. Regardless of what initiatives they embark upon they should ensure that they respect human rights in their own actions and those of their business relations, that is, **downstream and upstream value chains** (Ruggie, 2016). The *transportation case* illustrates the comprehensiveness and sometimes complexity of 'business relations'.

As the UNGC also refers to the UNGPs in its human rights guidance, businesses' integration of the UNGC Principles 1 and 2 is enhanced by knowledge of the UNGPs and understanding the managerial implications of human rights principles and obligations. The same applies to the application and integration of the UNGC labour Principles 3–6. The *passport-retention case* above illustrates how practices that may make economic sense to the manager must be undertaken with a broader appreciation of the human rights impacts.

TABLE 7.1 **Minimum age for employment**

Type of work	Developed countries (Years)	Developing countries (Years)
Light	13	12
Regular	15	14
Hazardous	18	18

(*Source*: UN Global Compact website, UNGC Principle 5, www.unglobalcompact.org/what-is-gc/mission/principles/principle-5)

To help the translation into a business context, it is recommended that students in regard to each of the Articles in the UDHR think about a situation in which a management practice could cause a violation of the right or rights protected by that Article, or a situation in which a company might be complicit of a violation. This engages students in applying UNGC Principles 1 and 2, and in thinking about the difference between the two principles. To support the 'translation' of human rights to business practices, it is further recommended that students also read the ICESCR and ICCPR, and reflect on the guidance that those texts provide for the manager in understanding the human rights implications of business practices.

Framing the four UNGC labour rights principles, the ILO fundamental conventions are brief but detailed. ILO conventions deal specifically with one topical right (such as the right to form trade unions and engage in collective negotiations). For example, ILO conventions 138 and 182 set explicit age limits for types of work permitted for youth and children. As Table 7.1 shows, this means that a commitment to avoid child labour does not mean that the company is left to its own discretion or to broad social expectations as to what constitutes child labour. It follows from the conventions that if national law provides for higher standards, the higher standards should be complied with.

Neither the UNGC nor the UNGPs are equipped with specific remedy institutions. For practical purposes, remedy institutions such as some National Human Rights Institutions or the National Contact Points (NCPs) under OECD's Guidelines for Multinational Enterprises provide remedies and facilitate their implementation. NCPs are national grievance institutions in countries that have acceded to OECD's Guidelines, but importantly, have extraterritorial reach: the NCP based in the home state of a company can deal with a complaint on a violation of OECD's Guidelines, if the host state where the alleged violation occurred has not acceded to the Guidelines. As the Guidelines are primarily acceded to by OECD states in the Global North, for practical purposes this provides the guidelines with application in the numerous other states in which many Global North-based companies conduct business, invest, produce or contract with suppliers. Providing evidence on the importance of this, the *transportation case* was considered by the home-state NCP but concerned actions in another country.

Summing up: Implications for management education

Human rights matter to business from a range of perspectives, including the social license to operate, managing economic and reputational risks, and ensuring that efforts to do well do not inadvertently cause human rights abuse. For this reason, managers need to know about human rights. The UNGC Principles 1–6 relate to human rights, and the UNGC refers to the UNGPs on Business and Human Rights, which set out the Corporate Responsibility to Respect Human Rights. The three cases above illustrate the challenges and importance of adhering to the human rights principles in the practical management context. For this reason, management education should introduce students to the International Bill of Rights and ILO's core labour standards, and invite students to reflect on management practices that risk infringing on the human rights protected by those international law instruments.

Many CSR-related teaching cases are also useful for teaching BHR; while they often do not treat human rights issues explicitly, many do contain human rights issues and students may be invited to identify those, drawing on the UNGPs, the International Bill of Rights and ILO's core labour standards. Students can be encouraged to analyze the cases from the perspective of the UNGPs to assess the adequacy of a corporate human rights policy. They can be encouraged to apply a human rights due diligence process in accordance with guidance contained in the UNGPs to identify human rights risks and discuss how those may be prevented or mitigated, and implications for corporate policies and internal as well as external communication.

While the UNGC has recently shifted some of its focus to the SDGs, the Ten Principles remain in place. This calls for retaining an emphasis on human rights when teaching how businesses may implement the UNGC. Teaching human rights in a business and management context complements general instruction on CSR, especially as broader CSR instruments have adopted and broadened the application of the risk-based due diligence approach elaborated by the UNGPs.

Educational institutions that have committed to the Principles for Responsible Management Education (PRME), which are developed to promote the UNGC, have a particular responsibility to consider how human rights may be included in management education. Teaching human rights issues in a management context helps faculty prepare their students to practice their professions responsibly with regard to human rights. Human rights in a business and management context should be taught at Bachelor's, Master's and Executive levels. Targeted courses offer best opportunities for comprehensively addressing human rights and their implications for business, but these topics should also be included in general courses on CSR, corporate governance, strategy, human resources and value chain management.

Further reading

Deva, S. (2012) *Regulating Corporate Human Rights Violations: Humanizing Business*, New York, NY: Routledge.

Monash University, Human Rights translated http://2.ohchr.org/english/issues/globaliza tion/business/docs/Human_Rights_Translated_web.pdf

References

Buhmann, K. (2015) 'Business and Human Rights: Understanding the UN Guiding Principles from the perspective of Transnational Business Governance Interactions', *Transnational Legal Theory* 6 (1): 399–434.

Buhmann, K. and F. Wettstein (2017) 'Business and Human Rights: Not just another CSR issue?', in J. Moon, M. Morsing and A. Rasche (eds) *Corporate Social Responsibility*, Cambridge, UK: Cambridge University Press, pp. 379–404.

Danish NCP/Maeglings- og klageinstitutionen for ansvarlig virksomhedsadfaerd (2014) Statement on retention of employees' identification papers, at http://businessconduct. dk/decisions (accessed 31 January 2017).

International Labour Organization (ILO) (1998) Declaration of Fundamental Principles and Rights at Work, http://ilo.org/public/english/standards/decl/declaration/text/ (accessed 31 January 2017).

Knox, J. H. (2012) 'The Ruggie Rules: Applying human rights law to corporations', in R. Mares (ed.) *The UN Guiding Principles on Business and Human Rights*, Antwerp, Belgium: Brill, pp. 51–83.

Ramirez, J. (2013) Vestas and the Indigenous Communities in Oaxaca, Mexico: Clean energy gets messy, Copenhagen Business School www.thecasecentre.org

Ruggie, J. (2013) *Just Business*, Boston, MA: Norton.

Ruggie, J. (2016) Keynote delivered to the 2016 UN Forum on Business and Human Rights, 14 November 2016, www.shiftproject.org/resources/viewpoints/globalization-sustainable-development-goals-business-respect-human-rights/ (accessed 31 January 2017).

UK NCP (2008) *Statement: DAS Air*, http://oecdwatch.org.cases/Case_14 (accessed 31 January 2017).

United Nations. (1948) Universal Declaration on Human Rights, available at www.un.org/ Overview/rights.html (accessed 31 January 2017).

United Nations. (1966a) International Covenant on Economic, Social and Cultural Rights, available at www.ohchr.org/EN/ProfessionalInterest/Pages/CESCR.aspx (accessed 31 January 2017).

United Nations. (1966b) International Covenant on Civil and Political Rights, www.ohchr. org/Documents/ProfessionalInterest/ccpr.pdf (accessed 31 January 2017).

United Nations. (2008) Protect, respect and remedy: A framework for business and human rights, UN Doc. A/HRC/8/5 (2008), 7 April 2008.

United Nations. (2011) Guiding Principles on Business and Human Rights: Implementing the United Nations 'Protect, Respect, Remedy' Framework. UN Doc. A/HRC/17/31, 21 March 2011.

Karin Buhmann is Professor with special responsibilities for Business & Human Rights. Employed at Copenhagen Business School (CBS), a Danish business university with a commitment to Corporate Social Responsibility and Sustainability, her research and teaching focus on human rights and social sustainability, public-private regulation and the juridification of CSR.

Section 3

Institutional
perspectives

8

Business and human rights

Learning experiences of an emerging agenda at a business school in São Paulo[1]

Marcus Vinicius P. Gomes
University of Exeter Business School, UK

Amon Barros
FGV-EAESP, São Paulo, Brazil

Maria Jose Tonelli
FGV-EAESP, São Paulo, Brazil

Abstract

This chapter describes the emergence of the human rights agenda at the Getulio Vargas Foundation Business School (FGV) in São Paulo and presents reflections on the pedagogical practices and research developed in collaboration with the FGV School of Law to address the human rights related impact of mega infrastructural projects in Brazil . It presents also organizational aspects of a joint elective course for three undergraduate programmes and the respective learning outcomes of the specific students' participative learning methods applied. The respective challenges and solutions on integrating human rights into business, public management and law-related education are presented. Recognizing the complexity of the issue, the chapter emphasizes the opportunities related to the implementation of Principles for Responsible Management Education, encouraging management educators in other countries to share their practices and learning.

Introduction

The importance of encompassing human rights as a central concern for business emerged in Brazil especially after the announcement that mega events (e.g., the 2014 FIFA World Cup and the 2016 Rio de Janeiro Olympics) would take place in the country. Besides that, Brazil has been experiencing a surge of huge infrastructural projects that added pressure to the capacity of the state to regulate its impacts on the communities and deliver essential services in the fulfilment of basic human rights. Under such a context, a window of opportunity to stress business' responsibilities to human rights was open.

In Brazil, the meaning of human rights was built around the struggles against the military dictatorship conducted by left-wing organizations. Such political context has contributed to foster human rights as an issue associated with left-wing ideologies. Therefore, the topic appeared as something that was not of general concern but rather of those who see themselves as part of the left in the political spectrum. This human rights trajectory holds similarities to the corporate social responsibility (CSR) agenda (Peña, 2014).

The chapter has two objectives. The first is to discuss the process of consolidating the field of human rights in a school of management that is one of the top-rated schools in Latin America and the most traditional in the country: FGV – Business School in São Paulo (FGV-EAESP). It is important to say that the school counted on the support from Direito São Paulo (FGV Law School). The experience related to developing the first course brought up the need to deal with pedagogical choices that could boost business and students' interest in the topic of human rights. The relevance of pedagogical aspects was necessary because this theme tended to be considered of minor concern in management courses. A way to promote interest on the topic was needed; the course also reflected the desire of the team involved in the project to stimulate critical thinking.

The second objective is to present some of the difficulties in institutionalizing the subject within business and management academia. They occurred in part because of the absence of other groups working and researching this theme. This context imposes even more difficulties in establishing debates with other business schools and business academics in the country.

Human rights and business

The initiative of approaching business and human rights has not yet been fully settled, even though huge steps have been taken in the last 15 years. Under the United Nations (UN) framework, such discussion started in 1999 when the then UN's Secretary-General Kofi Annan proposed the United Nations Global Compact (UNGC), to push forward business standards on human rights.

John Ruggie, a Human Rights and International Affairs professor from the John F. Kennedy School of Government at Harvard University, appointed in 2005 as the UN Secretary-General's Special Representative for Business and Human Rights, was in charge of laying the foundations and developing the guiding principles on business and human rights. During his mandate, Ruggie struggled to find a consensus around the business' responsibilities and duties regarding human rights. Finally, in 2011, the UN *Guiding Principles on Business and Human Rights* (UNGPs) were launched (Ruggie, 2013).

UNGPs were not the first attempt of the UN to tackle the issue of human rights and corporations. Such an idea was originally institutionalized as the UNGC, which is now the major CSR-related agreement in the world. The UNGC served as an inspiration for the UNGPs. While Ruggie was one of the leading designers of UNGC, corporations around the world had feared that if they had not taken action, governments would have tried to regulate their operations, creating barriers to free trade. Kofi Annan addressed such concern in his speech for the release of the Global Compact initiative at the World Economic Forum in Davos in 1999 (Annan, 1999).

Further discussions around the establishment of the UNGC related to business' human rights' responsibilities were attempted. However, the norms were considered too rigid since they were mandatory and corporations did not agree with binding responsibilities (Deva & Bilchitz, 2013). UN member states were also concerned about the possibility of losing their sovereignty over regulating business in their respective territories or losing competitiveness that could drive investments to other countries.

In his capacity as the Special Representative on the Issue of Human Rights and Transnational Corporations and Other Business Enterprises (SRSG), Ruggie directed his work towards the forging of a consensus (Ruggie, 2013). His approach was negotiated, aiming at building trust, especially among the business representatives. The idea was that without mandatory rules, with efforts on the gradual adoption up a learning curve, it would be easier to have business accepting the tri-factor related to their responsibility on human rights: *respect, protect* and *remedy*.

However, some think that the concessions to businesses went too far, leaving out some aspects of human rights ideas to gain broad acceptance within the business community (Deva & Bilchitz, 2013; Voiculescu, 2009). The main argument is that if the approach on human rights is too soft, it incurs the risk of giving the impression that human rights are just another form of CSR (Nolan, 2014). Yet, criticising initiatives directed at amplifying business responsibilities towards human rights is not the same as saying that they have no value at all. It is always better if the subject is on the table and there is ongoing discussion about how the approach can be improved.

Mega-projects and human rights course

Brazil faces a challenging environment that highlights human rights as an issue related to business practices. Because of the economic development and the infrastructure required for hosting both the 2014 FIFA World Cup and the 2016 Summer Olympic Games, many mega-projects (e.g. big stadiums, subway lines and port infrastructure) had been commissioned throughout the country.

The course on Human Rights and Mega-projects was a joint venture of FGV-Law School and FGV-EAESP, and involved students in management, public administration and law undergraduate courses. The course started in the second semester of 2014 and stimulated the students to conduct fieldwork on a project associated with the Football World Cup held that year in Brazil, specifically, a stadium built in the city of São Paulo. Throughout the semester the fieldwork took the form of the views of different stakeholders to achieve a proposition for action to deal with the challenges found.

The course was dedicated to promoting student reflection, but it also served the interest of the research group that was being formed at the same moment at FGV-EAESP. Moreover, it was possible to underline the complex relationships brought to light when performing stakeholders' analysis linked to major urban interventions.

The class discussions had kicked off after the mandatory reading of the UNGPs (Ruggie, 2013). This document was presented as a cornerstone of the current discussions on business and human rights, after the consolidation of the topic under the UNGC. The approach allowed the students to discuss the limits and possibilities of such proposal, especially when developing a diagnosis on its implications on human rights.

The course was designed with an active learning perspective, where students played an important role in building their knowledge. It was built around inter-actions among students and lecturers and included the discussion of real-life problems in the context of human rights and mega-projects. Examples of such real-life case studies are the impacts of the 'Itaquerão' Stadium on the fulfilment of children's rights; the responsibilities of big corporations about the use of natural resources; and how a Brazilian company explored the traditional know-ledge from communities in the Amazon forest to develop beauty products, which, consequently, disrupted the supply of those natural resources to the traditional communities.

Pedagogical aspects

Faculty from both the Law School and the Business School discussed how to develop a course that could take into consideration the complexity of the mega-projects' impacts on human rights and at the same time put in place an active learning approach (Bonwell & Eison, 1991). Since the beginning, there has been clarity about the need to break the teacher-centred approach and promote an environment in which students could take an active part in developing their knowledge. Moreover, the whole dynamic in the classroom was based on their research development.

Following such an active learning perspective, the course focused on the analysis of the impact on human rights. Three lecturers were responsible for the course. Each of them was present in every class, stimulating debate among the students and lecturers from the perspective of their original backgrounds, e.g., business management, public management and law.

This multidisciplinary approach encouraged students to debate on the mega-projects' human rights' impacts on local communities. The course aimed to develop awareness regarding the socio-environmental impacts of such large enterprises in the surrounding communities, by connecting the students with the actual stakeholders (i.e., individuals who were directly involved or affected in the studied case). The objective was to inspire and encourage students to develop alternative solutions that ensure human rights protection and reduce business risk.

The course was an elective component in the undergraduate programmes on: (i) Business Management; (ii) Public Management; and (iii) Law, and connected to the learning objectives of the three programmes. The intended learning outcomes of the course were:

1 Encourage critical thinking from a complex and specific context;

2 Develop research skills (such as collecting and analyzing data); and

3 Stimulate students to assume a well-grounded position on a particular case.

The final task for the student was to deliver a position paper containing an intervention proposal, offering diagnostics and solutions to the identified problems.

Working in the field

The students were required to study the Arena Corinthians construction's impact on its surroundings, especially the rights of children and teenagers. Thirty students had enrolled in this course, ten from each of the three mentioned undergraduate programmes.

The lecturers adopted three strategies to connect students with the research environment. The first one was to *organize a visit* to 'Comunidade da Paz', which suffered most of the impact from the construction of the Arena Corinthians stadium. Students had the opportunity to interview the staff from a non-governmental organization (NGO), public officials and people engaged with demonstrations against this mega-project.

The second strategy focused on *stimulating research activities*. To do so, the course comprised 60 hours per semester, half of them related to extracurricular activities. Students were required to collect data systematically – by conducting interviews with relevant actors from the Federal Prosecutor's Office, companies, state agencies, politicians and people engaged in demonstrations against the World Cup, or by researching a secondary source of data – and to analyze and present such data.

The third strategy was a *discussion with experts*: three experts on topics related to human rights violations were invited to give lectures and discuss the case at hand with students.

These three strategies allowed the students to reflect on the knowledge they were gaining and engage with the context to generate a proposal for intervention (a position paper was required as a final essay), combining both theory and practice.

Getting in touch with activists and communities affected by megaprojects helped students learn that big projects deliver huge externalities that have to be managed. In addition, students realized that spectacles such as the World Cup come at a great cost for local people, while the rest of the world may be enjoying the events. Therefore, it is difficult to assess the cost-benefit of such mega-projects, since on the one hand, they involve propaganda enjoyed by the host countries and exponential revenues for some companies, while on the other hand, such projects cause major disruptions in local communities.

Furthermore, the students learned that mega-projects have unintended consequences that might not have been captured by the media. It was clear for them that the negative effects were not restricted to those often showed in the media, such as corruption and public debt and also involve disruption of the way people live in communities, usually without due compensation. The most vulnerable populations also had to face some challenges such as the increase in child abuses prompted by the influx of population. It is fair to say that those impacts do not occur only in projects inside cities, as was the case of the stadiums, but are true for most interactions between big infrastructural projects and local populations.

Organizing classes and learning experiences

The course was designed in three blocks. The first block focused on discussing a theoretical framework on human rights. The second block put students in contact with the analyzed case and its context. Such a contact occurred through the interaction with the stakeholders of the case, focusing on examining their respective interests and expectations, as well as portraying the impacts of the project on each category of stakeholders. Finally, the third block sought to encourage students to assess the diagnosis they have made and propose possible interventions.

The students were divided into groups, sharing their research findings and opinions with teammates through the discussion facilitated by the lecturers, who also guided students on the next steps of their research. Based on participatory and student-centred methodologies, the course comprised lectures, research activities and fieldwork. The classes were not intended for knowledge acquisition exclusively via lectures. Concepts were presented through problems or situations discussed and experienced by the students. Classes were interactive, and this perspective was reflected in the layout of the classroom, with the students seated in roundtables with their group.

Some classes were designed to align the research findings and define the next steps of each group. In these classes the lecturers took a mediating role, promoting debate about what each group had found. Based on these interactions students created an actors' map, which displayed the context of the actors involved and their respective interactions. Such maps supported the definition and objectives for each group. Therefore, groups were sharing work tasks and information.

The presence of three lecturers in all classes required a lot of coordination. In each class, one lecturer would be responsible for coordinating the activities, while the other two facilitated students' interventions, including through coordinating time and allowing all who wished to participate and express their views. These roles were rotated for each class. Moreover, it was also decided that lecturers would sit among the students, not staying at the front or focusing on one area.

During the course, each group prepared a diagnosis regarding human rights violations. Based on this report, students developed a position paper, in which they took stands on the problems identified. At the same time, they elaborated on possible solutions and improvements aimed at human rights protection.

After a few sessions, the students become more proactive, taking responsibility for the execution of the suggested activities and sharing with their colleagues the conclusions and questions that arose during their research. Moreover, many of the students had no idea where Itaquera and Paz Communities were located within the city and how the construction of the stadium impacted these locations.

For a better understanding of this experience, two relevant aspects need to be emphasized: (i) FGV-EAESP and FGV Law School have a majority of elite students and most of them have no idea about the megalopolis they live in; and (ii) pedagogical practices that promote interactions with the environment are not usual in the Brazilian context, where lectures and in-classroom activities prevail. Besides that, the discussion of human rights on business environment is incipient and uncommon in the Brazilian context. By the end of the course, the complexities of management in a big metropolis and the diversity of environments present in the city became part of the repertoire of the students' knowledge and understanding. Along the way, students made visits on their own to the Itaquera region. This helped them build an awareness and proactive attitude, which have contributed positively to the realization of their work.

To sum up, it was possible to identify the following learning impacts:

- The engagement of the students during the course was visible; they became increasingly proactive, especially after the fieldwork and the contact with stakeholders;

- The complexity of human rights and the mega-project was highlighted. The students were able to identify that actors from different sectors create impact on how human rights violations are perceived. Such complexity materialized on the need to coordinate impact planning efforts among such a variety of actors;

- While developing their position papers, students acquired important skills to elaborate viable action plans. They had to identify the problem in a clear and specific manner and to highlight the stakeholders involved.

Lessons learned for addressing human rights in business school curricula

This section summarizes how the main challenges related to the new course were overcome, and suggests new opportunities for teaching human rights that emerged from contemporary society in the business schools.

Challenges

The fact that national and international accrediting agencies have been demanding that business schools address the topic creates a positive environment for the development of various business- and human-rights-related courses. It also develops awareness of the need to deal with human rights issues even though details and/or prescriptions are not provided. The lack of prescriptions and/or standards in this respect could be seen as a space of freedom in which the discussion of human rights could be adapted regarding the specification of a given context (Principles for Responsible Management Education (PRME) Principle 1 – Purpose and Principle 2 – Values).

As the world increasingly demands responsible and conscious managers and businesses, opportunities are created for teaching human rights. Moreover, since regulations are still being developed, students should learn both the consequences for businesses that such governance mechanisms bring and the impact of their consequences on human rights. An active learning approach is essential to engage students on the complexity of human rights, as well as its consequences for businesses. This experience showed, in practice, that when students are exposed to this topic, they could learn and incorporate such repertoire into their discourses. If the course was not offered (even though as an elective discipline), they would not have the opportunity of exploring such subjects. As elite students are prepared to assume leadership positions in companies, they could have a better idea of the impact of megaprojects on the local population and the necessity of humanitarian logistics for the reorganization of communities.

One challenge in designing and implementing the course on the subject of mega-projects and human rights in the Business School was the lack of literature in the field, especially in Portuguese. To respond to the challenge, discussions were organized around CSR, governance and, more specifically, the UNGC. Also, a research group was established within the Business School. The group mapped publications about the subject with a bibliometric study and noticed that the interest in the subject had broadly increased over the last 5 years. In Brazil, relevant publications in Portuguese are starting to appear, but still in small numbers. There is still a long way to go: Brazil has just experienced one of the largest environmental catastrophes in the world with the rupture of a tailing dam operated by Samarco mining company in the city of Mariana. After a couple of months of attention, the topic almost vanished from the media coverage, barely returning again upon the anniversary of the disaster.

The choices that were made during the course emphasize the importance of research (PRME Principle 4). Research is pivotal for advancing the understanding of how human rights violations took place in the "Comunidade da Paz" and of how to develop a mechanism to avoid it happening again. The research principle goes hand-in-hand with the method employed in the course (PRME Principle 3, Method), as it empowered the students to learn and develop their individual perspectives regarding the topic.

What they have learned from the case studied is not a universal solution. During the research and teaching/learning process, it was clear that such a complex topic as human rights and business should be tackled by actively involving other stakeholders [PRME Principles 5, Partnerships; and 6, Dialogue]. No single government, nor corporation, will be able to prevent human rights violations. This is the reason why governance mechanisms are arising, and why partnership and dialogue become essential.

Another challenge lies in the fact that human rights are a transdisciplinary topic and confining it to only one course does not allow its full potential to be realized. Management subfields will also face specific challenges regarding addressing human rights. A course in logistics may take into consideration the supply chain and its working relations, while a course in finance could discuss money laundering, tax evasion and other issues that may be associated with human rights violations.

The final challenge derives from the fact that human rights are not yet institutionalized within management literature. Consequently, academics have little incentive to study and teach it. Students, too, do not demand that human rights should be covered in their curriculum. In this sense, discussion of human rights may seem totally detached from pragmatic interests. Human rights are part of change that is already happening in governance arenas, which will require that local and global businesses adapt. Such a challenge is associated with the UNGC Principle 2 (Purpose), as students should develop skills and capacities for designing businesses that consider future generations, assuming that human-rights-related values go beyond that of considering their violation as an operational and reputational risk.

Opportunities

Human rights will gain importance in the world of business as the UNGC framework develops and raises more supporters. Social movements will increase pressure for better practices regarding business, social and environmental impacts. New governance mechanisms will be created, which will require businesses to comply and face these challenges. In such a context, the human-rights-related education should not be framed only as a business technique but rather as preparation for citizenship.

The course emphasizes how it is possible to integrate human rights and management learning. This experience promoted the debate on the human rights in a leading national business school that can be replicated in other schools in Brazil as well as in other countries. Both the experience and articles that have been produced in the Brazilian context offer a huge opportunity to expand the debate in the country. More generally, there is enough evidence that innovative approaches to learning are essential for preparing students for complex situations both here and abroad. Looking retrospectively, the PRME principles, particularly when examined in all their aspects, as was the case in the course described, come as a useful tool to guide the context-specific approach described in the chapter.

This may also encourage management educators in developing and developed countries to engage in further dialogue and share the respective learning experiences aimed at fostering the importance of human rights as a curriculum topic and more importantly as a guiding principle for business.

References

Annan, K. (1999). Secretary-general proposes global compact on human rights, labour, environment, in address to World Economic Forum in Davos. Retrieved at: http://un.org/press/en/1999/19990201.sgsm6881.html.

Bonwell, C. C. and Eison, J. A. (1991). *Active learning: Creative excitement in the classroom.* Washington DC: Association for the Study of Higher Education.

Deva, S., & Bilchitz, D. (2013). *Human rights obligations of business: Beyond the corporate responsibility to respect?* (Vol. 1). Cambridge, UK: Cambridge University Press.

Nolan, J. (2014). Refining the Rules of the Game: The Corporate Responsibility to Respect Human Rights. *Utrecht Journal of International and European Law, 30*(78), 7–23.

Peña, A. M. (2014). The Political Trajectory of the Brazilian CSR Movement. *Critical Perspectives on International Business, 10*(4), 310–328.

Ruggie, J. G. (2013). *Just business: Multinational corporations and human rights* (1st edn). New York-London: Norton & Company.

Voiculescu, A. (2009). Human Rights and the New Corporate Accountability: Learning from Recent Developments in Corporate Criminal Liability. *Journal of Business Ethics, 87*(0), 419–432.

Marcus Vinicius P. Gomes is currently a lecturer in Organization & Sustainability at University of Exeter Business School. He received his doctorate from FGV-EAESP (Brazil, 2014). Marcus is interested in critical perspectives on Business and Society. His research focuses on how organizations influence the context in which they are embedded.

marcus.gomes@exeter.ac.uk

Amon Barros received his PhD in management from UFMG (Brazil). He is currently a lecturer in organization studies at FGV-EAESP in São Paulo. Amon's research interests are in management history and the construction of the managerial knowledge and the impacts of business on society.

amon.barros@fgv.br

Maria Jose Tonelli has an undergraduate degree in Psychology and has a PhD in Social Psychology from PUC-SP. Since 1988 she is a professor at FGV-EAESP. Professor Tonelli held some administrative posts at FGV, and she has been playing an active role in Brazil's academic life in the management field.

maria.jose.tonelli@fgv.br

9

Shaping the PRME research agenda

A case study on students' engagement and contribution in applied sciences

Lutz E. Schlange

University of Applied Sciences Eastern Switzerland, Switzerland

Abstract

This chapter elaborates on the process of implementation of the Principles for Responsible Management (PRME)-related research by developing a comprehensive and topical research agenda for a given tertiary education institution. Its purpose is to share experiences gained regarding the motivation, initiation, provision and supervision of diverse sustainability-related academic activities. It highlights some key lessons, in particular, regarding the role of student-initiated research, and its linkages with prevalent research activities by the formally acknowledged institutional actors such as the university board, its head of research, its research grant commission and research faculty. While tying in PRME, the case illustrates some key mechanisms how its fourth principle, Research, may become instrumental for operationalising and realising the ideals and values embodied in the principles of the UN Global Compact and PRME at large.

Background

The fourth principle of the Principles for Responsible Management Education (PRME), Research, emphasises the need for business schools *"to engage in conceptual and empirical research that advances our understanding about the role, dynamics, and impact of corporations in the creation of sustainable social, environmental and economic value*".[1] Since its inception, the principle has stood somewhat on the side line when compared with the attention the other five principles have gained, in particular, the first (*Purpose*), second (*Values*) and third (*Method*), which centre on the core purpose of business schools, i.e. reorienting the education of future business leaders. Through the sharing of information on progress mechanism (PRME sharing information on progress (SIP) reports), over the last decade PRME signatories have been reporting substantial research output in the fields of corporate social responsibility and sustainability. However, only a few PRME signatory schools have shared specific experiences that they may have made when integrating the responsible management education (RME)-related research into their institutional agenda from the bottom up.[2] They point out the need to adopt an institutional approach by having a school's management define clear strategic priorities, allocate related funding, and create respective institutional arrangements (e.g. Donaldson, 2013). However, for many PRME signatories there are good reasons to question the viability of this approach. The required change effort may consist of rewriting the DNA of established research paradigms and programmes. Under commonplace conditions, respective defensive routines may impede effective progress and make it more likely that research activities, by and large, will continue to adhere to a 'business as usual' mode.

Meanwhile, within the PRME network, academic reception of research on RME has seen volunteering efforts such as the self-organizing activities of working groups and/or regional chapters organizing theme-focused workshops, seminars, conferences and book projects. Recently, this development has led to the organization of RME Research conferences as regular components of the PRME annual agenda. Supported by some of the PRME regional chapters and working groups, the conferences are expected to evolve into the fora, which could serve the particular needs of researchers, such as professional exchange on thematic priorities, networking with peers, and developing prospective channels for publication.

Research activities, however, inform state-of-the-art education and involve students in many ways.[3] They appear to offer a great variety of opportunities to expose students to a more value-driven form of exploratory learning. This chapter argues that research at higher education institutions deserves a second look as a means to encourage and drive change, specifically under conservative institutional settings that are averse to change and risks.

Therefore, the purpose of this chapter is to share specific experiences from the process that includes motivation, initiation, provision and supervision of diverse RME-related academic research activities in a specific institution of higher education, the University of Applied Sciences HTW Chur, Switzerland. A formerly teaching-oriented institution, the case of HTW Chur exemplifies the struggles when building a research agenda while at the same time introducing and integrating the hitherto disregarded idea of RME. It derives some key lessons by giving evidence of the mechanisms that underpin an emerging landscape of theme-focused research projects, which are contributing to adjusting and reframing the institutional agenda.

Institutional context

Research at the University of Applied Sciences HTW Chur today is focused on six fields: entrepreneurial management; tourism and leisure; regional economic policy; architecture and civil engineering; information and communication; and, as of late, photonics and ICT. Over the last two decades, the University has organized its applied research activities in institutes that cover the respective thematic domains.

In the course of its evolution, research in the areas of corporate responsibility and sustainable development was not assigned a high priority. Rather, in line with the view of knowledge generation as a human activity, whose primary purpose is to serve economic progress and human well-being, these two areas were seen as negligible addenda to the conventional agenda. When HTW Chur became a PRME signatory in 2009, its research was hardly reflecting these newly adopted, value-based principles at all. By mere coincidence, a few projects had some weak linkages with the concept of sustainable development, in particular in the areas of tourism and architecture research, while in the management field research on corporate responsibility was largely neglected. As a result, in the early days the research community at HTW Chur did not view PRME as a platform to inform its activities.

In order to comply fully with the Swiss federal law governing the universities of applied sciences, HTW Chur was established in 2000 through a fusion of two previously independent schools of business and engineering. Ever since, the University has seen a high cadence of consecutive change initiatives involving all of its parts. The Federal law required development of a programme of applied research activities, which was putting the predominantly teaching-focused institution under pressure. In order to meet the formal requirements for obtaining external funding for research grant allocation, Swiss universities of applied sciences are legally obliged to concentrate on applied research and knowledge transfer, which must be delivered in cooperation with partners from industry.[4] While in the early days, the new research mandate was implemented in a rather incoherent and ad-hoc manner, the results of the on-going efforts to establish institutional structures and processes to support the emerging research activities were gradually materialising.

Consequentially, upon signing with PRME, the critical challenge was to integrate the respective principles into the institutional change processes, specifically those in the area of research. Triggered by its first PRME SIP report in 2010, the role of corporate responsibility and sustainability for HTW Chur gained impetus. The first two SIP reports were instrumental in highlighting the relevance of these topics for the institution.

The 'HTW Chur Research Map 2012–2016', which overlapped with the preparation of the two SIP reports and was introduced as an instrument to better align research activities, turned out to be another milestone for establishing RME-related research as legitimate part of the institutional agenda. In particular, researchers from the management, tourism and economic policy institutes claimed their stakes in these topical areas and were therefore eager to put their respective future research interests on the map. As a result, the final version of the document formally acknowledges the domains of 'corporate responsibility' in management and 'regional sustainable development' in economic policy and tourism research. Since this map presupposes potential access to internal research grants, securing funding for projects in the respective thematic fields has been significantly facilitated.

Notwithstanding these important achievements, scepticism still prevails regarding whether value-driven research at HTW Chur can obtain sufficient funding, either from internal or, more importantly, from external sources, to achieve a significant share in its research output.

Emerging institutional research agenda

While the discursive process of devising an institutional research map clearly reflected preliminary board support, the assignation of corporate responsibility and sustainability as 'cross-sectoral' research areas also conveyed the message that they were far from being established and still needed further development to gain a wider acceptance. On the contrary, this approach was advantageous as it proved to be quite compatible with the prevalent organizational culture. Not 'beating the drums' too loudly for the matter at stake actually helped to open a new, hitherto unpaved avenue, which made it possible to build the research agenda in a rather tacit manner. Doing otherwise might have merely enhanced the reluctance by proponents of a more conventional approach.

As a result, the following RME-related research activities received institutional support at the HTW Chur.

In the field of *entrepreneurial management,* echoing the UN Global Compact's 10th Principle (*Anti-Corruption*), as well as related research themes, the first, and the most important activity stream was developed. Adopting a business view, in a seminal project carried out together with Credit Suisse and Switzerland Global Enterprise, the corruption-related risks were investigated in order to derive strategies for the Swiss SMEs operating abroad (Becker *et al.*, 2012; Hauser, & Kronthaler, 2013; Hauser & Hogenacker, 2014). Next, a project involving Transparency International Switzerland examined business students' perception of corruption-related risks (Becker *et al.*, 2013). In continuing this approach by involving TATA Interactive Systems AG and Siemens Schweiz AG as business partners, an integrated training tool 'HONEST' was developed to help prevent corruption among young professionals (Hauser & Nieffer, 2016).[5] Consecutive research projects examined the risks associated with the use of big data as well as determinants for a successful implementation and execution of in-house whistle-blower reporting systems. The latter approach has been transferred to the public domain in a project investigating whistle-blowing in the media in Switzerland (Dahinden *et al.*, 2016). As of late, a new research stream has started focusing on ethical challenges of big data and the risks associated with their proper handling.

In a related work stream, in line with the UN Global Compact's Principles 9 (*Environmentally Friendly Technologies*) and 10 (*Anti-Corruption*) research projects included subjects such as sustainable management practices, supply chain governance and the conceptual development of sustainability-driven entrepreneurship (Schlange, 2007, 2009). 'Circular economy and sustainable service design' involve business partners from the mobility, new renewable energies and recycling industries under the title 'SusQual – Sustainable Quality of services from a customer perspective' (Schlange *et al.*, 2016).

In the field of *tourism and leisure science*, referring to UN Global Compact's (UNGC) Principles 7 (*Environmental Challenges*), 8 (*Environmental Responsibility*) and 9 (*Environmentally Friendly Technologies*) research projects dealt with the impact of climate change on the tourism industry and its respective resilience (e.g. Wyss *et al.*, 2015), circular economy and energy systems, sustainable development of tourism destinations simulating qualitative growth and, more in general, sustainability assessment methodologies for mountainous regions (e.g. Luthe & Silberberger, 2015).

Correspondingly, research in the field of sustainable *regional economic policy* covered food and agriculture industries, potential synergies between organic agriculture and the tourism industry. A Swiss National Science Foundation funded project is currently looking at Swiss energy futures, in particular the corporate responsibility of hydropower companies regarding the long-term future (Hediger, 2016).

In a number of the above-mentioned projects, students played an important role in supporting the formally acknowledged institutional actors, i.e. research faculty. Since the Swiss higher education legislation reserves doctoral programmes only for the traditional universities, prospects for junior researchers at the universities of applied sciences are less favourable. Nonetheless, the HTW Chur students showing a stronger interest in academic research may be regarded as an important complementary resource. Going beyond their collaboration in specific projects run by the research institutes, they have proven to be constructive also for the development of the institutional research agenda.

The role of student-initiated research

Since 2008, the advent of the Masters of Science (MSc) programmes at the Swiss universities of applied sciences has triggered the admission of students showing interest in research. Besides being formally integrated into research projects, it has become current practice that these students select their MSc thesis topics on subjects that are related to, or build upon, current institutional research projects. In this context, providing MSc students with a listing of the ongoing research themes has shown to be an effective model:

i   to develop an initial outline of distinct ideas for future research before formally approaching funding partners (probing);

ii to elaborate on distinct aspects of an already running, fully or partially funded project, to extend its scope (widening); and

iii to build upon the findings of a completed project in order to apply and deepen its outcomes (refining).

In sum, the combination of ongoing efforts to create a diverse, though coordinated, agenda with bottom-up initiatives from loosely coupled groups of researchers catalysed the emergence of an overriding axis on corporate responsibility and sustainable development, which has been echoed by the overall institutional research map.

Challenges and opportunities for students' involvement

Coordinating student-led research in line with the emerging research agenda and integrating it into the different work streams poses two important challenges: first, from the perspective related to research subjects and timing, and second, from the quality assurance's point of view.

Research subjects and timing

The first challenge involves coordinating research projects that are partially funded, or are highly likely and/or expected to receive funding, as well as those that are fully funded. For the projects based on support from internal research grants, financial resources are quite restricted. Therefore, research staff has a strong incentive to involve students as collaborators. Researchers, who teach as well, have shown an inclination to promote actively their subjects to attract students from their teaching modules as research assistants. Experience has shown that in topics related to corporate responsibility and sustainability, students find an additional motivation to engage in the respective assignments to define their individual research theme while extending it beyond the initial mandate. For instance, in a project on ethical challenges of big data, a group of MSc students was assigned to prepare some basic considerations catering to the project needs. Similarly, in an MSc thesis project referring to Schlange (2009), characteristics of sustainability-driven entrepreneurship were empirically tested.

In contrast, fully funded research projects typically rely on grants from external sources. These offer opportunities to initiate research activities by students who are taking part as scientific collaborators. In this situation, however, the likelihood of coordinating research subjects in a way that would be more conducive to meeting the interest of different partners has risks that students may be deterred from the potential 'win–win' due to time constraints set by their compact learning agendas. For instance, in a fully funded research project on sustainable service design, which is a core subject in the MSc curriculum, it has proven difficult to engage interested students during the respective project timespan. There are chances that once this project has been completed, there will be follow-up steps to further refine the original research results, where students will find it worthwhile to continue.

Thus, while resources are scarcer for internally than externally funded research, both situations call for an improved coordination of the theme-specific timelines around the specific project requirements. Strategies to meet this challenge included pro-active communication with incoming MSc students, promotion of corporate responsibility and sustainable development as core research topics (including engagement in PRME), and responsiveness to the needs of students who are showing inclination to engage themselves for these topics.

Above all, any initiative from the students' side in this regard was duly considered. For instance, in one of the most prominent cases, an MSc student asked for support to define a thesis subject around her experiences from on-the-job training with GIZ[6] in Dhaka, Bangladesh. The resulting thesis (Blumer, 2015) not only showed how student-initiated research could be integrated in the institutional research agenda and initiate activities in the corporate responsibility and sustainability realms, but also demonstrated how high-quality standards could be achieved. This may inspire the research community of a given institution, thereby addressing the second main challenge, i.e. quality assurance.

Quality assurance

Defining thorough scientific quality standards is a particularly important issue within applied research. In many ways, applied research has been despised as the "ugly sister" of basic research. Building on the seminal work of Dubin (1978) and Lynham (2002), Swanson and Chermack (2013) have developed a framework for theory building in applied sciences, which has proven to comprise a suitable guideline for student-led research projects. As a methodological concept, their proposed five-phase framework, consisting of (1) conceptualising, (2) operationalising, (3) confirming, (4) applying and (5) refining, was instrumental to a seminal MSc thesis project, which has reached the highest qualitative standards.[7] A number of other thesis projects have also been applying this methodological framework as a firmly grounded scientific base. While not all of them have managed to reach similar high-quality levels, they all have provided a sound methodological base and proved to be compatible with academic expectations.

Since requirements of sound research practice are an important quality issue at universities of applied sciences in general, it should merit attention as such. Experience has shown that the institutional internal research community will take notice of excellent research practice. In addition, it helps to render additional impetus for research activities related to corporate responsibility and sustainability as precursors of high-quality academic work.

Key lessons and conclusion

The emerging process of organization and implementation of the research agenda in the fields of corporate responsibility and sustainability at HTW Chur have led to three key lessons: first, the role of a coordinated, though inconspicuous effort by all parties interested in furthering the cause; second, the existence and value of a latent, untapped potential for student engagement in research; and third, the necessity of patiently persisting in reaching the overarching objective, i.e. the installation of corporate responsibility and sustainability as formally and institutionally acknowledged fields of scientific ambitions.

Regarding coordination, it has been found to be of utmost value to regularly report the respective research achievements, both internally and as part of the institutional obligations as a PRME signatory. The biannual reporting procedure has facilitated developing an overview of the respective activities, thereby providing a coherent picture of what the various actors have been researching.

With respect to student engagement, it has been instrumental in triggering, exposing, amplifying and highlighting research achievements. Triggering insofar as students may question distinct curricular presumptions, for instance in connection with responsible business conduct, and bring in their own ideas for research. Exposing their innovative ideas upon completing their research, students may act as potential guest lecturers in related teaching subjects such as business in society, corporate responsibility and responsible management, thereby amplifying their approaches in the classroom discussion.

As the final point, highlighting the academic quality assurance needs to be given a high priority. The supplementary recognition gained from peer reviews may further increase the importance of these subjects.

In summary, student-led research renders additional momentum to the activities of academic staff. Moreover, it leads to self-reinforcing activities as student demand for supervision in the fields of corporate responsibility and sustainability has been gradually increasing over the years.

Finally, persistence, coupled with a patient attitude, has been key for the successful implementation of the described emerging research agenda. The most important success factor in this regard lies in the networking activities within the internal research community, which enabled sharing the results of mutual efforts and making them visible at university board level.

To conclude, this chapter delineates an emergent strategy for the institutional implementation of research in corporate responsibility, sustainability, and RME. The experiences and insights into the case suggest that it is possible to make breakthroughs in the development of an RME research agenda even in those business schools where the respective research subjects have been challenged by conservative mindsets and prevalent assumptions that can obstruct this agenda. In this context, engaging students has proven to bring new opportunities.

In addition, while building on selected UNGC principles, it demonstrates how the specific role of research may be conducive to improve integration of PRME principles regarding teaching methods, partnerships and dialogue, and, finally, to promote purpose and values of PRME.

It is hoped that the chapter will inspire colleagues who are striving to implement their coordinated research activities under similar institutional conditions.

Notes

1 www.unprme.org
2 Audencia Nantes School of Management, France; Euromed Management, Marseilles, France; University of Stellenbosch Business School, Bellville, South Africa (PRME 2012); Yunus Centre for Social Business and Health, Glasgow Caledonian University, Scotland, United Kingdom (PRME 2013).
3 For instance, Frondigoun (2013) gives an account of how involvement in community projects may help advance a better understanding of students of the role of research in a real-life context.
4 In particular, the Swiss Federal Commission for Technology and Innovation (CTI).
5 This was featured in the PRME Anti-Corruption working group's "PRME Anti-Corruption Toolkit". http://actoolkit.unprme.org/
6 GIZ (Deutsche Gesellschaft für Internationale Zusammenarbeit) is a provider of international cooperation services for sustainable development (www.giz.de).
7 In fact, Blumer's (2015) thesis won the 2015 Swiss Entrepreneurship Award (cf http://bit.ly/1qCReJg).

References

Becker, K., Hauser, C. and Kronthaler, F. (2012). Auslandskorruption bei Schweizer Unternehmen. *Die Volkswirtschaft/La Vie Économique.* 85(10).

Becker, K., Hauser, C. and Kronthaler, F. (2013). Fostering management education to deter corruption: What do students know about corruption and its legal consequences? *Crime, Law and Social Change.* 60(2): 227–240.

Blumer, H. (2015). *Internal Communication in Bangladeshi Ready-Made Garment Factories and its Connection to Labor Unrest.* BestMasters, Berlin: Springer.

Dahinden, U., Francolino, V., Hauser, C. and Nieffer, R. (2016). *Whistleblower und Medien in der Schweiz – Situationsanalyse und Empfehlungen für die Zukunft,* Chur, Switzerland: HTW Chur Verlag.

Donaldson, C. (2013). Researching poverty alleviation through third-sector initiatives in Scotland. *Inspirational Guide for the Implementation of PRME: Second Edition – Learning to go Beyond,* Sheffield, UK: Greenleaf Publishing, pp. 143–148.

Dubin, R. (1978). *Theory building.* Revised edition, New York: Free Press.

Frondigoun, L. (2013). Social science student community engagement. *Inspirational Guide for the Implementation of PRME: Second Edition – Learning to go Beyond,* Sheffield, UK: Greenleaf Publishing, pp. 135–142.

Hauser, C. and Hogenacker, J. (2014). Do firms proactively take measures to prevent corruption in their international operations? *European Management Review.* 11(3–4): 223–237.

Hauser, C. and Kronthaler, F. (2013). Neue Märkte, neue Risiken – Empirische Evidenz zum Korruptionsrisiko für den international aktiven Mittelstand. *Zeitschrift für Betriebswirtschaft (ZfB).* SI 4: 37–60.

Hauser C. and Nieffer, R. (2016). Korruptionsprävention mittels eines computerbasierten Planspiels. In: Wolf, S. and Graeff, P. (eds): *Korruption und Korruptionsbekämpfung – Die Vermittlung in Lehre, Unterricht und Weiterbildung,* Wiesbaden, Germany: Springer.

Hediger, W. (2016). The Corporate Social Responsibility of Hydropower Companies in Alpine Regions – A Welfare-economic Approach. *39th Annual IAEE International Conference* (19–22 June), Bergen, Norway.

HTW Chur (2012). *PRME sharing information on progress report #2* (Chur), http://bit.ly/V8FxHw.

HTW Chur (2014). *PRME sharing information on progress report #3* (Chur), http://bit.ly/1COBcP2

Luthe, T. and Silberberger, J. (2015). Assessing and communicating urban sustainability: Comparing the Ecological Footprint and the CERCLE multi-criteria indicator set. In: Condie J. and Cooper A. M. (eds): *Dialogues of Sustainable Urbanisation: Social Science Research and Transitions to Urban Contexts.* Penrith, Australia: University of Western Sydney. pp. 84–90. Available online at: www.victoria.ac.nz/hppi/images/Dialogues-of-Sustainable-Urbanisation.pdf.

Lynham, S. A. (2002). Quantitative research and theory building: Dubin's method. *Advances in Developing Human Resources.* 4: 242–276,

Principles for Responsible Management (PRME) (2012). *Inspirational Guide for the Implementation of PRME – Placing Sustainability at the Heart of Management Education,* Leeds, UK: GSE Research.

Principles for Responsible Management (PRME) (2013). *Inspirational Guide for the Implementation of PRME: Second Edition – Learning to go Beyond,* Sheffield, UK: Greenleaf Publishing).

Schlange, L. E. (2007). What drives sustainable entrepreneurs? *Indian Journal of Economics and Business,* 7(2): 35–45.

Schlange, L. E. (2009). Stakeholder identification in sustainability entrepreneurship. *Greener Management International,* 55:13–32.

Schlange, L. E., Jüttner, U., Schaffner, D. and Bothe, S. (2016). Customer value perceptions of sustainable services – Findings from four cases. *IRSSM7* (12–13 August), Bangkok, Thailand.

Swanson, R. A. and Chermack, T. J. (2013). *Theory Building in Applied Disciplines,* San Francisco, CA: Berrett-Koehler.

Wyss, R., Luthe, T. and Abegg, B. (2015). Building resilience to climate change: The role of cooperation in alpine tourism networks. *Local Environment: The International Journal of Justice and Sustainability.* 20(8):908–922.

Lutz E. Schlange, PhD, is Professor of entrepreneurial marketing and academic head of PRME, University of Applied Sciences HTW Chur, Switzerland; Speaker of PRME regional chapter DACH; Lectures, researche and deals with publications about corporate responsibility and organizational learning, futures studies, marketing, sustainability entrepreneurship, ecological management, and energy transitions.

lutz.schlange@htwchur.ch

10

Beyond the classroom

Embedding responsible
management principles,
practices, and possibilities
in our business schools

Anthony F. Buono
Bentley University, USA

Abstract

This chapter discusses a multi-pronged approach to implementing PRME
and a commitment to responsible management education, encompassing: (1)
the classroom [Principles for Responsible Management Education (PRME),
Principles 2: Values & 3: Method]; (2) campus life [Principles 1: Purpose 2:
Values and 7: Institutional]; (3) the production of knowledge [Principle 4:
Research]; and (4) outreach to the business and not-for-profit worlds [Prin-
ciples 5: Partnerships and 6: Dialog]. A case study is used to illustrate how a
business university is attempting to meet this challenge through the creation of
its Alliance for Ethics and Social Responsibility. Going beyond curricular
innovation per se, the focus is on how the PRME principles can be embedded
throughout the institution by working on the implicit dimensions of the
educational experience.

PRME implementation challenge

As business schools are being increasingly challenged to instill a 'beyond-the-bottom-line' mind-set in their orientation and practices, it is useful to examine the ways in which these institutions approach the ideal of responsible management. While much of the discussion in higher education surrounding the implementation of the United Nations Global Compact (UNGC) and its Principles for Responsible Management Education (PRME) focuses on curriculum innovation and faculty development (e.g. Fort, 2016; Hockerts *et al.*, 2015; Shrivastava, 2010), it is important to realize that these are only two, albeit critically important, components of the process. As research in this area suggests, although some business schools have added a broad array of courses on ethics, corporate responsibility and sustainability in their curricula, the majority of these courses are electives that are disconnected from core business disciplines (e.g. accounting, finance, operations) and institutional practices (Rasche *et al.*, 2013; Solitander *et al.*, 2012; Sterling, 2004). In fact, some observers contend that although business schools appear to be responding to increasing pressures and expectations (e.g. emerging accreditation criteria, social commentary criticism and student activism) to incorporate responsible management education through the creation of new courses, centres and committees, many of these efforts are decoupled from day-to-day institutional realities (Rasche and Gilbert, 2015).

Drawing on a case study of the creation of a campus-wide network of programs and initiatives focused on ethics, social responsibility, civic engagement and sustainability, the chapter examines how a multi-pronged approach to the PRME principles can build on the implicit dimensions of the educational experience – what has been referred to as the 'hidden curriculum' (Blasco, 2012). In an attempt to fully meet the *purpose* (Principle 1: Purpose) of PRME, the underlying challenge is to integrate those core areas – from what faculty do in the classroom and their research, to how organizational members live their lives on campus and interact with external stakeholders – in ways that can enhance the meaning of responsible management for our students and ourselves.

Towards a holistic approach to responsible management education

The PRME emphasize the need for a holistic approach to responsible management education (Forray and Leigh, 2012; Kell and Haertle, 2011). However, largely out of respect for contextual differences in institutional norms and practices across its global signatories, the initiative has stopped short of offering specific guidelines for how this might be accomplished (Rasche, 2010;

Waddock *et al.*, 2010). While dedicated courses across the curriculum are clearly an important part of responsible management education, the need to look beyond the classroom itself should be just as obvious. As Blasco (2012) has argued, the myriad signals that students are given about appropriate conduct – communicated in many subtle ways – go well beyond formal curricular content. These inherent dimensions of the education process – codes of conduct and honour codes, socialization routines and extracurricular activities, testing and assessment procedures, faculty comments and behaviours in and out of class – significantly influence student values, attitudes and behaviours (Blasco, 2012; Gair and Mullins, 2001; Trevino and McCabe, 1994). Reflecting Argyris and Schön's (1978) distinction between espoused values (what people say they do) and 'theory-in-use' (i.e. enacted values that reflect what they actually do), the notion of the hidden curriculum differentiates the 'curriculum as designed and curriculum in action' (Barnett and Coate, 2005, p. 3; Blasco, 2012).

As analyses of corporate scandals and unethical business activity suggest, the culture of a community or organization is a far more significant determinant of moral behaviour than any set of requirements, laws, regulations or guidelines (Lowenstein, 2004). Cheating and cutting corners, for example, which appear to be ubiquitous phenomena in American life, are rampant on college campuses (Callahan, 2004; Trevino *et al.*, 2012). If the culture and operation of business schools do not fully embrace an ethical and responsible approach to business education, it is hardly surprising that later in their careers these same students will be likely to cut corners and engage in questionable behaviours – especially when the stakes are that much greater. Since school campuses are where students hone their learning about enacting ethical practices in their day-to-day lives (Swanson, 2004; Trevino and McCabe, 1994), a cross-institutional approach is necessary to infuse reflection about responsible conduct into all activities. These considerations also reflect the commitment of PRME signatories to ensure that their organizational practices (as Principle 7: Institutional) 'serve as examples of the values and attitudes we convey to our students' (PRME, 2016, p. 30).

Building an alliance

Within this context, the chapter examines the creation of the Bentley University Alliance for Ethics and Social Responsibility (referred to as the Alliance), emphasizing an underlying process-oriented framework that other schools and programs can draw on to enhance the role that PRME can play on their campuses. It is written from both an institutional and personal perspective, reflecting a challenging, ongoing journey.

As one of the original signatories of the PRME initiative, Bentley's commitment is reflected in the University's mission to 'educate creative, ethical, and socially responsible organizational leaders by creating and disseminating impactful knowledge within and across business and the arts and sciences.' The Alliance, which has been the main institutional mechanism for implementing and supporting PRME, is a collaborative effort dedicated to encourage and promote an institution-wide commitment to ethics, social responsibility, sustainability and civic engagement. While many successful initiatives in these areas were already under way at the institution, they were often isolated and disconnected from each other. It was apparent that they would benefit collectively from further collaboration, coordination and a clear direction.

A unique feature of the Alliance is its integrative focus, which reflects the PRME initiative's commitment to inspire responsible management and responsible management education. Its mission is to amplify and extend the work of the core centres and initiatives on campus that are focused on ethics, social responsibility, sustainability and civic engagement, supporting and encouraging greater awareness of, respect for, and commitment to these areas in faculty research, curricula and campus culture. The Alliance is dependent on the commitment of a broad range of internal and external stakeholders, including Bentley faculty, staff, students and alumni as well as business executives, corporate and community partners, and relevant associations in an effort to enhance and disseminate PRME's ideals across the institution.

The challenge at Bentley, as with many colleges and universities embarking on any cross-institutional initiative, was to seek out and build on the dedication and creativity of individuals throughout the organization. This section of the chapter details the key steps involved, beginning with the idea of management by 'talking around' and 'preaching to the choir' – starting with those faculty across the institution who were already committed to PRME's goals. Emphasis is also placed on efforts to leverage institutional strengths, draw on social capital and create 'small wins' (see Weick, 1984) as a way of building communities of practice.

Management by 'talking around'

The underlying approach to creating the Alliance can be thought of as management by *talking around*, beginning with one-on-one conversations with key players across campus, and gradually building to one-on-two, one-on-three, two-on-two and so forth interactions. These discussions focused on understanding and honouring the past, conceptualizing potential linkages across campus and thinking about ways to engage key stakeholders both on and off campus. The underlying idea was to build on these smaller interactions to transition to wider community conversations with the goal of, what organization development guru Marvin Weisbord referred to as, 'getting the whole system in the room' (Weisbord and Janoff, 2010).

To illustrate this process, two of the critical pillars of the planned Alliance were Bentley's Center for Business Ethics (CBE; founded in 1976) and the Bentley Service-Learning Center (BSLC; founded in 1990), each of which have had a long and influential presence on campus. A basic goal was to honour their past contributions and leverage their visibility and impact on the institution, and explore how those endeavours might further contribute to and benefit from collaboration with other programs, centres and initiatives on campus. A series of 'Bringing the Centers to the Center' programs were held, where the directors of these different initiatives had the opportunity to share their past, present and future activities and plans with faculty, staff and students across campus.

The 'talking around' strategy also helped to create an initial benchmark for what had been accomplished in this area, from gathering information on the number of faculty involved in ethics-, social responsibility- and sustainability-related research and course development, to creating a web-based repository of information (which also served as the basis for the University's first PRME Communication on Progress report).

Preaching to the choir

As part of the 'talking around' strategy, emphasis was initially placed on *preaching to the choir*, starting with faculty across the institution that were already committed to PRME's goals as a way of building communities of practice. The idea was to build on the energy and enthusiasm of these individuals, providing support and visibility for their efforts and linking them with like-minded colleagues in different departments. The resulting 'small wins' from these interactions and conversations led gradually to a tipping point, where the beliefs and energies of this critical faculty group began to influence a gradual conversion to a PRME-oriented mindset across campus. Over time, a small group of motivated individuals can generate pockets of commitment that can influence large-scale institutional change (see Kim and Mauborgne, 2003).

Providing context, creating content

The next phase focused on ways to (1) enhance individual learning as a foundation for organizational learning, and (2) envision new ways of thinking about responsible management. In terms of context, early on it was determined that faculty would need support if they were going to meaningfully incorporate ethics and responsible management-related concepts into their discipline-based courses. As a way of facilitating this process, the Business Ethics 'Gadfly' Workshop was created, with the intent of 'seeding' every academic department on campus with 'ethical gadflies' who would develop and share materials for their courses and encourage their departmental colleagues to do the same.

The goal of the Gadfly Workshop is to assist faculty to feel more comfortable with ethical concepts, analysis and application so that they are better able to work with students in raising their ethical awareness and ability to make rational and ethical choices. In the workshop and accompanying readings, an attempt is made to balance exposure to ethical theory and frameworks with hands-on practice in analysing cases and other teaching materials (such as films, simulations, role plays and service learning) from an ethical as well as discipline-based perspective. The mix of faculty from different departments and disciplines – sharing their ideas, experiences and concerns about these important issues – further contributes to a rewarding and developmental experience.

As an example of further supporting this contextual effort with content, the work of Bentley's marketing professor Raj Sisodia and his co-authored book *Firms of Endearment: How World-Class Companies Profit from Passion and Purpose* (Sisodia *et al.*, 2007) were drawn upon. This work, which led to the development of Conscious Capitalism, reflects a new way of thinking about the role of business that emphasizes commitment to a higher purpose (beyond profits per se) and a multi-stakeholder engagement orientation, supported by conscious leadership and the development of a facilitative culture (Mackey and Sisodia, 2013). Sisodia's research found that these 'firms of endearment' paid their rank-and-file employees much better than their peers, had suppliers who were profitable, invested heavily in their communities, paid taxes at a higher rate than their corporate counterparts, provided remarkable customer service, invested in making their operations more environmentally sustainable and did not externalize costs onto society. As other observers have also noted (Schwartz, 2013; Simpson *et al.*, 2013), while such spending would suggest that there would simply be less left for investors, the opposite was true. These companies had dramatically outperformed the market over a 15-year period. Beyond financial wealth, these companies also created many other kinds of societal wealth: more fulfilled employees, happy and loyal customers, innovative and profitable suppliers, thriving and environmentally healthy communities and more (Buono and Sisodia, 2011). The essence of this approach – which highly resonates with the UNGC principles on human rights, labour, environmental protection and ethical business practices – lies in stark contrast to traditional approaches to business, providing strong evidence of the utility of a conscious orientation towards business.

Making it real

Finally, as a way of solidifying this effort, it was important to 'make it real,' linking PRME-related goals with other structures, systems and processes on campus (Buono and Sisodia, 2011). As examples, this step included integration with Bentley's Academic Integrity System, institutional ethics policy and related ethics committees, Institutional Review Board (focussing on ethical issues in research with human subjects), students as colleagues initiative (engaging them in community projects, domestic and international service-learning and research initiatives) and related institutional programs, initiatives and experiences. The goal was to ensure that PRME's ideals were reflected not only in the classroom but also in faculty research, campus life and engagement with external stakeholders.

A unified approach to responsible management infusion

The result of the collective effort described above was the Bentley Alliance for Ethics and Social Responsibility (see Figure 10.1). The Alliance's mission is to *amplify and extend the work of the autonomous centres and initiatives on campus, supporting and encouraging greater awareness of, respect for and commitment to ethics, service and social responsibility in faculty research, curricula and campus culture.* Reflecting PRME's guiding principles, the initiative seeks to:

- support and encourage collaborative, trans-disciplinary applied *research* that has the potential to significantly affect current practice (Principle 4: Research);

- influence *curriculum* development and pedagogical innovations intended to make our students more ethically sensitive and socially aware (Principles 2: Values and 3: Method);

- ensure a broader application of these principles and ideals in *campus life* (Principle 7: Institutional);

- attempt to foster life-long *civic engagement* and a commitment to *responsible management* among our students (Principle 1: Purpose) and

- work closely with external organizations – *partnering* with academic and professional associations, corporations and civil society organizations in pursuit of these goals (Principles 5: Partnerships and 6: Dialog).

As illustrated in Figure 10.1, the Alliance was built on four key centres in the Bentley community that continue to operate as autonomous entities but collaborate under the aegis of the initiative:

- *Center for Business Ethics (CBE)*: founded in 1976, the CBE promotes ethical leadership, conduct and cultures as critical to an effective and legitimate role for business in society.

- *Bentley Service-Learning Center (BSLC)*: established in 1990, the BSLC seeks to promote academic learning, develop socially responsible working professionals and assist community partners in serving the human needs and interests of their constituencies.

- *Center for Women and Business (CWB)*: initially created as the Women's Leadership Institute in 2003, CWB focuses on assisting women reach their full potential in the workplace and helping corporations engage the full potential of talented women leaders.

- *Valente Center for Arts & Sciences*: created in 2007, the centre's mission is to help make the arts and sciences a vital, integral and challenging aspect of undergraduate and graduate education at Bentley.

FIGURE 10.1 The Bentley Alliance for Ethics and Social Responsibility

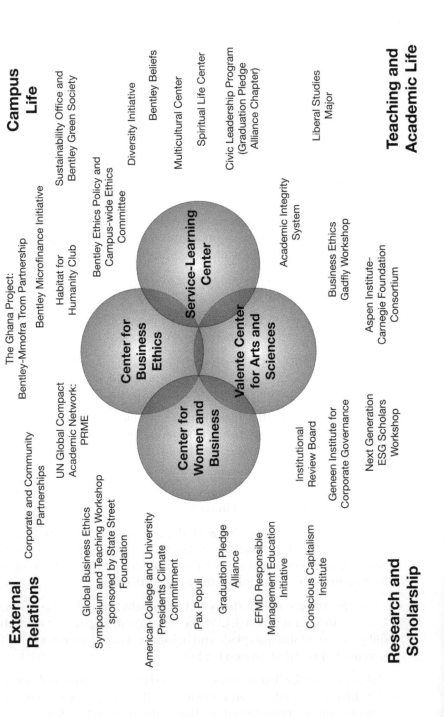

Combined with a series of programs and activities across the institution (captured in Figure 10.1), this initiative has led to a multi-pronged approach that attempts to shape and influence a sense of ethics, service, responsibility and sustainability in: (1) the classroom; (2) campus life; (3) the university's research agenda and (4) outreach to the academic, corporate and not-for-profit worlds.

The classroom

As a way of influencing curriculum development (Principles 2: Values and 3: Method), in the late 1980s, CBE began working with the academic chairs of the accountancy, law and computer information systems departments, providing them with assistance in integrating ethics into their departmental courses. The subsequent work with these departments – and its success in elevating the visibility of ethics in their curricula and stimulating faculty research in this area – prompted CBE to transform this initiative into a formal workshop.

Initially referred to as the Business Ethics 'Gadfly' Workshop, the intent is to encourage faculty to address ethical issues and questions of corporate responsibility and sustainability in courses across the curriculum. The Gadfly reference dates back to Socrates, who described himself as a 'gadfly,' whose purpose was to 'sting' the citizens of Athens out of their ignorance and intellectual complacency. By 'seeding' each academic department with such gadflies, the goal is to develop a core group of faculty who would prod and influence their colleagues to incorporate informed discussions of ethical issues and corporate responsibility in their classes. As illustrated in Figure 10.2, a basic objective is to broaden the ways in which faculty think about drawing discussions of ethics and responsible behaviour into their discipline-based courses.

As part of the Alliance's mission to amplify and extend such initiatives, the Business Ethics Teaching Workshop went global in 2004. Through the generous support of the State Street Foundation, each year visiting scholars from other colleges and universities around the world join Bentley faculty to explore ways to incorporate these perspectives into their courses. Reflecting on the impact of the program, a senior executive from State Street Foundation noted: 'We are committed to supporting this program because good behavior needs to be modeled and encouraged; we know all too well what happens when values are ignored.'

Our 'gadfly' experience suggests that by addressing pedagogical tactics and approaches to incorporating ethical and social responsibility issues into different courses, such workshops can stimulate a greater comfort level across the faculty – to the point where a growing number of faculty report capturing 'teachable moments' to bring these ideals to life. With more than 200 Bentley faculty who have gone through the program – and over 120 external 'alumni' – it has enabled the institution to influence the ways in which ethics-related issues and topics

FIGURE 10.2 **Business ethics pedagogy infusion continuum**

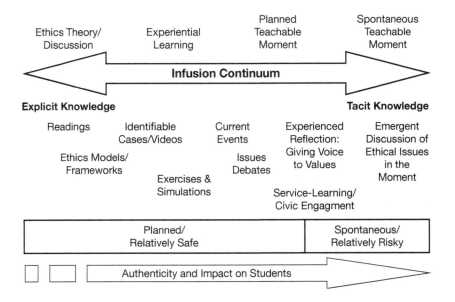

Business Ethics Infusion: Pedagogy ~ Bentley's "Gadfly" Program

are incorporated into courses across the curriculum, from accounting and finance to marketing, operations management and human resource management to organizational behaviour and strategy. The program has had a clear influence on the content of Bentley's curriculum – in addition to building a growing network of committed scholars across the globe.

Campus

As part of an attempt to maintain and nurture the college community and to maximize the potential for learning, the institution embraces what is referred to as the *Bentley Beliefs*, a set of principles intended to govern conduct in classrooms, residence halls and places of work. Emphasis is placed on 'treating one another with respect, acknowledging and learning from our differences, acting with integrity and honesty, and seeking to further the growth and learning of each member of our community and ourselves.'

Building on the *purpose* of PRME (Principle 1), the next dimension of the strategy was to go beyond the classroom and curriculum, supporting discussions of ethics and responsible management through extracurricular activities (the 'hidden curriculum'). Among its myriad initiatives, for example, CBE hosts the annual Raytheon Lectureship in Business Ethics, whereby in each semester a prominent CEO comes to campus to talk about ethics, sustainability and corporate responsibility in his or her company (Principles 3: Method, 5: Partnership and 6: Dialog). CBE also hosts the Verizon Visiting Professor of Business Ethics – for one week each year a prominent business ethics scholar is invited to campus, giving public lectures, visiting classes and, in general, promoting greater awareness of responsible management. The other centres in the Alliance also sponsor a series of speakers and events that reinforce issues of ethics, corporate responsibility and sustainability.

Through the Alliance, the issue of ethics and personal responsibility became the foundation for Bentley's new Academic Integrity System (AIS). Developed jointly by students, faculty and administrators, the AIS sets and regulates standards of academic integrity throughout the university. An Academic Integrity Coordinator (AIC) oversees and facilitates the system's procedures for insuring fair and effective implementation. The AIC also provides educational outreach to students and faculty about the importance of academic honesty and integrity. The underlying goal is to instill a commitment to ethical behaviour as part of business education (and subsequent practice).

The visibility of the Alliance on campus has also prompted undergraduate students to get more actively involved through the Bentley Civic Leadership Program (BCLP), which is Bentley's chapter of the Graduation Pledge Alliance. The BCLP, which is student-initiated and led, has three foci: campus involvement (facilitating the ability of students to become a leader within their immediate community), civic engagement (facilitating student appreciation of the importance of the greater community) and ethical and responsible behaviour in their lives.

Students also have the opportunity to directly immerse themselves in the surrounding community through the BSLC. Each year, the service-learning program has averaged roughly 700 students in 90 credit-bearing courses taught by over 60 faculty members in a broad range of courses. As such, service-learning – and the self-reflection that is part of the process – has become a critical component in the management education of Bentley students (see Salimbene *et al.*, 2005; Principles 3: Method, 5: Partnership and 6: Dialog).

Finally, a campus-wide commitment to these ideals has further renewed the college's emphasis on the protection of human participants in research through the Institutional Review Board, and supported the institution's campus-wide College Ethics Policy and Oversight Committee. In addition, the Alliance supports diversity workshops for faculty, staff and students (e.g. 'Day–to-Day Diversity', 'Becoming an "Ally" on Sexual Identity Issues') and a series of campus-wide panels and presentations on current issues, from peer-to-peer file sharing to business ethics and the arts.

While any of these initiatives might be found at many other colleges and universities and each exerts a positive influence on campus life, the combination of these programs through the Alliance reflects an integrated and systemic intervention.

The production of knowledge

In addition to the research interests of individual faculty, Bentley's strategy also encourages and sponsors applied trans-disciplinary research, emphasizing collaborative projects that involve faculty members across different academic departments and research streams that have the potential to significantly affect current practice (Principle 4: Research). With the ideal of thought leadership in mind, the Alliance supports interdisciplinary research on governance, strategy and corporate integrity, and sponsors campus-wide panels and presentations on current issues. The University's annual research colloquium draws together faculty and doctoral student researchers across campus to share their work around a given theme that reflects responsible management practices. The 2015 Colloquium, for example, focused on 'Sustainable Worlds,' emphasizing the UNGC Sustainable Development Goals agenda.

Outreach to the external world

The final component of the Alliance's integrated strategy is outreach to other colleges and universities, relevant associations, the corporate sector and the institution's community partnerships and the not-for-profit world (Principles 5: Partnerships and 6: Dialog). As an extension of Bentley's 'Gadfly' workshop, for example, a day-long symposium focused on ethics, responsible management and sustainability that is open to the public was added. The intent of the Symposium is to bring together international experts for in-depth discussions of current practices and challenges in business ethics, corporate responsibility and sustainability. Emphasis is placed on uniting business and higher education in the common goal of building a strong ethical foundation from which to serve our many constituencies and communities.

Working with the Ethics Officer Association, which was initially established through CBE, the Alliance's CBE also offers a 'Managing Ethics and Organizations' (MEO) program. Since 1995, well over 400 ethics and compliance officers and graduate students have completed the five-day MEO course. Over the years, the course has provided attendees with practical advice and tools for creating and managing an effective ethics and compliance initiative.

Institutionalizing PRME

A unique feature of Bentley's Alliance for Ethics and Social Responsibility is its collaborative and integrative focus, drawing together an emphasis on ethics, social responsibility, civic engagement and sustainability across the entire campus. The initiative has helped to solidify the role of PRME on campus – ensuring that the overall experience at the University reflects its mission and commitment to responsible management education. The Alliance has also increased the visibility of many of these activities and programs, both on campus and with external stakeholders. As the University continues to move forward – in essence, continuing a journey towards responsible management in all facets of the educational experience – the current plan is to continue to explore and assess the overall effectiveness of this strategy. At present, it clearly appears to be a step in the right direction.

References

Argyris, C. and Schön, D. (1978) *Organizational learning: A theory of action perspective*, Menlo Park, CA: Addison-Wesley.

Barnett, R. and Coate, K. (2005) *Engaging the curriculum in higher education*, Berkshire, UK: Open University Press.

Blasco, M. (2012) 'Aligning the hidden curriculum of management education with PRME: An inquiry-based framework,' *Journal of Management Education, 36*(3): 364–388.

Buono, A. F. and Sisodia, R. (2011) 'A conscious purpose,' *EFMD Global Focus, 5*(2): 56–59.

Callahan, D. (2004) *The cheating culture: Why more Americans are doing wrong to get ahead*, New York, NY: Harcourt.

Forray, J. M. and Leigh, J. S. A. (2012) 'Primer on the principles of responsible management education: Intellectual roots and waves of change,' *Journal of Management Education, 36*(3): 295–309.

Fort, T. (2016) 'Adding ethics to the classroom,' *BizEd, 15*(1): 48–49.

Gair, M. and Mullins, G. (2001) 'Hiding in plain sight,' in E. Margolis (ed.), *The hidden curriculum in higher education*, New York, NY: Routledge, pp. 21–41.

Hockerts, K., Borgbo, P., Srkoc, T., Goldberg, E. S. and Chaudry, R. (2015) *Faculty development for responsible management education*, New York, NY: PRME Champions Report.

Kell, G. and Haertle, J. (2011) 'UN global compact and principles for responsible management education: The next decades,' *Global Focus, 5*(2): 14–16.

Kim, W. C. and Mauborgne, R. (2003) 'Tipping point leadership,' *Harvard Business Review*, March–April: 37–47.

Lowenstein, R. (2004) *The great bubble and its undoing*, New York, NY: Penguin Press.

Mackey, J. and Sisodia, R. (2013) *Conscious capitalism*, Boston, MA: Harvard Business School Press.

PRME. (2016) *Transformational model for PRME implementation*, New York, NY: UN Global Compact. Available online at http://unprme.org/resource-docs/PRMETransformational ModelPrint.pdf.

Rasche, A. (2010). *The Principles for Responsible Management Education (PRME): History, Purpose, and Content*. Paper presented at the Academy of Management Annual Meeting, Montreal, Canada, August.

Rasche, A. and Gilbert, D. U. (2015) 'Decoupling responsible management education: Why business schools may not walk their talk,' *Journal of Management Inquiry, 24*(3): 239–252.

Rasche, A., Gilbert, D. U. and Schedel, I. (2013) 'Cross-disciplinary ethics education in MBA programs: Rhetoric or reality?' *Academy of Management Learning & Education, 12*(1): 71–85.

Salimbene, F. P., Buono, A. F., LaFarge, V. and Nurick, A. (2005) 'Service-learning and management education: The Bentley experience,' *Academy of Management Learning & Education, 4*(3): 336–344.

Schwartz, T. (2013, April 4) 'Companies that practice "conscious capitalism" perform 10x better,' *Harvard Business Review.* Available online at https://hbr.org/2013/04/companies-that-practice-conscious-capitalism-perform (accessed 28 October 2016).

Shrivastava, P. (2010) 'Pedagogy of passion for sustainability,' *Academy of Management Learning & Education, 9*: 443–455.

Simpson, S., Fischer, B. D. and Rohde, M. (2013) 'The conscious capitalism philosophy pays off: A qualitative and financial analysis of conscious capitalism firms,' *Journal of Leadership, Accountability and Ethics, 10*(4): 19–29.

Sisodia, R., Wolfe, D. B. and Sheth, J. N. (2007) *Firms of endearment: How world-class companies profit from passion and purpose,* Upper Saddle River, NJ: Wharton School Publishing.

Solitander, N., Fougère, M., Sobczak, A. and Herlin, H. (2012) 'We are the champions: Organizational learning and change for responsible management education,' *Journal of Management Education, 36*(3): 337–363.

Sterling, S. (2004) 'Higher education, sustainability and the role of systemic learning' in P. B. Corcoran and A. E. J. Wals (eds), *Higher education and the challenge for sustainability: Problematics, promise and practice,* Dordrecht, the Netherlands: Kluwer Academic, pp. 47–70.

Swanson, D. (2004) 'The buck stops here: Why universities must reclaim business ethics education,' *Journal of Academic Ethics, 2*(1): 43–61.

Trevino, L. K. and McCabe, D. (1994) 'Meta-learning about business ethics: Building honorable business school communities,' *Journal of Business Ethics, 13*: 405–416.

Trevino, L. K., McCabe, D. and Butterfield, K. D. (2012) *Cheating in college: Why students do it and what educators can do about it,* Baltimore, MD: John Hopkins University Press.

Waddock, S., Rasche, A., Werhane, P. H. and Unruh, G. (2010) 'The principles for responsible management education,' in D. L. Swanson and D. G. Fisher (eds), *Towards assessing business ethics education,* Charlotte, NC: Information Age, pp. 13–28.

Weick, K. (1984) 'Small wins: Redefining the scale of social problems,' *American Psychologist, 39*(1): 40–49.

Weisbord, M. and Janoff, S. (2010) *Future search: Getting the whole system in the room for vision, commitment, and action,* San Francisco, CA: Berrett-Koehler.

Anthony F. Buono is professor of Management and Sociology and founding director of the Alliance for Ethics and Social Responsibility at Bentley University, which he oversaw from its inception in 2003 through 2013. He has been actively involved in the PRME initiative, at Bentley and working with the PRME Secretariat.

abuono@bentley.edu

Section 4
Country and regional perspectives

11

Designing a management education platform for the twenty-first century learner

The experience of La Salle schools in the Philippines

Andrea Santiago

Asian Institute of Management, Philippines

Abstract

This chapter documents how nine business schools belonging to the network of institutions owned and managed by the La Salle Christian Brothers in the Philippines strove to integrate the Principles for Responsible Management Education and the United Nations Global Compact Principles into a framework to be used by member schools as they redesigned their business curricula. While the framework was collectively designed by representatives of each school, the challenge is seeing how the framework translates into the actual curricula, subject contents and classroom activities of these business schools that are operating in different contexts. The framework is still in its early stages of implementation but the fruits of integration are slowly being felt at all the schools in the network, albeit at different levels.

The call for responsible management education

The 2030 Agenda for Sustainable Development is a call to correct the disequilibrium in, and address the injustices of, the experiences of marginalized and differently-abled global citizens. It is a worldwide collective action endeavour that aims to meet 169 targets in seventeen thematic goals so as to achieve a better world and sustainable planet for all. Its success lies in cooperative action to be taken by all sectors of society. One such sector is business.

The business sector had begun to accept its responsibility towards sustainable development. In 2000, the United Nations Global Compact (UNGC) was officially launched as a voluntary corporate sustainability initiative that called for business organizations to operate ethically and sustainably. Sixteen years later, almost 9,000 businesses in 166 countries had joined that commitment. The numbers, however, are still small compared to more than 235 million registered businesses in 200 countries as of 2013[1].

The business sector needs help and academia can do its part in shaping the attitude and mindsets of its students so that when they graduate, they are able to become responsible citizens who can positively influence how businesses operate (UNGC, 2007). In 2007, the United Nations Principles for Responsible Management Education (PRME) was founded as a voluntary global initiative among business schools. Ten years later, 650 institutions from eighty countries have signed with PRME, arguably a small number. However, for any change to happen, action must start somewhere.

Even when there is a compelling reason to take action, the response of academe has not been swift. The resistance may come from the fundamental debate of whether shareholder maximization is still the primary objective of business or whether other stakeholders should be considered (Mauboussin & Rappaport, 2016; *The Economist*, 2015). Thus, more traditional business schools may continue with the status quo.

It is also possible that resistance to embed ethics, corporate social responsibility (CSR) and sustainability into the business curriculum may stem from a lack of knowledge of how to go about it or even from sheer lethargy of some faculty members who do not want to learn and adapt. Faculty buy-in is, indeed, one of the major challenges to overcome (Escudero *et al.*, 2012).

Some business schools have, however, risen to the challenge. A number of business schools worldwide have adopted separate courses, either required or as electives, or have integrated the subject matter into individual courses (Christensen *et al.*, 2007; Solitander *et al.*, 2012; Stubbs & Schaper, 2011; Wright & Bennett, 2011). Others have favoured experiential learning through immersion programs (Weber *et al.*, 2013). However, for real transformation to take place, a multi-level approach that considers the institution, curriculum and course offerings may be the direction to take (Setó-Pamies & Papaoikonomou, 2016).

This chapter explores how a group of schools in the Philippines took the challenge of embedding UNGC and PRME principles into their business curricula.

With full support from the presidents of nine business schools, deans colla-boratively developed a business education framework, with the intention of redesigning courses and learning spaces so that its graduates become socially responsible citizens. First and foremost, this chapter addresses PRME's third principle ('Method'), that of developing frameworks to enhance the learning environment of students so that they become 'future generators of sustainable value for business and society at large and to work for an inclusive and sustain-able global economy.' It also highlights areas in which the other five PRME principles ('Purpose' (Principle 1); 'Values' (Principle 2); 'Research' (Principle 4); 'Partnership' (Principle 5) and 'Dialogue' (Principle 6) pertain to the LaSalle School experience.

The response of La Salle business schools in the Philippines (PRME 'method' principle 3)

The Commission on Higher Education (CHED) is the governing body over the public and private higher education in the Philippines. Of the 2,400 higher education institutions, 71.5 per cent are owned and managed by the private sector[2]. A fifth of the private schools are managed by religious groups, a number of which belong to the Brothers of Christian Schools.

The Brothers of Christian Schools, known as La Salle Brothers, established their presence in the Philippines a hundred years ago with De La Salle University (DLSU) as their first school. To date, there are now sixteen schools that have come together under the five-year-old umbrella organization – De La Salle Philippines (DLSP). It is the task of DLSP to facilitate collaboration among the La Salle schools in the country so that the mission of the founder, St. John Baptist de La Salle of providing human and Christian education, is fulfilled.

Of the schools belonging to the network, nine offer business programs. Four of the nine schools are PRME signatories, namely DLSU, University of St. La Salle (USLS), De La Salle University Dasmariñas (DLSU-D) and De La Salle Lipa (DLSL). Two more schools expect to be signatories in the near future: the De La Salle College of Saint Benilde (DLS-CSB) and La Salle University (LSU). The three remaining schools are working hand-in-hand with DLSU on their PRME commitment; these are De La Salle Araneta University (DLSAU), La Salle College Antipolo (LSCA) and De La Salle John Bosco College (DLSJBC). The business deans and the school presidents are working together on these initiatives.

In 2014, DLSP established the Professional Learning Community (PLC) for business so that the nine business schools would be able to offer comparable quality programs regardless of their environmental context. Of the nine schools, only two – DLSU and CSB – are located in the capital city of Manila on the island of Luzon. The other schools are also city-based, although three (USLS, LSU and

JBC) are located in the island groups of Visayas and Mindanao (See Appendix A). Because of their locations, the schools cater to different types of students with respect to learning aptitude and attitude as well as their paying capacity. The schools also attract faculty members possessing varying qualifications.

Members of PLC for Business, who are business deans and department heads, decided to design a Lasallian Business Curriculum that differentiates a La Salle business education from those offered by all other schools in the country. In the design stage, the PLC members took note of internal, national and international environments. The following is the context of the discussion:

- Within the DLSP umbrella are schools with business programs that are progressing at different paces, with differing student and faculty populations, varied minimum teaching load requirements and diverging access to financial and personnel resources. It made sense that schools that were more advantaged would help those at the opposite side of the spectrum by providing access to academic resources as a means of leveling off academic standards.

- The introduction of a twelve-year basic education program in the Philippine system effective academic year 2016 would mean lower enrollment at the tertiary level. This is because students who would have graduated from high school would have to enroll in Grade 11 and then in Grade 12 before going to college. (More details and implications of this change are provided later in the chapter.) This would have two effects. First, there would be an undersupply of students and an oversupply of faculty for at least two years. Financially challenged institutions would be further challenged by having to continue to pay the salaries of tenured faculty. Second, the current curriculum would become partially irrelevant since some of the subjects previously taught in earlier grades would be taught in Grades 11 and 12. This would necessitate a change in curriculum by the academic year 2018.

- The introduction of a twelve-year basic education program requires a change in the curriculum of higher education institutions. This period can be an opportune time to review the business curriculum of all colleges to focus on courses and subjects that would produce the kind of graduates who are in keeping with the Lasallian values.

- Internationally, there is a clamour by the UNGC and the UN PRME to produce management graduates who are to become true global citizens, working towards inclusive development. The Lasallian values of the spirit of Faith, zeal for Service, and Communion in mission (FSC) closely align with the principles espoused by PRME and the UNGC, specifically on responsible and sustainable inclusive development.

Process of developing an integrated framework (PRME 'dialogue' principle 6)

The PLC for Business undertook a two-stage process with an intervening event to develop an integrated framework. The first stage brought together in 2014 the business deans or their respective representatives to present their schools' vision/mission and curriculum. There was then a session on PRME and UNGC principles as well as the teachings from the Vocation of the Business Leader[3] to bring participants to the same starting point. During this session, participants were asked to reflect on how the PRME and UNGC principles could be integrated into the curriculum by first ensuring that it forms part of expected student learning outcomes.

From discussions, there was a convergence towards developing students to become socially responsible citizens (PRME 'Purpose' (Principle 1)). Thus, this became one of the desired attributes of a Lasallian graduate. In addition, the PLC participants expect that Lasallian graduates, similar to other business graduates, must also be critical and creative thinkers, effective communicators and reflective life-long learners (See Figure 11.1). However, to differentiate a Lasallian graduate from other graduates, the four attributes were brought together by the need to make ethical decisions; thus, ethics is the underlying foundation. Further, the attributes are bounded by the need to be faithful to God,

FIGURE 11.1 **The Lasallian business education framework**

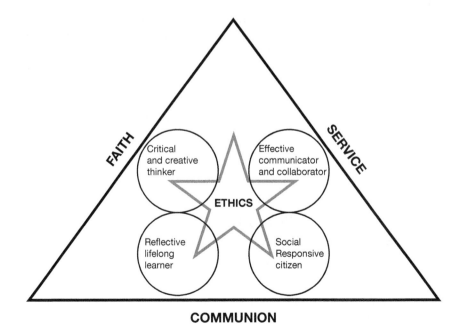

to be enthusiastic in service and to work within, for, and with support from, a community.

A subsequent workshop led to the development of twelve student-learning outcomes, one for each of the four graduate attributes cross-tabbed with the Lasallian values (See Appendix B). This approach was inspired by Pepperdine University, as gleaned from its published documents.[4] The PLC also described the learning environment to support the achievement of each of the outcomes (See Appendix C).

The output of the first stage was presented to the participants of the International Association of Lasallian Universities (IALU), a network of Lasallian higher education institutions around the world, in a meeting held in early 2015 in Manila. The outcome of this meeting emboldened the PLC for Business to commit to its framework by formally organizing Lasallian Educators and Administrators in Business and Accountancy (LEAD in BA), and encouraging all business faculty members to be involved in the LEAD in BA. This opened the door for the next stage.

In the second stage, more business faculty from the nine schools, including the deans and department chairs, were invited to a two-day workshop to determine the acceptance of the framework and to move the learning outcomes to the subject level. Instead of directly presenting the framework, the participants went through the process of becoming familiar with the PRME and UNGC principles as well as the working document on the UN Sustainability Development Goals (SDGs), which at that time had not yet been released. The participants also went through an exercise of defining their ideal Lasallian graduate after group and plenary discussions on what they believed to be curriculum drivers. Curriculum drivers refer to phenomenon and events happening at the global, regional and national levels as well as with the Lasallian community. The global call for more inclusive development that provides equal chances free from corruption was the one driver identified. There was also the 2015 establishment of the Association of Southeast Asian Nations (ASEAN) Economic Community that allows for greater mobility of resources that necessitates the development of a more responsive business curriculum. After securing consensus, the nine schools were able to articulate a common vision and mission statement (See Appendix D).

Expected graduate attributes and learning outcomes of a Lasallian business education in the Philippines (PRME: 'Values' (principle 2) and the UNGC principles)

The inclusion of learning outcomes in the syllabi of business courses among the La Salle schools began in 2010 and reached the consciousness of business faculty by 2013. This forced business faculty to view desired results and then to eventually identify Lasallian graduate attributes. The articulated attributes were, however, not exclusively Lasallian. Eventually, four graduate learning attributes were identified: (1) Critical and creative thinker, (2) effective communicator and collaborator, (3) reflective lifelong learner and (4) social responsiveness. It was emphasized that all these attributes have as their central theme sound ethical decision-making.

To differentiate the more common graduate attributes, the PLC determined that the core values of every Lasallian should serve as the guiding principle. The Spirit of Faith calls for Lasallians to 'Live Jesus in Our Hearts Forever'. This is to see God in every human and thus to treat others kindly and with respect. 'Zeal for Service' implies that Lasallians serve, not as part of compliance but to do so enthusiastically and infectiously. More importantly, following the footsteps of St. John Baptist de la Salle, this core value directs service orientation to the 'last, lost, and least'. Lasallians, therefore, are called upon to help society first before thinking of personal and financial interests[5]. This core value clearly supports the principles espoused by PRME and UNGC.

Finally, the third core Lasallian value calls for Communion in Mission. This means that Lasallians should work with others in pursuit of the common good. Lasallians are encouraged to be collaborative and to work towards reaching out to others so that they, too, work for the betterment of society.

The Lasallian core values must be imbibed live while the business students are in their academic institutions. Consequently, the learning environment must be supportive of the need for internal transformation. It is in this context that the PLC worked towards describing how each Lasallian graduate attribute, woven into each of the values of Faith, Service and Communion, could be enriched within and outside the confines of the classroom. It is only in providing this environment where the student learning outcomes can be achieved and later witnessed.

Implementing the Lasallian business framework

There were two major challenges that the nine schools faced. The first involved the need for schools to comply with the Philippine business education curriculum that dictated the minimum number of subjects and credits per degree program. The second pertained to how the schools would incorporate the Lasallian guiding principles as well the principles of PRME and UNGC at the subject level.

The shift in the basic education system in the Philippines necessitated a change in the higher education system. In 2010, the Philippines adopted the K12 system, adding two years to basic education to make the number similar to all other countries. This meant that the general education subjects previously taught at the tertiary level were brought down to grades 11 and 12. When DLSP began designing a unified framework in 2014, the Philippine business curriculum was still being crafted. Consequently, some deans were hesitant to discuss the business curriculum in case the CHED was to make drastic changes. Other deans, however, felt that the La Salle schools should set the standard for the Philippine business education and thus continue to proactively prepare its curriculum, possibly influencing the government-required minimum standards. It was no surprise that the deans who hesitated were not as fast in implementing the changes in the curriculum.

The LEAD in BA agreed that the business curriculum that would be mandated by the CHED would be the minimum standard and that the La Salle schools will either infuse each subject with lessons on responsible management or add subjects beyond the Ethics and Social Responsibility previously mandated by CHED. The deans agreed to adopt the Lasallian Business Framework, although this would be contextualized in their environments. Using the framework as the foundation, each La Salle business school would then design its own course offerings and syllabi. The smaller schools, as well as those located in provincial cities, looked to the bigger schools to guide them even at this level.

Even with the framework available, there was a need to constantly monitor the progress of implementation with each of the deans. Some deans were more enthusiastic than others, particularly those with higher social capital in their institutions. Thus, deans who had held their positions for longer and were expected to retain their positions were able to strongly influence the early adoption of the framework. Certainly there were deans who had greater difficulty with faculty buy-in.

To integrate the PRME, UNGC and Lasallian guiding principles at the subject level, the first hurdle was to manage teacher resistance. There were faculty members unwilling to invest time in developing new subjects, and there were those who frowned upon changing the learning environment and integrating principles of good practice. They felt that adding the dimension of ethics and sustainability would reduce the number of hours to teach the core lessons with which they were familiar. For instance, some Finance professors were more comfortable teaching the mechanics of financial complications and were unwilling to spend a session or two to explain that financial manipulation is unethical. Some Operations professors emphasized the need of efficiency and taught techniques on computing productivity but resisted having to take time to explain that efficiency should not come at the expense of unethical workplace practices.

Faculty buy-in is a work-in-progress. In anticipation of the resistance, many faculty coming from the nine schools were invited to participate in a teaching and learning session on Lasallian business education. The four-day live-in workshop conducted by Lasallian professors demonstrated the type of teaching style and learning environment espoused by the framework. The overall approach was for faculty participants to take a critical view of themselves as teachers and to experience learning in an environment that infused the core values of Faith, Service, and Communion. With varied individual, group and class activities, participants learned to shake away their angst, inhibitions and even their sense of superiority, so they were able to participate effectively as teachers and learners in the Lasallian learning community.

The teaching and learning sessions proved to be helpful to those who participated in a live-in workshop. In subsequent meetings with them, almost all expressed how they were able to integrate great portions of the lessons learned in the sessions. It was easy for them to adopt the lessons because they were made to feel what the learning environment should be like. Instead of lectures of the 'should' and 'should not' variety, participants were exposed to simulated scenarios. For instance, participants had to act out ethical dilemmas that students were exposed to and discuss practical solutions. Teachers also were asked to reflect on, and discuss, dilemmas they faced such as receiving gifts from students. Then they were asked to translate this to the business environment. Subsequently, they had to develop teaching techniques so that their students learn that potential conflict of interest may arise due to gift giving and receiving.

Early outcomes of framework implementation

An early champion in the adoption of the Lasallian Business framework was the Management and Organization Department (MOD) of DLSU. In 2015, DLSU was acknowledged by the CHED to be a centre of excellence for business education in the country. The recognition of excellence by the CHED is an affirmation of the excellent performance of the business school in educating students so that they become responsible and productive citizens. Sharing in this honour with DLSU is CSB, which was also recognized for its innovative programs.

As part of integrating the Lasallian guiding principles and the principles of PRME and UNGC, MOD had earlier revised its vision and mission statements encapsulated in the slogan – Bridging Faith and Management Practice. The department had also re-focussed its research agenda in themes that supported the slogan, namely in business ethics, CSR, corporate governance, sustainable organizations and spirituality in the workplace. Consequently, it was very natural to work with the framework and move deeper into developing a learning environment that would aid in influencing the hearts and minds of its undergraduate and graduate students to be more cognizant of their responsibility towards inclusive development.

Undergraduate students taking their internship were being evaluated not only on their ability to meet the technical demands of the workplace but also by their ability to influence the workplace for positive change in society (PRME 'Partnership' (Principle 5) and 'Dialogue' (Principle 6)). The choice of thesis topics also centred around MOD's research agenda, thus heightening awareness for responsible management. Doctoral students also selected dissertation topics along the same lines, while Master's students undertook action research projects, introducing change in their sphere of influence (PRME 'Research' (Principle 4)).

At all levels, stand-alone subjects on CSR, corporate governance and humanistic workplace were introduced, while business subjects were reinforced with strong stress on ethics and sustainability.

Previously, the MOD had begun to see students shift their line of work when their value system is compromised or opt to work with social enterprises. It is expected that over time more graduates would become positive change agents in organizations they eventually join. The likelihood of producing more graduates who will become positive change agents is expected to rise as the business education provided by MOD centres around responsible management. As a principal mover, MOD faculty hope to influence other La Salle business schools to do the same by providing the training needed by other faculty.

Lessons learned from the collaborative experience

The move of DLSP to have nine business schools of La Salle come together to craft a Lasallian business curriculum was bold, but timely. The business deans felt a strong need to synergize at a time when the Philippine education was entering a state of flux. Yet attempting to produce a unified business curriculum in diverse business school contexts was a challenge.

There was a suggestion to keep lines of communication open, especially for institutions that were not located on the main island of Luzon. This proved difficult since the schools outside Manila had: (1) slower and erratic internet connections; (2) fewer financial resources, and (3) employed teachers that were not all fully qualified since it was difficult to attract better teachers to distant places. However, the workload of bigger and more progressive schools did not allow the deans time-off to stay in touch. Without communication, the pace by which projects and programs can be developed and delivered in support of a unified business curriculum will certainly be hampered.

The other challenge was for the business faculty to commit to redesigning their course syllabus based on the need to integrate responsible management principles as espoused by UNGC and PRME and to provide a learning environment that would allow students to reflect and transform the way they think and act. Maloni *et al.* (2011) identified faculty resistance as a key deterrent in the integration of the principles of responsible management. Training was identified as one approach to overcome teacher resistance. In the DLSP experience, academics who attended the four-day workshop conducted by in-house PRME and integrity champions were more encouraged to introduce changes in the classroom. If more faculty members can be trained, then the chances of integration within the curriculum would improve. The role of dean in encouraging widespread participation is important.

For any real impact, the integration of UNGC and PRME principles should permeate throughout the institution and should be manifested in the curriculum, courses and the manner by which faculty teach the courses. There needs to be a deliberate move to mobilize academics and champion the idea that individuals, institutions and countries must work together to address global concerns of inequity and world preservation. Business schools produce graduates who eventually may become key decision makers in business and society. The promise of change lies in academe.

Notes

1 https://en.wikipedia.org/wiki/Dun_%26_Bradstreet
2 http://api.ched.ph/api/v1/download/422
3 This is a document prepared by the Pontifical Council for Justice and Peace in 2012. www.pcgp.it/dati/2012-05/04-999999/Vocation%20ENG2.pdf
4 See http://oie.pepperdine.edu/assessment/ilos.aspx
5 http://dlsu.edu.ph/inside/lasallian-guiding-principles/formation.asp

References

Christensen, L. J., Peirce, E., Hartman, L., Hoffman, W. M. and Carrier, J. (2007) 'Ethics, CSR, and sustainability education in the Financial Times Top 50 Global Business Schools: Baseline data and future research directions', *Journal of Business Ethics*, 73:347–368.

Commission on Higher Education. (2015) 'CHED centres of excellence.' (23 December). Available online at http://ched.gov.ph/wp-content/uploads/2016/03/CMO-No.-38-Series-of-2015-for-COE-and-COD.pdf (Accessed 11 August 2016).

The Economist. (2015) 'The business of business: An old debate about what companies are for has been revived', *The Economist* (21 March).

Escudero, M., Albareda, L., Alcaraz, J. M., Weybrecht, G. and Csuri, M. (Eds.) (2012) *Inspirational guide for the implementation of PRME: Placing sustainability at the heart of management education*, Leeds, UK: GSE Research.

Maloni, M., Shane, S. and Napshin, S. (2011) 'A methodology for building faculty support for the United Nations principles for responsible education', *Journal of Management Education*, 36(3): 312–336.

Mauboussin, M. and Rappaport, A. (2016) 'Reclaiming the idea of shareholder value', *Harvard Business Review*, July.

Setó-Pamies, D. and Papaoikonomou, E. (2016) 'A multi-level perspective for the integration of ethics, corporate social responsibility and sustainability (ECSRS) in management education', *Journal of Business Ethics*, 136: 523–538.

Solitander, N., Fougère, M., Sobczak, A. and Herlin, H. (2012) 'We are the champions: Organizational learning and change for responsible management education', *Journal of Management Education*, 36(3): 337–363.

Stubbs, W. and Schapper, J. (2011) 'Two approaches to curriculum development for educating for sustainability and CSR', *Curriculum Development*, 12(3): 259–268.

United Nations Global Compact (UNGC). (2007) *The principles for responsible management education*, New York, NY: United Nations Global Company.

Weber, J., Green, S. and Gladstone, J. (2013) 'Responding to the call: Changes in graduate management curriculum's attention to social and environmental issues', *Teaching Ethics*, Spring: 138–157.

Wright, N. and Bennett, H. (2011) 'Business ethics, CSR, sustainability and the MBA', *Journal of Management & Organization, 17*: 641–655.

Prof. Dr. Santiago is a full-time professor at the Asian Institute of Management. Prior to joining the Asian Institute of Management, she worked at De La Salle University and was given a special assignment with De La Salle Philippines, the umbrella organization of sixteen La Salle Christian Brothers schools in the Philippines. She has written several published materials on social responsibility, responsible management education, poverty alleviation and social inclusion in the Philippines.

asantiago@aim.edu

Appendix A: Approximate Location of Nine La Salle Business Schools in the Philippines

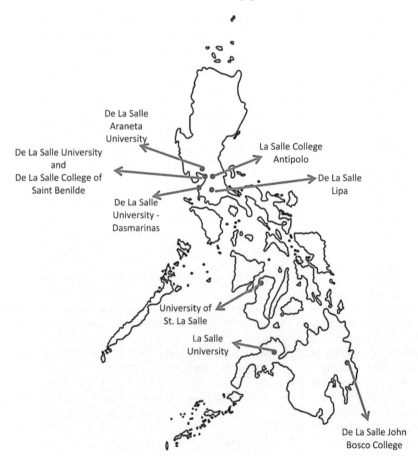

Appendix B: Lasallian Learning Environment

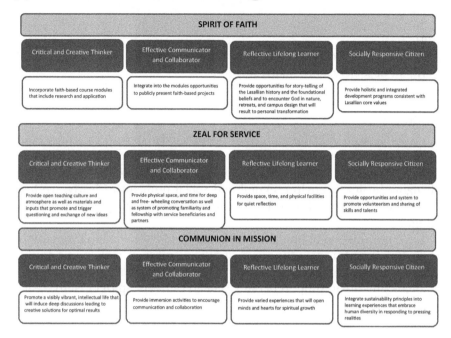

Appendix C: Lasallian Student Learning Outcomes

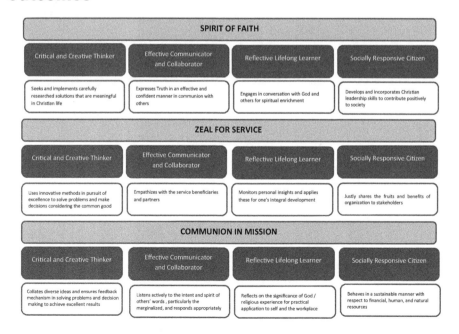

Appendix D: LEAD in BA Vision/Mission

Vision

Our vision is to develop future business leaders who will use their talent for the betterment of society, particularly the poor.

Mission

Our mission is to provide the young adults entrusted to us with a learner-centred education that encourages self-reflection as well as independent, critical and creative thinking, all necessary to help find innovative solutions to pressing and challenging business, environmental and social problems. Clearly, we foster environmental, social and ethical responsibility as the guiding posts in decision-making.

It is also our mission to prepare our future business leaders to listen intently to the opinion and respect the views of others and to articulate in a truthful, confident and clear manner.

All these aims are in support of our Lasallian values of Spirit of Faith, Zeal for Service and Communion in Mission.

12

Canadian academic uptake of the PRME

Sheila Carruthers
Sustainability Resources Ltd., Canada

Meenakshi Kakkar
Sustainability Resources Ltd., Canada

Carla Davidson
Sustainability Resources Ltd., Canada

Lisa Fox
Sustainability Resources Ltd., Canada

Abstract

To include sustainability and social responsibility in management education requires a change in perspective and practice. In ten years, just eighteen of Canada's academic institutions committed to follow the Principles for Responsible Management Education (PRME) and report on their efforts to integrate/ implement the principles. This low number of signatories compelled the chapter's authors to research utilization and effectiveness of the PRME within Canadian academic institutions. The PRME are most often embedded into specific academic programs and external stakeholder initiatives, but not into the entire institution. Effective integration of the PRME into curricula depends on the knowledge and dedication of faculty: simply incorporating sustainability into curricula is insufficient. The most significant barrier in Canada appears to be a lack of awareness and understanding among faculty. We conclude that signatory schools may be better at integrating the PRME into their institutions than non-signatories due to signatories' awareness of its resources and benefits.

The PRME

In a 2006 Global Compact Forum, academic leaders recognized the need to develop tools to teach business students the ten principles of the United Nations Global Compact (UNGC) in a business context. A task force was formed to develop an engagement platform that would give management schools the tools required. In 2007, the task force released the six principles that comprise the Principles of Responsible Management and Education (PRME). Since this time, management and business schools throughout the world have had the opportunity to endorse and adopt these principles in their curricula and research.

The purpose of this chapter is to assess the integration of the UNGC principles into management education; to examine how Canadian business schools and management institutes are (or not) preparing students to integrate business strategy with sustainability strategy and to explore whether faculty members are incorporating the topic of sustainability into their business-focussed curricula and research.

Post-secondary PRME signatories

Out of more than 650 post-secondary business schools and management-related academic institutions from over eighty-five countries around the world that are signatories of the PRME, just eighteen academic institutions are from Canada (see Appendix A). Moreover, two of these current Canadian signatories are indicated to be non-communicating participants, i.e. have not shared information on their progress with the PRME secretariat for more than two years, and thus will lose their signatory status. Just one Canadian signatory is listed as a PRME Champion, the University of Guelph, which means that it has been invited by the UNGC to contribute case studies and articles on responsible management education that fit with the United Nations Sustainable Development Goals (SDGs). Ten of the Canadian signatories are listed as being Advanced Signatories, which means they are sharing progress information with the PRME and have paid its annual service fee. The final five Canadian signatories are sharing information on their progress to the PRME. Appendix B lists Canadian colleges and universities that offer business education but have not signed on to either the UNGC or PRME.

The PRME is well-positioned to assist academic institutions in creating both internal and external awareness of how their curriculum aligns with the UNGC, help define direction and strategy, and encourage the creation of new synergies and collaborations among faculty. The preparation of biennial reports has been noted by signatories to be a 'powerful catalyst' for continued change on campus.

Drawing from the PRME, related public reports and academic papers, this chapter offers a balance of general and specific insight. The research team reviewed the Communication on Progress (CoP) reports that signatories are required to submit to the PRME, and analyzed key knowledge, understanding, resources and leadership that caused the Canadian signatories to commit to the PRME and UNGC.

Examples from Canada's signatories

Using the framework of the six PRME, Canada's current signatories have reported a variety of initiatives that are briefly summarized here to inspire others. Their full reports can be found on the PRME website.

Principle 1 | Purpose

A commitment to sustainability is embedded into many of these institutions' vision and mission statements, and long-term sustainability strategies are integrated into academic and institutional plans. One school gives every student a copy of its Corporate Social Responsibility (CSR) pledge and oath during orientation. Signatories also run community/business outreach activities to engage students in practical experiences that benefit local needs and the students by directly aligning the purpose with their studies.

Principle 2 | Values

The topic of CSR, sustainability, ethics and/or indigenous business are being added to curricula, and certifications and accreditations are offered in these specializations. Involvement in sustainability challenges and competitions is encouraged, as is interdisciplinary curricular innovation, and schools are converting their facilities to operate in more environment-friendly ways.

Principle 3 | Method

Workshops, symposia, debates, case studies and other pedagogical tools focussed on CSR, ethics and sustainability are used by faculty in undergraduate, graduate and executive education. Student interns are being placed in sustainability positions in businesses and in the non-profit sector. Hosting sustainability expert guest speakers is frequently cited as a way to expose students and faculty to these topics. Independent or faculty-led sustainability institutes, centres, hubs, endowed chairs and social innovation incubators are other methods being used.

Principle 4 | Research

Faculty are encouraged to write scholarly articles and books on sustainability, including the UNGC and PRME. Research is undertaken by undergraduate and postgraduate students as well as faculty on topics that include CSR/social responsibility, sustainability, ethics, workplace diversity, civil society engagement, environmental management systems, health and safety, recycling, social innovation, consumer power, labour management, non-profits, privacy, cybercrime, law and tourism.

Principle 5 | Partnership

Faculty and students are partnering with business and community leaders and organizations by engaging in initiatives on social entrepreneurship, offering a business advice clinic and delivering publicly accessible presentations in-house, hosted by a local business, and through webinars. A cross-institutional learning hub is an innovative method to partner with other faculties.

Principle 6 | Dialogue

Speaker series, business school-led corporate roundtables, cross-enterprise leadership workshops, winners' presentations from business ethics/case competitions and faculty serving on academic ethics and research boards and committees are all methods being used to engage people in dialogues to promote the PRME.

Research process

In 2014, the research team from Sustainability Resources Inc. participated in a survey led by leading sustainability experts and coordinated by the Canadian Business for Social Responsibility (CBSR) of sustainability practitioners from across Canada that was assessing people's attitudes towards the availability of training on CSR and sustainability. The research results of that study overwhelmingly indicated a need and demand for more training in this area.

Building on that research, Canadian academics, professionals and business schools were surveyed in early 2016 by the Sustainability Resources Inc. research team to determine how the UNGC, in concert with the PRME, were being integrated into post-secondary education courses and faculty training. The questions were conceptualized through the team's combined practical experience in advancing CSR and sustainability, literature reviews and inferences drawn from previous research. The survey was brief (Appendix C). Respondents were asked to identify their focus area of CSR and/or sustainability in business management and to answer questions under the following subset of topics:

1 Knowledge of UNGC and PRME

2 Approach to teaching responsible business management

3 Integration of PRME into higher education faculties

Contact information for deans, or their administrators, was identified in each school. These contacts were invited to participate in the online survey

(Appendix C). Each individual was emailed at least twice and called at least once to encourage his or her participation. In total, fifty-eight institutions were contacted; thirteen signatories and forty-five non-signatories to either the PRME or the UNGC. Participation in the study was voluntary and participants were required to give informed consent before initiating the survey. The team endeavoured to make it clear that the survey was intended to assess attitudes and not to generate a report card or evaluation of their programs.

In keeping with the Greenleaf Publication Ethics Best Practices Guidelines and Canada's Tri-Council Policy Statement, 'Ethical Conduct for Research Involving Humans', an informed consent form was emailed to all business schools along with a link to the survey. Target participants were made aware of the goals of the study, how their responses would be reported and their ability to remove themselves and their data from the survey at any time.

The responses that are cited in this chapter have not been attributed to any particular organization or person to ensure individual confidentiality.

Survey results

Awareness

Of the fifty-eight universities that were contacted, twenty-three (40 per cent) responded to the survey, of which just two were signatories. However, not every respondent fully completed the survey. Each question had an average of six to ten responses, with open-ended (written) questions having a lower response rate. This left too small a sample for a quantitative analysis, although many interesting responses were submitted. This chapter summarizes the important themes that emerged.

The survey probed respondents' familiarity with the UNGC, the PRME and the UN SDGs. Of the ten respondents, eight were aware of the UN SDGs, seven were aware of the UNGC and PRME and six stated that their organization had embraced the principles of the UNGC and PRME.

Integrated principles

Survey participants were asked how they use the PRME to promote research at their academic institution and how they facilitate dialogue around sustainability with fellow educators and knowledge networks. Nine respondents shared specific examples of how the principles are utilized at their institutions. Notably, one (non-signatory) respondent stated the PRME goals are part of his or her institution's mission, vision and strategic plan. Another described the deepening integration of PRME within his or her institution, which was an early signatory to the PRME in 2009. Annually at this institution, a faculty member interviews faculty to assess PRME activity and set goals. A progress report is shared with all employees and circulated to faculty and staff. By 2015, the school was highlighting PRME in at least half of its weekly communiques, which were posted on the website and distributed to all employees, some senior university administrators and other engaged stakeholders. Since 2015, this institution has used the PRME as a framework for its annual review of school activities.

Typically, respondents say the PRME are embedded into specific academic programs but not integrated into the entire institution (six respondents). One respondent stated that the PRME are embedded into his or her school's CSR/Sustainability Certificate Program but could not say whether there was awareness of, or use of, the principles elsewhere in the university.

On the question, whether their institution was partnering with other stakeholders such as business, government, and/or civil society organizations to integrate sustainability based on the UNGC principles, three out of four respondents identified projects or initiatives that involved other stakeholders in UNGC-related initiatives.

One promising approach was the formation of a stakeholder group to advise program curriculum and course delivery. This university is creating a cross-institutional learning hub for sustainability and CSR education and is in the process of entering into agreements with national civic and business associations to collaborate on sustainability and CSR education. At another business school, faculty members are partnering with municipal and community leaders as well as non-government organizations (NGOs), working collectively to address local poverty issues.

Although most respondents did not have specific mechanisms for engaging with people and organizations outside the academic institution, some have established unique and local solutions to integrate UNGC both within and outside the academic community. However, little to no specifics were shared, indicating potential loss of opportunities to benefit from the experiences of others.

Curriculum integration

The way in which the PRME are integrated into course curricula varied for each responding institution. Interestingly, none of the respondents indicated what specific topics of the UNGC or PRME are taught in their institution. This includes both signatories and non-signatory participants. However, respondent institutions do offer courses that contain CSR and/or topics such as environmental assessment, regulations and reclamation, social responsibility and innovation, ethics and financial management (including audits and ESG). Each institution delivers a combination of courses, certificate programs, diplomas and Masters-level studies that are specifically designed around CSR and/or sustainability-relevant topics. Some have gone so far as to establish centres/institutions that are dedicated to the study of CSR/sustainability. Interestingly, of the forty-five non-signatory schools, six had an institute or centre devoted to sustainability/sustainable business.

The effectiveness of integrating the PRME into curricula appears to depend on the knowledge and dedication of faculty. One institution uses blog posts, regular department meetings and communiques to engage its faculty, employees and community stakeholders. Other institutions have creative methods for increasing the capacity of faculty to use the PRME. For example, one participant's faculty members are supported by a network of business advisors that assist delivery of workshops to promote an understanding of the principles. Four institutions indicated they have mandatory courses on responsible management, while one institution has compulsory courses in ethics, social responsibility and sustainable development for all students at the undergraduate level.

The methods used to ensure effective integration of sustainability in curricula were not clearly outlined. Few institutions use audits, guidelines, checklists or frameworks to ensure CSR, and/or sustainability is integrated into the curriculum. The institutions' methods to assess student competencies in this area vary from brief quizzes to large projects such as partnerships with local businesses. Implementation methods differ depending on the nature of the curriculum. For example, a course on entrepreneurship partners with local businesses.

Institutional integration

Human rights, anti-corruption and environmental sustainability are issues that are deeply intertwined. All have outcomes and are impacted by decisions made by business. Therefore, these issues, covered by the ten UNGC principles, are better confronted when they are interwoven throughout all curricula in all relevant disciplines. Assessments of survey participants on their views of the interaction between PRME issues and common business practices were conducted. When asked about correlations between sustainability issues and business management, most respondents cited there to be a correlation between human rights, labour practices, gender equality, environmental concerns and governance on the one hand, and business practices and management education on the other. Most agreed that it is important to embrace sustainability. Some feel business has 'gone global' and students must consequently become more aware of cultural differences, differing business practices, supply chain challenges and ethics. One survey respondent noted that 'fully embedding sustainability and CSR into business practices which includes social and environmental considerations is the future of business.'

Consistent with the findings of the survey on curricula, the topics of human rights, anti-corruption and environmental sustainability still tend to be considered separately from the rest of business education and there was little indication of how consideration for these topics are being translated into business, administrative and operational functions in the institutions. One respondent noted the case for a systems approach to creating shared value in business and education, explaining that for each of these elements (comprising the principles) they can make the business case for reduced reputational risk, increased profitability (increased sales), increased productivity and engagement and reduced costs. However, when asked, to what extent business practices are designed to balance the growing concern for social, environmental and humanitarian aspects of corporations, responses reflected the respondents' specific academic interests. Interestingly, all five respondents espoused the importance of sustainable business practices, while four shared sentiments stating the process was in its early stages. One respondent stated: 'I think business involvement/integration of social, environmental and humanitarian issues is growing, and I believe the extent of the involvement/integration varies widely among businesses.' Others suggested that the integration of sustainability practices has more traction in some industries than others. For example, another respondent stated:

> [T]he extent to which business practices are trying to balance the growing concern varies across countries as well as industry type and company's size and ownership. It will be very difficult to assess, classify or generalize these attempts apart from the impossibility to separate genuine intentions from PR conformity.

By comparison, a signatory assessed its integration of sustainability in its curriculum and reports on the PRME website, indicating that of its 113 courses, sixty-five have a sustainability component. Three of these courses focus on sustainability. Interestingly, the school admits that most of the sustainability content in these courses exists in isolation, i.e. not fully integrated throughout the course but instead a single chapter in a thick course textbook and maybe a few questions on a quiz.

The topic of integration of sustainability into education highlights two key influencers: (1) professional development, and (2) institutional culture. Faculty need opportunities to learn about sustainability and innovate to embed concepts and competencies into curricula and co-curricular activities (Tilbury and Wortman, 2008). Business schools and other management programs can commit to 'proactive ethics', where they actively engage stakeholders in teaching, research and community outreach that promotes social responsibility and is supported by faculty development, rigorous planning, direct communication between project partners, creation of a shared vision among project participants and a collaborative culture of learning (Cornelius-White, 2007; Moratis *et al.*, 2006).

Each respondent recognized the sea change that fully adopting the PRME is in its infancy. Integrating sustainability principles into business practice is perceived as being complex.

Innovative projects and practices

An abundance of tools for teaching sustainability cannot be assumed to automatically imply that such topics will impact practice. In fact, some respondents suggested that such curriculum incorporation might not improve students' readiness for implementing the PRME in their future careers.

Many respondents stated that their courses use typical tools of course work, quizzes and case studies. However, others have utilized more in-depth tools for encouraging learning in this area. One respondent's institution established an 'undergraduate sustainability challenge'. Students form groups in partnership with an international student and then design a socially responsible business idea that benefits the international student's home country. The student groups then pitch their idea to a panel of judges drawn from faculty, community and business leaders.

Tools for integrating PRME in the academic institution or community include efforts to support knowledge transfer between the institution and the community. Not only does this highlight where curricular improvements and course content updates are needed to meet the demands of a dynamic job market but it also informs both the institution and the surrounding community on attitudes towards sustainability principles in business education. More commonly, institutions that undertake to teach sustainable or socially responsible business practices establish centres and institutes dedicated to supporting and researching sustainability. These internal centres are focused on communicating and developing methods of incorporating CSR and sustainability throughout course curricula, faculty research, governance and operations. The ubiquity of this approach suggests that it is an effective support for PRME-related education.

Challenges and opportunities

Although some survey respondents had impressive success stories of integrating the PRME in their curricula, they cited the following challenges:

- Few Canadian institutions have become signatories to the PRME, and the fact that few survey respondents felt their students were adequately equipped to deal with these topics speaks of the challenges of fully integrating the PRME into business education. Crucially, while the survey was devised to assess why the non-signatory schools in Canada had not signed on to the PRME, it turned out that, until it was mentioned, the schools had no knowledge of the principles or had little interest in CSR. This is different from if those schools had made the conscious decision that either the principles were inconsistent with their academic vision or there was insufficient demand for such curriculum to warrant inclusion. However, the low rate of response to the survey, especially among non-signatory schools, hampers our ability to determine why the PRME has not had wider adoption within Canada.

- The most significant barrier to implementing the PRME in business and management education in Canada appears to be a lack of awareness and understanding among faculty. For example, one respondent noted:

    > It is a challenge to ensure that all faculty members have an understanding of the Principles that is deep enough for them to feel comfortable

discussing them in the classroom. It might also be a challenge to educate the faculty members on the depth to which contemporary business must and does deal with issues of sustainability and social responsibility.

- The inclusion of sustainability and social responsibility in management and business education represents a change in perspective and practice. At the same time, these new topics must compete with what is already being taught in Canadian business schools.

- The PRME encourage engagement with the business community and all participants had methods to gauge employer satisfaction with their graduates; and student feedback is also collected. However, respondents indicated, there still remains a gulf in the ability of their graduates to navigate the PRME.

- Some businesses may not yet realize the benefit of adopting sustainable and socially responsible practices. This challenges academic institutions, particularly business schools that are balancing competing priorities. It is, however, crucial if Canadian academic institutions are to catch up with their global peers.

There are also a number of opportunities for Canadian business and management schools:

- For schools that have strong ties with the business community, priorities often are influenced by the businesses' interests; thus, the opportunity for the school to show leadership in responsible management practices may be limited. However, one might argue that schools with strong ties in the business community are more likely to be able to influence businesses by sharing corporate responsibility and sustainability research results and by engaging dialogue on the topics between business leaders, students and faculty. One respondent offered such insight:

  > [A] key challenge is simply competing priorities in terms of required content and overall review of curricula with this objective in mind. . . . We . . . have many programs where program content is aligned with industry requirements for achievement of industry designations adding pressure on hours and structure of content.

- A cited lack of resources, including up-to-date textbooks, implies a 'lone wolf' trying to foment change. But common among all responses was the importance of making the business case to institution decision-makers that incorporating the principles of sustainable and socially responsible business practice is worthwhile. Survey respondents understand the importance of these issues. As one stated:

  > Fully embedding sustainability and CSR into business practices which includes social and environmental considerations is the future of business. Companies need and in many cases are looking for the "shared value" value proposition.

The evidence indicates an opportunity to convince senior administrators that incorporating these principles in business education is not only worthwhile but is also the future of business education.

- Only two of the six participants believed that their graduates were well prepared to deal with PRME-related issues. This indicates that there may be a significant difference between students that are required to study PRME-related issues and those for whom such study was optional. The opportunity exists to further research this assumption.

- The PRME website provides extensive guidance on how to become a signatory. There are also community of practice networks such as the Global Compact Network and the International Society for Sustainability Professionals providing postgraduate and professional management support. These networks demonstrate the success of institutions that are adopting the PRME and integrating them into management education. However, notwithstanding all the readily available information, res-pondents to the survey indicated that there remains a gulf in the ability of their graduates to navigate the PRME, suggesting there is opportunity to improve the efficacy of PRME education and postgraduate support.

- Implementing significant change in management education requires sustained and varied methods of building capacity. There are oppor-tunities for more education resources such as textbooks and learning modules based on the PRME to be added to curricula.

Conclusions and recommendations

Ten years have passed since the establishment of the UNGC's PRME and yet relatively few Canadian business schools have become signatories. A significant barrier appears to be a general lack of awareness and understanding of the PRME existence and purpose as well as the need for a clear business case for academic institutions to adopt the PRME.

Based on survey results covered in this review and the authors' independent research, we conclude that signatory schools appear to be better at integrating corporate responsibility and sustainability education and management practices into their institutions than non-signatories as a result of the institution decision-makers' commitment to the PRME.

Business schools that want to develop responsible future leaders can use the three enablers of change, i.e. (1) transformative learning, (2) issue-centred learning and (3) reflective practice and field work (Muff *et al.*, 2013). Both Canadian PRME signatories and non-signatories, as well as this chapter, offer examples of these three enablers and they were mentioned by some survey participants. However, there is a difference between developing responsible future leaders and incorporating the PRME into administration and curricula. Canada's academic institutions need to decide to what extent they will be thought leaders and to what extent they will fully integrate the PRME into their administration and curricula.

Our recommendation is that for the PRME to be adopted by Canada's business schools, a sustainable awareness strategy is needed that includes not only the sharing of educational materials and innovative knowledge mobilization tools to track progress and success but also both a high-impact promotion (similar to the launch of UN SDGs in 2016), affirming initiatives such as public recognition, support for establishing internal centres of CSR and sustainability excellence, and the development/distribution of case studies that showcase measurable and successful implementation and integration of PRME into Canadian academic institutions.

Bibliography

Cornelius-White, J. (2007) 'Learner-centered teacher-student relationships are effective: A meta-analysis'. *Review of Educational Research*, 77:1, 113–143.

CSR Strategies Inc. (2014) 'CSR & sustainability survey results report'. Available online at www.csrstrategies.ca/uploads/strategies/pdfs/CSR%20BOK%20and%20Certification%20Survey%20Report%20FINAL.pdf (accessed 21 June 2016).

DNV GL. (2015) 'Impact: Transforming business, changing the world. The United Nations Global Compact.' Available online at http://globalcompact15.org/report (accessed 21 June 2016).

International Society for Sustainability Professionals (ISSP). (2016) Available online at www.-sustainabilityprofessionals.org/ (accessed 21 June 2016).

Moratis, L., Hoff, J. and Reul, B. (2006) 'A dual challenge facing management education: Simulation-based learning and learning about CSR'. *Journal of Management Development*, 25:3, 213–231.

Muff, K., Dyllick, T., Drewell, M., North, J., Shrivastava, P. and Haertle, J. (2013) *Management education for the world: A vision for business schools serving people and planet.* Cheltenham, UK: Edward Elgar, GRLI Foundation 2013.

PRME: Principles for Responsible Management Education. (2016a) 'History.' Available online at www.unprme.org/about-prme/history/index.php (accessed 21 June 2016).

PRME: Principles for Responsible Management Education. (2016b) 'Signatories.' Available online at www.unprme.org/participants/index.php (accessed 21 June 2016).

PRME: Principles for Responsible Management Education. (2016c) 'Six principles.' Available online at www.unprme.org/about-prme/the-six-Principles.php (accessed 21 June 2016).

PRME Secretariat. (2016a) 'A basic guide to the sharing information on progress (SIP): For current and prospective signatories of the principles for responsible management education. Version 1.0.' Available online at www.unprme.org/resource-docs/SIPToolkit FINALWeb.pdf (accessed 21 June 2016).

PRME Secretariat. (2016b) 'Management education and the sustainable development goals: Transforming education to act responsibly and find opportunities.' Available online at www.unprme.org/resource-docs/SDGBrochurePrint.pdf (accessed 21 June 2016).

Six Principles of Responsible Management Education (PRME). Available online at www. unprme.org/about-prme/the-six-Principles.php (accessed 21 June 2016).

TCPS. (2010) 'Tri-council policy statement: Ethical conduct for research involving humans.' Available online at www.pre.ethics.gc.ca/pdf/eng/tcps2/TCPS_2_FINAL_Web.pdf (accessed 15 December 2015).

Ten Principles of the United Nations Global Compact (UNGC). Available online at www. unglobalcompact.org/what-is-gc/mission/Principles (accessed 21 June 2016).

Tilbury, D. and Wortman, D. (2008) 'How is community education contributing to sustainability in practice?' *Journal of Applied Environmental Education & Communication*, 7:3, 83–93.

UN GLOBAL Compact. (2016) 'The ten principles of the UN global compact.' Available online at www.unglobalcompact.org/what-is-gc/mission/Principles (accessed 21 June 2016).

UN Global Compact Network. (2016) 'About the Global Network Canada.' Available online at www.globalcompact.ca/about-us/about-the-global-compact-network-canada (accessed 21 June 2016).

Sheila Carruthers, MBA, CMC, senior associate with Sustainability Resources and owner of CSR Strategies Inc., specializing in communications and Corporate Social Responsibility (CSR). Sheila instructs CSR in the Continuing Education Faculty at the University of Calgary and is a trainer for the Canadian Association of Management Consultants.

Meenakshi Kakkar, MPhi, PhD, senior associate with Sustainability Resources after an accomplished career as general manager (sustainability) at Steel Authority of India Ltd. She is an elected member of the Stakeholder Council of the Global Reporting Initiative (GRI), where she contributed to the development of the GRI-G4 sustainability reporting guidelines.

Carla Davidson, PhD, senior associate with Sustainability Resources and owner of Endeavour Scientific Inc. Carla has a BSc in Ecology and Environmental Studies from the University of Victoria, a PhD in Systems Biology (University of Calgary) and certifications: Post-Secondary Teaching (University of Calgary) and Knowledge Translation (University of Toronto).

Lisa Fox, BA Phil, is the founder and executive director of Sustainability Resources, a non-profit education and professional consortium dedicated to advancing solutions and building capacity for sustainability. She is an accomplished policy analyst and has worked with governments across Canada on issues relating to resource management and sustainability.

Appendix A: PRME signatory universities in Canada: Indicating signatory type

Academic Institution	Business School Name	Signatory Type
University of Guelph	College of Business and Economics	PRME Champion
Concordia University	John Molson School of Business	Advanced
Dalhousie University	Rowe School of Business	Basic
Grant MacEwan University	School of Business	Advanced
Laurentian University	Faculty of Management	Advanced
Queen's University	Smith School of Business	Advanced
Saint Mary's University	Sobey School of Business	Advanced
Simon Fraser University	Beedie School of Business	Advanced
University of British Columbia	Sauder School of Business	Advanced
University of the Fraser Valley	School of Business	Advanced
University of Victoria	Gustavson School of Business	Advanced
Wilfrid Laurier University	Lazaridis School of Business & Economics	Advanced
British Columbia Institute of Technology	British Columbia Institute of Technology	Basic
University of Calgary	Haskayne School of Business	Basic
University of Windsor	Odette School of Business	Basic
York University	Schulich School of Business	Basic
Ryerson University	Ted Rogers School of Management	Non-communicating
Western University	Ivey Business School	Non-communicating

Appendix B: PRME non-signatory colleges and universities in Canada

Academic Institution	Business School Name
Acadeia University	F.C. Manning School of Business
Algonquin College	School of Business
Arctic College	Business and Management
Aurora College	School of Business & Leadership
Bishop's University	Williams School of Business
Cape Breton University	Shannon School of Business
Capilano University	School of Business
Carleton University	Sprott School of Business
Centennial College	School of Business
Dawson College	Business Administration programs
Durham College of Applied Arts and Technology	School of Business
George Brown College of Applied Arts & Technology	Centre for Business
Holland College	Business Program
Humber College Institution of Technology and Advanced Learning	The Business School
Kwantlen Polytechnic University	Business Program
Lakehead University	Faculty of Business Administration
Lethbridge College	Business Program
McGill University	Desautels Faculty of Management
McMaster University	deGroote School of Business
Memorial University of Newfoundland	Faculty of Business Administration
Mount Royal University	Bisset School of Business
Nova Scotia Community College	School of Business
Okanagan College	
Olds College	Business Program
Robertson College	Business program
Royal Roads University	Faculty of Management
Saskatchewan Institute of Applied Sciences and Technology	School of Business
Seneca College	
Sheridan College	Business Program
Sheridan College	Pilon School of Business
St. Francis Xavier University	Gerald Shwartz School of Business
Thompson Rivers University	School of Business and Economics
University of Alberta/Alberta School of Business	Alberta School of Business
University of Lethbridge	Faculty of Management
University of Manitoba	Asper School of Business
University of New Brunswick	Faculty of Business Administration
University of Northern BC	The School of Business
University of Ottawa	Telfer School
University of PEI	School of Business
University of Regina	Paul J. Hill School of Business
University of Saskatchewan	Edwards School of Business
University of Toronto	University of St. Michael's College
University of Toronto	Rotman School of Management
University of Winnipeg	Faculty of Business and Economics
Vancouver Island University	Faculty of Management
Yukon College	School of Management, Tourism & Hospitality

Appendix C: PRME survey questions for academic institutions' business schools

Target: Academic institutions and business schools in Canada offering management education

Introduction

Sustainability Resources is conducting a survey to assess the integration of the UN Global Compact into management education. The results of this survey will be included in a chapter of the book titled *Redefining Success: Integrating the UN Global Compact into Management Education* being published by Greenleaf.

The six principles of PRME[1] provide a framework for engaging Higher Education Institutions (HEIs), especially management and business programs, to embed principles of corporate sustainability in education, research and campus practices.

The survey will only take about 15 minutes to complete. Business schools from Canada are taking part in this survey and we hope you can do it too. Participation is voluntary.

Please complete all questions. However, if you feel uncomfortable answering a particular question, you can skip to the next question.

Survey Questions

1. Please tell us about your organization

    (a) Title _____
    (b) Location_____
    (c) Focus area_____
    (d) Website_____
    (e) Contact person_____

    Have you heard about UNGC and PRME?

    • Yes
    • No
    • Not sure

2. Has your institution embraced the Principles of UNGC and PRME?

    • Yes
    • No

3. Have you heard about the United Nations Sustainable Development goals?

- Yes
- No
- Not sure

4. How do you define responsible management education?

5. How have the Principles of PRME been used to promote research and facilitate dialogue around corporate sustainability with fellow educators and knowledge networks in your business school or institution?

6. Is your business school or management institute partnering with business, government, civil society organisations and other stakeholders to integrate sustainability based on UNGC Principles?

7. Do you see any correlations between sustainability issues, such as human rights, labour practices, gender equality, environmental concerns and governance and their implications for business practices and management education?

8. To what extent are business practices trying to balance the growing concern for social, environmental and humanitarian aspects of corporations?

9. Which of the following do you teach in your business school or management institution? Select all that apply.

- CSR
- Ethics
- Responsible behaviour
- TBL – sustainability
- Stakeholder engagement
- Transparency and disclosure
- Sustainable consumption and production
- Labour issues
- Human Rights
- Anti-corruption
- Environmental sustainability
- Legal aspects of CSR
- Diversity, gender equality and non-discrimination policy
- Social accountability
- Fair trade
- UNGC and PRME
- UN SDG
- *Others:

10. Do you think that your students are well equipped to handle the issues and topics noted in #9 above in real life?

11. Have you had feedback from corporate or industry partners on the ability of students?

12. To what extent does your academic institute support faculty development to facilitate and disseminate research, teaching and outreach activities based on UNGC Principles?

13. What kind of innovative projects does your business school or management institute have? Are they relevant enough to come up with financially sustainable business solutions to real social issues?

14. Are there any mandatory modules on responsible management education in your business school?

   - Yes
   - No
   - Not sure

15. What are the challenges of, and solutions to, integrating the ten principles comprehensively and pragmatically into management education?

16. Would you like to share strategies, theories, case studies and examples of best practices and innovations, and resources for teaching and learning that can help integrate the ten principles of Global Compact into management education programs?

   (a) Please provide a link to any online resources that you would like to share:

17. What do you think of the responsibilities of business executives and management educators in defining and promoting multiple agendas, e.g. intellectual, research, educational, institutional and policy that address the social, environmental and humanitarian issues embodied in the ten principles?

18 Would you like to give any suggestions and demonstrations of how the Global Compact Ten Principles can best be integrated into management education consistent with the six principles of PRME?

19 Is your business school or institute of higher learning defining or revisiting their mission statement mirroring the mission of PRME (provide a link)?

Thank you for your contribution to advancing the capacity for a sustainable future.

13

Rethinking management education in Africa

Integrating the UN PRME

Ijeoma Nwagwu
Lagos Business School, Nigeria

Abstract

This chapter discusses the prospects and the challenges that management education institutions in Africa face in integrating the United Nations Global Compact and the Principles of Responsible Management Education standards on method, research and partnership. The chapter argues that while challenges exist in the implementation of these principles in African management education, solutions and opportunities are also increasingly evident. The chapter explores these challenges, solutions and opportunities as they play out across Africa's management education institutions in their teaching and research activities within a global economy, and at the same time defining their relevance to local conditions characterized by systemic poverty and the prevalence of informal markets.

Introduction

Responsible management education plays a major role in the drive towards achieving the UN Sustainable Development Goals (SDGs) and in influencing companies to follow the UN Global Compact principles, a prospect of particular significance in emerging economies. Business schools in African countries can play a critical role, for instance, in poverty reduction by educating business managers and executives on the implementation of inclusive business models, which provide opportunities for the poor while offering commercial benefits to business (Neal, 2016; Rigoglioso, 2012a; Stanford Graduate School of Business (SGSoB), 2014a).

Thirty management education institutions from eleven countries in Africa identify with the UN Global Compact and are signatories to the PRME (UN PRME, 2016) (see Appendix). The UN Global Compact and PRME provide frameworks for integrating ethics and responsibility in the management education of present and future business leaders. The potential for management schools to play a role in driving the emergence of responsible business – 'business that serves and empowers the poor' – is particularly relevant in most African countries where the bulk of the population falls within the demographic described as the 'Bottom of the Pyramid' (BoP) (Nwagwu, 2017; Prahalad, 2006).

Because of the unique features of BoP markets, ensuring that teaching, research and methods in management education are structured in a manner that caters to learners from BoP markets poses certain challenges. A key challenge is that this business model within the BoP market is largely an uncharted territory, which management education institutions have only recently started engaging on a largely preliminary and experimental basis. The subject of this engagement – business models within the BoP market – is itself evolving even as scholars and practitioners are examining it (Garcia-DeLeone and Taj, 2015:139; Karamchandani *et al.*, 2011:6; Nwagwu, 2017; Prahalad, 2012:7). Management educators are in the process of understanding these trends through research, distilling them for teaching in the classroom, and generating alternative models to suit the largely weak macro-institutional contexts in many African countries. The pace is slow considering the extent of the challenges and the PRME maxims offering a systemic framework for accelerating action towards sustainable development through management education. The adaptation of PRME goes hand-in-hand with efforts under the UN Global Compact to establish standards on labour, anti-corruption and human rights as core business precepts. Business schools can play a key role in adapting these frameworks to the emergence of responsible business: Business that serves and empowers the poor.

Although business schools can work towards developing responsible leaders by activating all six principles of PRME, this chapter focuses on only three: **Method** (#3), **Research** (#4) and **Partnership** (#5).

- **Method**: Adopting innovative educational frameworks to impart responsible business skills to entrepreneurs.

- **Research**: Focusing on research and documentation of successful inclusive businesses.

- **Partnership**: Advocating alternative and inclusive business models through conferences, informal meetings and other interactions with business leaders and managers.

Rigoglioso (2012b) posits that research and teaching methods provide the foundation tools for alleviating poverty within the BoP populations. That is, while researchers examine ideas and results for tackling extreme poverty, faculty members and students can pursue answers to crucial questions that are essential to understanding poverty reduction and economic growth within the BoP market (Rigoglioso, 2012b; Stanford Graduate School of Business, 2014b). However, it would require a thoughtful and systematic approach that considers cultural and environmental factors in the relationship between the management school and society (Rigoglioso, 2012a). African business schools can play a role in fostering innovative research, teaching methods and partnerships that seriously engage the challenges of economic growth and poverty in the broader society.

Africa has a vast network of business schools and universities that teach management courses and train students on how to run businesses. However, most of these institutions are unregistered and unaccredited; they compete with accredited management education institutions for participants (Furlonger, 2014; Jenvey, 2013). The result is that leading business schools have maintained their focus on educating managers for larger, publicly quoted businesses, which have more formal structures (Soni *et al.*, 2015).

Africa also has very few business schools dedicated solely to improving and positively shaping how business is practiced (Furlonger, 2014). The Association of African Business Schools (AABS) is an association of leading business schools in Africa that promotes excellence and responsibility in business and management education through capacity-building, collaboration and quality improvement (Association of African Business Schools (AABS), 2012). It is also one of the ten members of the PRME Steering Committee – the body that guides the strategic intentions and activities of the whole PRME community (UN PRME, 2016). AABS provides member schools with an endorsement of quality, an opportunity to learn from peers and access to a worldwide network (AABS, 2012).

Association of African Business Schools was formally established in 2005 and registered as a non-profit organization in 2007 (AABS, 2016). Its mission is 'to enable all business schools in Africa to contribute towards inclusive economic and social development in the continent by promoting excellence and responsibility in business and management education' (AABS, 2012). AABS conducts study visits, peer reviews, workshops and conferences as well as organize consultant visits to schools. It also runs an annual case-writing competition in collaboration with Emerald Publishing Limited (AABS, 2012). AABS has thirty accredited schools and forty-three member institutions across fourteen countries in Africa (see Figure 13.1 and Appendix).

FIGURE 13.1 Mapping Africa's management education institutions

Key: Black-AABS member schools Grey-AABS accredited Schools

Source: www.aabschools.com

Institutions such as the American University in Cairo (2015), Gordon Institute of Business Sciences (GIBS), Lagos Business School, Strathmore Business School, University of Stellenbosch Business School and University of Cape Town's Graduate School of Business stand out globally as business education institutions setting the pace in their societies (PRME Signatories, 2016; Webometrics, 2016). Through the training of current and future leaders in their home markets, these business schools can play a crucial role in laying the groundwork for sustainable development. This change in management education focus has led to courses and programs on Corporate Social Responsibility (CSR), ethics, corporate sustainability and social entrepreneurship being integrated into the core curriculum of many African business schools and universities (Purushottam and Rwelamila, 2011).

Opportunities to integrate the UN Global Compact in management education

The PRME provide a framework through which management education institutions can implement effective practices to drive the understanding and practice of UN Global Compact's principles in business organizations. This section discusses three key arenas to integrate the UN Global Compact and PRME maxims on method, research and partnership.

Innovative education models on doing business at the BoP and emerging economy context

(PRME Principle 3: Method)

Given the importance of small businesses to a nation's economy and their vulnerability to early failure due to management issues (Okpara and Wynn, 2007), business schools in Africa have a large untapped market of prospective students who need to be educated on the management of small- and medium-size enterprises (SMEs) in local environments (Gibb, 1996; Ladzani and van Vuuren, 2002). This is juxtaposed with large multinationals requiring managers with competencies for doing business in particular emerging economy contexts (Gordon, 2008).

Central to capturing the value and opportunities represented by doing business at the BoP and emerging economy contexts is the 'telling of the story' of business life in the local context apart from the mainstream markets. For instance, while the BoP market offers promise of great economic gains for companies, these rewards are only attainable if companies are able to implement innovative localized solutions to issues such as procurement and distribution. For instance, fast-moving consumer goods (FMCG) multinationals have evolved in Nigeria to surmount infrastructure challenges. In the absence of reliable roads that support the large-scale haulage companies, many of these FMCG companies, such as the Tolaram Group and Diageo, have established their own logistics support companies and decentralized their manufacturing operations to serve different regions of the country (Nwagwu, 2017). Hence, there is a need for field-based education in business schools, so students explore such contextual issues.

There is a wide knowledge gap, which African business schools have been striving to close. Management educators provide life support to local businesses, leaving little time to document more comprehensively the management knowledge derived from their business practices. For instance, The Pan African University's Lagos Business School in Nigeria incubated an innovative education model to address learning gaps. The model evolved into an independent centre called the Enterprise Development Centre (EDC). The EDC is dedicated to equipping small-, medium- and micro-scale businesses and aspiring entrepreneurs with basic accounting, inventory management, human resource and capital management skills.

This model has seen the emergence of hundreds of new entrepreneurs as well as a vibrant ecosystem of entrepreneurial networks. It is working to the extent that BoP entrepreneurs who initially lacked the requisite knowledge and business structures to access finance are surmounting these obstacles. Other entrepreneurs have been connected to these 'networks of opportunity', making it possible for business managers to be integrated in the value chain of big businesses and access opportunities through peer businesses. Further progress in integrating the UN Global Compact in this context would involve documenting these businesses in teaching case studies, enabling future cohorts of business students to become engaged with UN Global Compact principles on human rights, labour standards and anti-corruption. Other examples include the following:

University of Stellenbosch Business School (USB): The Academic Planning Committee of the USB oversees the integration of responsible leadership content into all curricula on offer. The USB also has been an active participant in the UN PRME anti-corruption working group over the last few years.

University of Kwazulu-Natal: The discipline of Management and Entrepreneurship developed a program known as E-Zone for students and academics to create a platform to write informative and practical articles to develop entrepreneurial and managerial thinking and competencies.

Graduate School of Business, University of Cape Town: The Groote Schuur Hospital Innovation Hub was launched in 2015 by the Bertha Centre for Social Innovation & Entrepreneurship[1]. Allan Gray Centre for Value-Based Leadership was established in 2011, which explores methods of learning, and new ways of doing business based on purpose, sustainability and responsible practices. There is also the MTN[2] Solution Space (comprising a learning lab, venture lab and exchange/network lab) which brings management educators and students in touch with real-world business problems.

The American University in Cairo (AUC): AUC offers a joint degree in sustainable development. There is also the AUC Venture Lab – launched in 2013 – to enable innovative start-ups to capitalize on AUC's intellectual capital, world-class facilities and research capacities. Goldman Sachs 10,000 Women Entrepreneurship and Leadership (WEL) program is also anchored in the institution.

Mzumbe University, Dar es Salaam: Mzumbe University has been one of the fourteen piloting business schools globally for testing and implementing the anti-corruption tool kit developed by the PRME anti-corruption working group. The contents of the tool kit have been integrated in different masters and undergraduate level courses.

Building the evidence base for inclusive business models

(PRME Principle 4: Research)

Business schools and institutional management educators have access to various leaders in business. Chief executive officers (CEOs) and senior management staff of various companies and organizations attend training and develop partnerships with these institutions. Researching and documenting inclusive business models, and integrating such research as cases and teaching resources in the curriculum of the schools' programs will go a long way to drive the value of inclusivity.

Case-focused research is but one level of the engagement required. Empirical research on business practices conducted consistently over the long term is essential to the durability of UN Global Compact principles in management education. Some of this work to address Africa's data-gap is already underway through dedicated research centres. The Lagos Business School as well as the University of Stellenbosch have 'sustainability centres', and the Strathmore University Business School runs a centre on sustainability studies, which increasingly links with business analytics and strategy. Other examples of African institutions implementing PRME, Principle 4 ('Research') include the following:

University of Stellenbosch (USB): There are various research centres at the USB, e.g. African Centre for Dispute Resolution; Base of the Pyramid Learning Lab; Centre for Applied Entrepreneurship; Centre for Business in Society; Centre for Corporate Governance in Africa and Centre for Leadership Studies.

Graduate School of Business, University of Cape Town: The Graduate School of Business, University of Cape Town launched the South African Education Innovator's Review, which seeks to explore working innovations in the education sector with a view to scaling up models for greater impact across emerging markets.

The American University in Cairo (AUC): The American University in Cairo maintains the *AUC Business Review* – the quarterly business magazine of the School of Business, which aims to bridge the gap between theory and practice. El-Khazindar Business Research and Case Centre provides case studies and educational services offering student participant-centred learning tools. Other research centres at AUC include the Gerhart Center for Philanthropy and Civic Engagement, Center for Entrepreneurship, Venture Lab and Entrepreneurs Society Student Club. They also host the BoP Local Office for Egypt, and are involved in the program Global Entrepreneurship Monitor (GEM).

Gordon Institute of Business Sciences (GIBS): To drive research at Gordon Institute of Business Sciences (GIBS), several research centres exist, including the Centre for Leadership and Dialogue, Centre for Business Analysis and Research and Centre for Dynamic Markets.

Strathmore University: @iLabAfrica is a research centre under the Faculty of Information Technology established to spearhead research, innovation and entrepreneurship at Strathmore University. @iLabAfrica collaborated with Safaricom, the leading integrated communications company in East Africa, and Vodafone to establish Safaricom Academy for developing mobile applications to exploit opportunities created by fast growing telecommunication industry in the country.

Stimulating multi-stakeholder collaboration

(PRME Principle 5: Partnership)

Management education institutions not only educate business leaders and managers but also represent a platform for businesses to engage with others on key principles of the UN Global Compact. Business school conferences and roundtables are being used to mainstream discussions and thought leadership on inclusive business, poverty, unemployment and related topics. Such forums are a viable platform to disseminate research findings and can help build avenues for dialogue between businesses and business schools. This would drive inclusivity from a subject in management academic literature to become a practice in Africa.

For example, Lagos Business School runs a research project, titled 'Sustainable Business Models for Delivering Digital Financial Services to Lower Income Unbanked Citizens of Nigeria,' supported by the Bill and Melinda Gates Foundation. The project seeks to understand better the delivery and access constraints the poor face in relation to the financial system, and explore appropriate Digital Financial Service (DFS) business models to enhance access and financial inclusion. The project features numerous stakeholder forums, bringing together industry practitioners, policy makers, academia, FinTech companies as well as financial sector experts to discuss opportunities and challenges in digital financial services for reaching the un-banked and under-banked.

Other examples of PRME, Principle 5 ('Partnership') implementation activities in various African management institutions include the following:

University of Kwazulu-Natal: The school recently set up a training program with IBM International University to train students for career-ready opportunities in the IT industry.

Mzumbe University: Mzumbe University maintains relationships with corporate managers and practitioners, partners with businesses, non-governmental organizations (NGOs) and other organizations. The university also maintains international strategic partnerships.

Rhodes University: Rhodes Business School runs 'Think like an Entrepreneur', a small business entrepreneurial skills workshop, in a community centre in undeveloped township areas. People who cannot get loans from banks attend this workshop and are guided on starting up their businesses.

The challenges

Management education in Africa has several challenges that relate to the UN Global Compact and the PRME goals. These include the following:

Research – The unique position of business schools and universities in management education hinges on their role not only as management education institutions but also as research institutions (Thomas *et al.*, 2016). Such intellectual research efforts help to shape the knowledge direction of the school as well as enhance business practices. Historically, there has been a lack of research focus in business schools, and consequently, limited scientific information on business in Africa, especially business models that are inclusive (Okonedo and Aluko, 2016; Thomas *et al.*, 2016). Moreover, this research must be 'very practice-oriented' (Bennis and O'Toole, 2005; Pfeffer and Fong, 2002; PRME, 2012; Thomas *et al.*, 2016).

Faculty – Management education institutions in Africa experience problems in the attraction, retention and development of qualified academic faculty and staff needed to build strong institutions and address the huge demand of Africans for management education (Klein and Ward, 2005). Faculty development is a challenge per se, and to deal with the challenges related tor research appropriate faculty development inter-institutional and international collaboration offers huge opportunities to deal with the challenges related to research and appropriate faculty development.

Globalization – African management education institutions experience issues involved with navigating focus on local and global relevance (Nkomo, 2015). That is, conditions in African nations are different from those in other countries of the world (Thomas *et al.*, 2016). Hence, the imperative to create African-specific content while maintaining global relevance continues to pose a challenge to management education in Africa (Klein and Ward, 2005; Thomas *et al.*, 2016).

Access – Conventional African business schools and management institutions are either inaccessible or not adapted to impoverished individuals (Thomas *et al.*, 2016). Further, business schools are inaccessible to small local businesses, as leading business schools have traditionally catered to the upper echelons of large multinational or publicly listed companies (Ndimande, 2006).

Infrastructure – It is critical for management education institutions to possess certain infrastructure (e.g. information and communication technology, legal and physical infrastructure). However, African management education institutions experience an absence or inadequacy of such infrastructure (Khan, 2015).

Broader Institutional environments – Broader institutional environments plagued by corruption and unstable economic policies and markets (Ezenyilimba, 2015) affect the prospects and viability of management education institutions in Africa (Thomas *et al.*, 2016).

Ndlovu-Gatsheni (2013) summarized these trends and challenges saying the following: 'Our challenge is ensuring that management education is relevant to the developmental priorities of the nation as well as to erasing the negative imprints of Africa's marginalization. Tellingly, the World Economic Forum 2015 Global Agenda survey points to education and skills development as the biggest challenges facing Africa. Most of the respondents suggested that business is the stakeholder and is most affected by Africa's educational challenges.

Solutions

To address these challenges, business schools and universities in Africa have taken proactive steps in developing strategies to deliver educational and research services that are relevant and reflect a determination to redirect Africa's emerging economies to a more sustainable future. Following are the examples:

Research: El-Khazindar Business Research and AUC's case centre develop case studies and educational services that provide students with participant-centred learning tools. Other research centres at AUC include the Gerhart Center for Philanthropy and Civic Engagement, Center for Entrepreneurship and the Venture Lab.

Faculty: Lagos Business School has, as one of its missions, to retain and recruit faculty with the highest standards and academic excellence who are devoted to teaching, research and mentoring students to solve societal problems. To further this mission, it collaborates with Instituto de Estudos Sociais e Economicos (IESE) Business School in Spain to expose its faculty to excellent pedagogical seminars and practical workshops. Its faculty members also participate in the Academy of Business Management's 'teaching business' workshops, which provide a setting for collaboration across Africa's business schools in the area of faculty development.

Globalization: An interesting example of local solutions emerging in a globalized context is the Africapitalism Research Project. This project involved a research partnership among the University of Edinburg, University of Birmingham, Nottingham University, University of Cape Town, Durham University, Strathmore Business School, International University of Grand Bassam and University of Bedforshire. It explores African understandings of entrepreneurship and capitalism against the backdrop of trends in global capitalism.

Access: Rhodes Business School students act as consultants to emerging businesses in Joza (a local poor township area) and provide training to assist the development of their business through 'Think like an

Entrepreneur' – a program that provides small business entrepreneurial skills workshops in a community centre in Grahamstown East. The business school welcomes the so-called 'unbankable people' who cannot get loans from banks to attend the workshops (see Table 13.1). Similarly, HEM Business School aspires to launch in the 2017 school year a new private university model, professionalizing and combining quality and fair price designed to train mid-management executives. It will target the middle class and will cover, in addition to a relatively moderate cost of studies, a complementary system of credit education.

Infrastructure: At Lagos Business School, training and lectures are delivered in 'purpose-built' learning facilities' developed as a collaborative philanthropic project between the founders of the school and businesses operating within the country environment. In addition, its facilities and learning environment are constantly being improved by staff specially trained to maintain the building and landscape.

Broader Institutional Environments: The AUC collaborates with the government in the Model Egyptian Economy Initiative as an example of a business school that is not only shaped by its macro-economic contexts but is also producing solutions to positively reshape its broader institutional context.

Conclusion

To achieve a shift towards more responsible and sustainable business practices across Africa, management education plays a vital role in articulating and guiding businesses towards adopting inclusive strategies to address the social and economic needs of the bottom billion. Three PRME maxims that provide opportunities to achieve this were discussed in this chapter – teaching methods, research and partnerships. First, in their teaching methods, schools should systematically provide innovative business case models to train entrepreneurs from, or catering to, the BoP on the basics of running SMEs and sensitize larger and more established firms on fostering inclusivity in their supply chain and business models. Second, emphasis should be placed on research, with specific focus on systematically documenting and disseminating the experience of inclusive businesses and companies that have adopted inclusive business model as part of their core business activities with positive results or challenges worth sharing. Third, business school conferences and roundtables can be utilized as opportunities for partnerships and dialogue to explore effective ways to meet social challenges. The platform for partnership would supplement earlier discussed possibilities around academia–business collaboration. When combined, teaching methods, research and partnerships could lead to innovative models to educate on doing business at the BoP and emerging economy context.

Notes

1   The Bertha Centre for Social Innovation & Entrepreneurship established in 2011 a hub for the promotion of social innovation and entrepreneurship in Africa.
2   MTN Group, is a mobile telecommunication company based in South and operates in many African, European and Asian countries.

References

Ain Shams University. (2015) *Sharing information on progress (SIP)*, report, Faculty of Commerce, Ain Shams University, Cairo, Egypt.

Al Akhawayn University. (2015) *Report on progress*. School of Business Administration, Al Akhawayn University, Ifrane, Morocco.

Association of African Business Schools (AABS). (2012) *Growing through quality management education*, Johannesburg, South Africa: AABS, p. 1. Available online at www.aabschools. com/cms/attachments/243/aabs_overview.pdf

—— (2016a) *Report of activities January–December 2015*, Johannesburg, South Africa: AABS, p. 3. Available online at www.aabschools.com/cms/attachments/391/annual_report_2016_2015_05052016_12pg_final_vf.pdf.

—— (2016b) 'AABS accredited and member schools.' Available online at http://aabschools.com/directory/schools.html (accessed 18 November 2016).

Bennis, W. and O'Toole, J. (2005) 'How business schools lost their way', *Harvard Business Review, 83*(5): 96–104.

Ezenyilimba, E. (2015) 'The challenges of tertiary management education and strategic learning panacea in Nigeria', *International Journal of Academic Research in Business and Social Sciences, 5*(6): 35–49.

Furlonger, D. (2014) 'Business schools in Africa: In it together', *Financial Mail*. Available online at www.financialmail.co.za/coverstory/2014/07/24/business-schools-in-africa-in-it-together.

Garcia-DeLeone, S., & Taj, S. (2015). A business model designed to tap into the bottom of the pyramid. *International Journal of Business, Marketing, & Decision Science, 8*(1): 136-149.

Gibb, A. A. (1996) 'Entrepreneurship and small business management: Can we afford to neglect them in the twenty-first century business school', *British Journal of Management, 7*(4): 309–321

Gordon Institute of Business Science. (2016) *Sharing information on progress (SIP)*. Pretoria, South Africa: Gordon Institute of Business Science, University of Pretoria.

Gordon, M. D. (2008) 'Management education and the base of the pyramid', *Journal of Management Education, 32*(6): 767–781.

Graduate School of Business, University of Cape Town. (2015) *Report on progress*, Cape Town, South Africa: Graduate School of Business, University of Cape Town.

HEM Business School. (2015) *Sharing information on progress (SIP)*, report, HEM Business School, Casablanca, Morocco.

Jenvey, N. (2013) 'Global rankings highlight African business schools', *University World News*, (279). Available online at www.universityworldnews.com/article.php?story=20130706 07385921.

Karamchandani, A., Kubzansky, M. and Lalwani, N. (2011) 'Is the bottom of the pyramid really for you?' *Harvard Business Review*, 1–6.

Khan, M. (2015) 'Business management education in reality', in M. Khan, D. bank, E. Okon, G. Al-Qaimari, S. Olivares and S. Trevino-Martinez (eds), *Diverse contemporary issues facing business management education* (1st edn), Hershey, PA: Business Science, pp. 130–146.

Klein, S. and Ward, M. (2005) 'An emerging market player in international business education: The case of WITS Business School', in I. Alon and J. McIntyre (eds), *Business education and emerging market economies: Perspectives and best practices* (1st edn), New York, NY: Kluwer, pp. 327–342.

Ladzani, W. M. and van Vuuren, J. J. (2002) Entrepreneurship training for emerging SMEs in South Africa, *Journal of Small Business Management*, 40(2): 154–161.

Management College of Southern Africa (MANCOSA). (2015) *Sharing information on progress (SIP)*. Durban, South Africa: MANCOSA.

Mzumbe University. (2015) *Sharing information on progress (SIP)*, report, Mzumbe University, Dar es Salaam, Tanzania.

Ndimande, B. (2006). Parental Choice: The liberty principle in education finance. *Perspectives in Education*, 24(2): 143-156.

Neal, M. (2016) *Learning from poverty: Why business schools should address poverty, and how they can go about it*, Academy Of Management Learning & Education, 16(1): 54–69.

Ndlovu-Gatsheni, S. J. (2013) Decolonising the university in Africa, *The Thinker, 51*: 46–51.

Nkomo, S. M. (2015) Challenges of management and business education in a 'developmental' state: The case of South Africa, *Academy of Management Learning & Education, 14*(2): 242–258.

Nwagwu, I. (2017) 'Reaching the bottom billion through inclusive business: Lessons from enterprises in Africa', in M. Gudić, T. K. Tan and P. Flynn (eds), *Beyond the bottom line: Integrating the UN global compact into business and management practice*, Saltaire, UK: Greenleaf, pp. 108–119.

Okonedo, E. and Aluko, T. (2016) 'The role of accreditation in overcoming the challenges of graduate management programs in Africa' in H. Kazeroony, Y. duPlessis and B. Puplampu (eds), *Routledge studies in international business and the world economy* (1st edn), New York, NY: Routledge, pp. 64–81.

Okpara, J. O. and Wynn, P. (2007) 'Determinants of small business growth constraints in a Sub-Saharan African economy', *SAM Advanced Management Journal*, 72(2): 24–35.

Pfeffer, J. and Fong, C. (2002) 'The end of business schools? Less success than meets the eye', *Academy of Management Learning & Education*, 1(1).

Prahalad, C. K. (2006) 'The fortune at the bottom of the pyramid: Eradicating poverty through profits', Upper Saddle River, NJ: Wharton School Publishing.

—— (2012) 'Bottom of the pyramid as a source of breakthrough innovations', *Journal of Production Innovation Management*, 29(1): 6–12.

PRME (2012). *Fighting poverty through management education: Challenges, opportunities, solutions*, report, PRME working group on poverty as a challenge to management education, Rio de Janeiro, Brazil.

—— (2016) 'PRME steering committee'. Available online at www.unprme.org/about-prme/steering-committee/index.php (accessed 11 August 2016).

PRME Signatories. (2016) 'PRME participants'. Available online at www.unprme.org/participants/index.php?sort=name&dir=asc&start=630 (accessed 18 November 2016).

Purushottam, N. and Rwelamila, P. D. (2011). 'Issues and strategies in management education: A South African perspective', in *8th AIMS international conference on management*.

Rigoglioso, M. (2012a) 'Can research and teaching help alleviate poverty?' Stanford Graduate School of Business. Available online at www.gsb.stanford.edu/insights/can-research-teaching-help-alleviate-poverty (accessed 11 August 2016).

—— (2012b) 'Field research as a tool for poverty alleviation'. Stanford Graduate School o of Business. Available online at www.gsb.stanford.edu/insights/field-research-tool-poverty-alleviation (accessed 10 August 2016).

Rhodes University. (2015) *Sharing information on progress (SIP)*, report, Rhodes University, Grahamstown, South Africa.

School of Management, IT and Governance, University of Kwazulu-Natal. (2015). *Sharing information on progress (SIP)*, report, School of Management, IT and Governance, University of Kwazulu-Natal, Durban, South Africa.

Soni, P., Cassim, N., RItacco, G. and Linganiso, X. (2015) 'Africa: The jury is out for African business schools', *Allafrica*. Available online at http://allafrica.com/stories/20150810 1128.html.

Stanford Graduate School of Business (SGSoB). (2014a) 'Stanford launches global development and poverty research initiative'. Available online at. www.gsb.stanford.edu/newsroom/school-news/stanford-launches-global-development-poverty-research-initiative (accessed 10 August 2016).

—— (2014b) *Stanford launches university-wide global development and poverty research initiative*, Stanford report, SGSoB. Available online at http://news.stanford.edu/news/2014/february/global-poverty-initiative-022014.html (accessed 11 August 2016).

Strathmore University. (2015) *Sharing information on progress*. Nairobi, Kenya: Strathmore University.

The American University in Cairo. (2015) *PRME sharing information on progress*, report, School of Business, The America University in Cairo, Cairo.

The British University in Egypt. (2015) *Sharing information on progress*, Faculty of Business Administration, Economics, & Political Science, The British University in Egypt, Cairo, Egypt.

Thomas, H., Lee, M., Thomas, L., and Wilson, A. (2016) *Africa: The management challenge*. Bingley, UK: Emerald Group.

University of Stellenbosch Business School. (2014) *Sharing information on progress*. Cape Town, South Africa: University of Stellenbosch Business School.

UN PRME. (2016) 'PRME – about us – six principles'. Unprme.org. Available online at www.unprme.org/about-prme/the-six-principles.php (accessed 11 August 2016).

Webometrics. (2016) 'Africa. Ranking web of business schools'. Available online at http://business-schools.webometrics.info/en/Ranking_africa (accessed 11 August 2016)

World Bank. (2016) Regional dashboard sub-Saharan Africa.

Dr. Ijeoma Nwagwu manages Lagos Business School's First Bank Sustainability Centre. She earned her doctorate in Law (S.J.D) and Masters in Law (L.L.M) degrees from Harvard Law School. A researcher, lecturer, speaker, and writer, she currently teaches corporate social responsibility, sustainability strategy, and social entrepreneurship at Lagos Business School.

inwagwu@lbs.edu.ng

Appendix

TABLE 13.1 Management Education Institutions in Africa

Name	Parent Institution	Country	PRME Signatory	PRME Communicating Member	AABS Member	AABS Accredited
1. Adalia School of Business		Morocco	Yes	Yes	No	No
2. Ain Shams University Faculty of Commerce	Ain Shams University	Egypt	Yes	Yes	No	No
3. Al Akhawayn University School of Business Administration	Al Akhawayn University in Ifrane	Morocco	Yes	Yes	No	No
4. American University of Nigeria (AUN)	American University Nigeria	Nigeria	Yes	Yes	No	No
5. Community Bible College & Seminary		Ghana	Yes	No	No	No
6. Copperbelt University Business School	Copperbelt University	Zambia	No	No	Yes	No
7. Deraya University		Egypt	Yes	Yes	No	No
8. Eastern and Southern African Management Business School		Tanzania	No	No	Yes	Yes
9. ESCA School of Management	ESCA Ecole de Management	Morocco	Yes	No	Yes	Yes
10. ESITH		Morocco	Yes	Yes	No	No
11. EUCLID	Euclid University	Gambia	Yes	Yes	No	No
12. Faculty of Business Administration, Economics, & Political Science	The British University in Egypt	Egypt	Yes	Yes	No	No
13. Faculty of Management Technology	German University in Cairo	Egypt	Yes	Yes	No	No
14. Ghana Institute of Management and Public Administration Business School		Ghana	No	No	Yes	Yes

TABLE 13.1 Continued

Name	Parent Institution	Country	PRME Signatory	PRME Communicating Member	AABS Member	AABS Accredited
15. Gordon Institute of Business Sciences (GIBS)	University of Pretoria	South Africa	Yes	Yes	Yes	Yes
16. Graduate School of Business	University of Cape Town	South Africa	Yes	Yes	Yes	Yes
17. Groupe Ecole Superieure de Commerce de Dakar		Senegal	No	No	Yes	Yes
18. Groupe Institut Superieur de Commerce et d'Administration des Enterprises	Institut Superieur de Commerce et d'Administration des Enterprises	Morocco	No	No	Yes	Yes
19. Harold Pupkewitz Graduate School of Business		Namibia	No	No	Yes	No
20. HEM (Institute of Higher Education of Management	HEM	Morocco	Yes	Yes	Yes	Yes
21. Henley Business School		South Africa	No	No	Yes	No
22. Institut African de Management		Senegal	No	No	Yes	Yes
23. Institut Superieur de Management de Dakar		Senegal	No	No	Yes	Yes
24. KCA University		Kenya	Yes	Yes	No	No
25. Lagos Business School	Pan Atlantic University	Nigeria	Yes	Yes	Yes	Yes
26. MANCOSA	Management College of Southern Africa	South Africa	Yes	Yes	Yes	Yes
27. Milpark Business School	Milpark Education (Pty.) Ltd	South Africa	Yes	Yes	Yes	No

No.	Name	Institution/Type	Country				
28.	Moi University School of Business & Economics		Kenya	No	No	Yes	No
29.	Mount Kenya University School of Business	Mount Kenya University	Kenya	No	No	Yes	No
30.	Multitech Business School	Makerere Business School	Uganda	Yes	Yes	No	No
31.	Midlands State University Graduate Schools of Business Leadership		Zimbabwe	No	No	Yes	Yes
32.	Mzumbe University	Mzumbe University	Tanzania	Yes	Yes	Yes	Yes
33.	Nelson Mandela Metropolitan Business School	Nelson Mandela Metropolitan University	South Africa	Yes	Yes	Yes	Yes
34.	North West University School of Business and Corporate Governance		South Africa	No	No	Yes	Yes
35.	Namibia Business School		Namibia	No	No	Yes	No
36.	October 6 University		Egypt	Yes	Yes	No	No
37.	Onitsha Business School		Nigeria	Yes	Yes	No	No
38.	Regenesys Business School	Stand-Alone Private Business School	South Africa	Yes	Yes	No	No
39.	Regent Business School		South Africa	No	No	Yes	No
40.	Regent University School of Business and Leadership		Ghana	No	No	Yes	No
41.	Rhodes Business School	Rhodes University	South Africa	Yes	Yes	No	No
42.	School of Business – JKUAT		Kenya	No	No	Yes	Yes
43.	School of Business	The American University in Cairo	Egypt	Yes	Yes	Yes	Yes

TABLE 13.1 Continued

Name	Parent Institution	Country	PRME Signatory	PRME Communicating Member	AABS Member	AABS Accredited
44. School of Management, IT, and Governance	University of Kwazulu-Natal	South Africa	Yes	Yes	Yes	Yes
45. Strathmore University	Strathmore University	Kenya	Yes	Yes	Yes	Yes
46. Sup' Management		Morocco	No	No	Yes	No
47. University of Stellenbosch Business School (USB)	University of Stellenbosch	South Africa	Yes	Yes	Yes	Yes
48. The Catholic University of Eastern Africa		Kenya	No	No	Yes	Yes
49. University of Botswana		Botswana	No	No	Yes	Yes
50. University of Dar es Salaam Business School		Tanzania	No	No	Yes	Yes
51. University of Ghana Business School		Ghana	No	No	Yes	Yes
52. University of Free State Business School		South Africa	No	No	Yes	No
53. University of Lagos Faculty of Business Administration	University of Lagos	Nigeria	No	No	Yes	Yes
54. University of Limpopo Turfloop Graduate School of Leadership		South Africa	No	No	Yes	No
55. University of Lusaka		Zambia	No	No	Yes	No
56. University of Nairobi School of Business		Kenya	No	No	Yes	Yes

57. University of South Africa School of Business Leadership	South Africa	No	No	Yes	Yes
58. University of the Witwatersrand Business School	South Africa	No	No	Yes	Yes
59. USIU Chandaria School of Business	Kenya	No	No	Yes	Yes
60. Zimbabwe Ezekiel Guti University	Zimbabwe	Yes	Yes	No	No

Note: There are PRME signatories who do not maintain a communicating relationship with the UN PRME body (i.e. communication through submitting PRME reports). AABS membership does not confer that an institution or program is accredited. AABS member schools must still pursue accreditation.

Sources: PRME Signatories. (2016); AABS (2016b).

Section 5
Looking ahead

14

Work-based learning

Students solving sustainability challenges through strategic business partnerships

Petra Molthan-Hill

Nottingham Business School, Nottingham Trent University, UK

Fiona Winfield

Nottingham Business School, UK

Jerome Baddley

Sustainable Development Unit (SDU), NHS England

Susan Hill

Nottingham Business School, UK

Abstract

The importance of partnerships between business schools, local companies and other organisations has grown in recent years and is the basis of Principle 5 (Partnerships) of the United Nations' (UN) Principles for Responsible Management Education (PRME). This chapter offers a replicable model that other business schools and universities could integrate into their core curriculum while also enriching their educational methods (PRME Principle 3). The focus of the described Greenhouse Gas Management project is on the UN Sustainable Development Goal (SDG) #13 (Climate Action), but the partnership model could also be used to address other SDGs. The model is based on the assumption that students can contribute to solving sustainable challenges. Instead of learning frameworks for later use in life, students directly apply the concepts they encounter in a real-life business. In this chapter, the deployment of such work-based learning in the core curriculum at Nottingham Business School is described, along with details of how this aids the development of employability skills of the participating students. Furthermore, the partnership, which won the Guardian University Award in Business Partnership 2015, is described, and recommendations are included on how to set up something similar in other colleges and universities.

Innovations in management education to support sustainable development

As recognised by the United Nations' (UN) Principles for Responsible Management Education (PRME) Principle 3: Method, education for responsible leadership is not simply about introducing additional information or issues to what is currently taught, it requires thinking about how we 'do' education: how we create educational frameworks, processes and learning environments by rethinking our methods, revising our courses, recasting our priorities and re-orientating our communities of practice (PRME, 2007). Innovations in responsible management education can then be facilitated through a combination and synergy of simultaneously applying several PRME principles, such as in this case, where establishing Partnerships (Principle 5) facilitates innovation in Educational Method (Principle 3), aimed at addressing one of the Sustainable Development Goals (SDGs).

Syvertsen (2008) suggests that business schools are in a position where the ability to innovate is regarded as a source of competitive advantage and, furthermore, innovation is being rewarded by higher education sustainability bodies. Examples of environment-related rewards include the 'People and Planet University League' award (People and Planet, 2015); the Environmental Association for Universities and Colleges 'Green Gown Awards' (The Environmental Association for Universities and Colleges (EAUC), 2016) and the 'Learning in Future Environments Award' (LiFE, 2016).

The significance of INNOVATION through strategic business partnerships in creating a more sustainable future is increasingly being recognised. The Association to Advance Collegiate Schools of Business (AACSB, 2011: 9), the largest accreditation body for business schools internationally, notes that '. . . the relationship between the business profession and the business academy is largely symbiotic: they support each other in various ways that advance the welfare of society'. Furthermore, Starkey *et al.* (2004: 1527) highlight that '. . . the business school stands at the fault line where the future of the university and the future of society interact.' This sentiment is emphasised by Principle 5 of PRME, which underscores the role of such partnerships to develop the capabilities of students to be future generators of 'sustainable value' for business and society (PRME, 2007).

There are various thematic areas of sustainable value as portrayed, for example, by the Principles of the UN Global Compact (UN, 2016a) and the SDGs (UN, 2016b). However, unlike the preceding Millennium Development Goals, the SDGs explicitly call on businesses to advance sustainable development.

Innovations through strategic partnerships

One major benefit of business–business school partnerships is that they can help co-create innovative solutions to current business challenges, and impact specific sustainability issues. This could be, for example, through the implementation of the UN Global Compact Principles (UN, 2016a) and the interpretation of the SDGs for business. The latter could identify future opportunities related to the SDGs through the provision of company-specific guidance for advancing SDG-related goals and measuring progress and impacts (PRME, 2015a).

Multi-stakeholder cooperation and partnerships are strongly encouraged by the UN Economic Commission for Europe's (UNECE, 2013) strategy on 'Education for Sustainable Development'. Furthermore, cooperation is at the heart of the European Commission's (EC, 2010) 'Europe 2020' strategy, which seeks to encourage development of innovative curricula while building stronger business partnerships.

Despite a seemingly logical affiliation between business schools and business, most observers would agree that the potential for collaboration has not been maximised (AACSB 2006a, 2006b). Within the UK, the Department for Business, Innovation and Skills (BIS, 2012), the Chartered Management Institute (Chartered Management Institute (CMI), 2014; McBain *et al.*, 2012) and the Quality Assurance Association for Higher Education (QAA, 2014) highlight the need for increased partnership to tackle the most complex problems facing our world. Partnerships can facilitate experiential, interactive and participatory activities that enable students to engage with sustainability issues at a number of levels, not only in relation to their discipline but also in terms of reflecting on their own values, attitudes and the accepted normative frameworks. Combined with collaborative working, students have the opportunity to develop their ability to communicate ethical issues (see, for example, 'Giving Voice to Values' (GVV); Gentiles, 2016) and to focus on developing 'decision-making in complex and unpredictable situations' (QAA, 2008: 21).

Students have expressed a desire for closer relationships with businesses and managers of business organisations. Many students claim there is a low correlation between much of what is studied at university and real-life work experience, and that universities tend to focus on theory, with little attention to the 'everyday' practice of business. In work-based learning (WBL) this gap is closed. As the EC notes, there is a wide range of vocabulary used, often inter-changeably, for the concept of WBL, including: problem-based learning, experiential learning, situated learning, competence-based learning, work-related learning, service learning and vocational learning (EC, 2013). The common thread in all of these is that students are exposed to relevant theories and apply them directly to practice in a client or employing organisation (learning *for* work). Furthermore, as Siebert *et al.* (2009) observe, in such an approach, students learn from their community of practice in their workplace as well as their peers at university (learning *through* work).

The Greenhouse Gas (GHG) management project at Nottingham Business School

An approach of comprehensively introducing one or several dedicated core module(s), through which to reinforce sustainability tools (knowledge, skills and mind-set) across the curriculum, is advocated by PRME (2015b), since it enables more than just superficial learning. The GHG management project at Nottingham Business School (NBS) is a good example of where Nottingham Trent University (NTU) is helping to make this happen.

At NBS, students learn about SDG #13 on Climate Action through a GHG management project in the core curriculum of their undergraduate business degree. They then apply this knowledge directly as consultants to local organisations. Within the module in question, 'Leadership & Employability', theory and practice are so intertwined that students encounter the theories in a lecture in one week, and apply each step directly afterwards to their allocated organisations. With the help of their tutors in the following seminar, they further consolidate their ideas and skills through discussion, feedback and reflection on the application of the theory and how the client's situation could be further improved. This approach enables students to produce their own solutions, becoming active participants in their learning and giving the process additional purpose and meaning. They sometimes realise that they have not fully understood the theory when they try to apply it, which encourages deeper learning when they go back to the classroom to fill the gaps in their knowledge and skills.

The strategic partner: NetPositive Ltd

In the case to be highlighted, at the heart of the success of this partnership with local businesses and councils, is another organisation: NetPositive Ltd[1], which is part of a nationwide not-for-profit accreditation scheme, Investors in the Environment (iiE). The students at NBS work in small teams with client organisations under the supervision of a tutor, alongside staff from NetPositive, helping their client work towards accreditation from the iiE.

The iiE programme is run as a franchise, owned in Nottinghamshire and Derbyshire by NetPositive Ltd, while nationally the network is run by Peterborough Environment City Trust (PECT)[2]. It is a three-part environmental management accreditation scheme (bronze, silver or green) and a local low-carbon business network. Members are supported to implement an Environmental Management System (EMS) and are encouraged to network and trade among themselves. The network has helped identify local suppliers and partners who are also interested in developing the 'low carbon' label as a unique selling point, supplying low-carbon products or services, or collaborating on projects.

NetPositive Ltd had worked for many years with public procurement departments such as National Health Service (NHS) trusts and local councils, to support the development and implementation of carbon reduction and resource efficiency (now linked to SDG #13 on Climate Action). As large organisations were becoming increasingly capable of identifying and reducing costs and emissions themselves, there was growing interest in encouraging this in their supply chain. There was, however, reticence to call for environmental management standards because of a fear that it would be too expensive and burdensome in implementation, thereby disadvantaging small and medium-sized enterprises (SMEs).

NetPositive was keen to support local low-carbon growth for social and environmental reasons while seeking a steady, predictable and revenue-generating means of maintaining cash flow in the periods between larger consultancy projects. While good publicly-funded projects appear fairly regularly, the reliance on time-limited funding meant that the support for SME low-carbon innovation, resource efficiency and environmental management was patchy and inconsistent in the local market. Very little support was accessed by SMEs to gain the type of visible accredited standards that could give confidence to procurers. The NetPositive team already networked closely with European Regional Development Fund[3] program providers, funders and major private sector organisations to identify opportunities, tenders, funding, partnerships and other support to local low-carbon businesses. The team, therefore, decided to take on the franchise for the iiE standard and running of the network as a low-cost, un-bureaucratic approach to support businesses to gain a green standard recognised by procurers. As the standard also requires businesses to reduce their impacts year on year, there was the added benefit that it encouraged them to buy resource-efficient products and services from one another. This internal trade and network facilitated a more interconnected, fertile and resilient local low-carbon economy.

The partnership

Early on in the establishment of the franchise, the NetPositive team and NBS decided to work closely together to build iiE into the 'Leadership and

Employability' final year module. Typically, 100–150 students take the module each year, with the involvement of twenty to twenty-five businesses. The program follows a successful GHG management project run by NBS since 2011; to date over 400 students and 100 organisations, from shopping centres to restaurants, have participated. Many local businesses have been able to take part due to support from the NTU 'Future Factory' (a European Regional Development Fund project supporting SMEs with sustainability).

NetPositive employees teach on the module alongside NBS academics, with students receiving support from both. The students potentially have two private sector job references at the end, and direct experience of working as consultants with a client in the interpretation of SDG #13, identifying future business opportunities and cost savings by providing guidance on setting GHG-related goals, measuring progress and assessing impact. The activity helps remove barriers to SMEs and micro businesses taking the first steps towards the low-carbon economy and encourages resource efficiency; specifically cost, skills and time. As a result of this collaboration, NBS and Nottingham Energy Partnership (now NetPositive Ltd) received the Guardian University Award for Business Partnership in 2015 (Thomas, 2015).

The client businesses benefit from acquiring an accredited EMS, enabling them to bid for contracts where this is increasingly required. Some have been shown how to identify areas where they can lower their overheads with improved resource efficiency. Others have gained valuable insight into how to leverage their accreditation through 'green' marketing strategies. The growth of the local low-carbon business network has also provided local procurers with greater confidence in the capacity of the market to respond to higher expectations of environmental performance.

From NBS's point of view, NetPositive has been very helpful in locating interested local clients. Each summer, the project is promoted to local organisations (public and private). Potential clients are told they can receive free advice from students in exchange for a small investment of time to provide data to the team. Before the partnership was created with NetPositive, the module leader approached NTU's 'Future Factory' team in order to find SMEs for the students. She also advertised through various local channels such as 'Nottingham Means Business'[4]. In 2013, one year before the partnership started, an insufficient number of organisations had signed up for an especially large cohort of students. In the first week of term, the students were therefore asked to act as full consultants, who had to source their clients, too! Amazingly, the students managed to recruit twenty companies during that week and no one had to carry out a desk-based study (the fall-back situation). Although this worked out all right in the end, it was felt better to have a more secure plan in place, hence the development of the relationship with NetPositive.

Recruiting companies through a partnership has further clear benefits. For two years now, NetPositive has prepared the companies for the work with the students. As every organisation is different in providing information (some very forthcoming, others have to be asked repeatedly), NetPositive tries to ensure that the necessary data are available. After being allocated to their client, the teams have to make contact and schedule a meeting four weeks later. In the intervening month, students receive an overview of the project, the nature of the consultancy work to be undertaken and they familiarise themselves with their client, preparing relevant questions to ask during their first site visit.

The curriculum and assessment

In the first years of running the project, the underpinning framework used was Lingl *et al.*'s (2010) book: *Doing Business in a New Climate*. In the last two years, however, the teaching content has been modified to integrate the required material for the iiE accreditation. Detailed information and teaching material are available from the authors of this chapter on request.

As the consultancy project is part of the core curriculum, the assessment methods need to be carefully conceptualised. After some trial and error, the current method seems to work well, confirming Brayshaw and Gordon's (2008) findings that WBL offers ways to get students to engage with assessment activities. Students have to prepare a poster for their clients summarising the main steps, calculations and recommendations. In a formative exercise, feedback is provided to enable students to improve their final poster presentations and reports, which are subsequently presented collectively to tutors and clients. That event is a hub of exciting ideas and one of the key low-carbon economy network events in the region. High-profile keynote speakers highlight main developments in the low-carbon sector, followed by talks from representatives of organisations which have taken part in the past, commenting on the impact the project had on *their* business. Afterwards, all attendees can review all the posters, collect ideas for their own organisation and network with the students and other businesses.

In order to progress to iiE accreditation, the clients also need a written report. The school's faculty, however, did not wish to over-assess the students, as this is just one of six modules in the final year. The weighting for the report is therefore just 20 per cent of the total grade, and the students are provided with a template to populate. This template was designed in cooperation between NetPositive and the module leader and covers all relevant information for the iiE accreditation; guiding the students through the process. They consequently place emphasis on the poster, and especially on the recommendations for the business. Their brief is to provide two recommendations based on their calculations, highlighting the highest potential to reduce CO_2 emissions with the associated costs, plus one recommendation based either on observations made during their site visits, requests from the company or their own preference.

Students develop very creative ideas adding to the existing knowledge of how to reduce GHG emissions. Groups have, for example, planned a community event for their client, designed a new logo, set up a carbon accounting system, developed a new method of how to incentivise employees to use more energy-efficient cars and designed a carbon-free Christmas decoration for a shopping centre. However, it would also be possible to design the assessment in such a way that report and poster presentation carry equal weight, this would depend on the context in which the project is embedded. Further ideas and inspiration on how GHG management is taught in this module, or could be taught elsewhere, can also be found in Dharmasasmita *et al.* (2014).

Client companies have commented positively on the professional work of the students, and their innovative ideas on how to reduce carbon emissions have been especially applauded. Richard Fuller (County Battery Services, UK) commented, for example, as follows:

> The students made suggestions regarding how we could lower our carbon footprint. Once the system is in place it is easy to measure the impact of improvements. iiE with the help of our students has lowered our carbon footprint and our energy bills, making us more profitable, more sustainable, [and] more marketable.

And Martin Rigley, MBE (Lindhurst Engineering Ltd, UK), noted as follows:

> The need to differentiate yourself from your competition has become ever more important to all businesses. The work with students from NTU Future Factory was a great boost in Lindhurst Engineering gaining the iiE award. This has allowed us to clearly demonstrate our commitment to environmental stability to our customers and stakeholders.

For students, this project is an opportunity to showcase their subject specialisations, combining academic work with practical application, for example, drawing on the theories of other subject areas such as marketing regarding how to influence buying decisions. The feedback has been very positive, as shown in the following testimonial given by one student, Ella McManus:

> It was a really enjoyable experience and has inspired me to investigate jobs in the energy/sustainability sector as a future career path . . . it was quite an eye opener discovering how a few simple changes could lead to a more environmentally-friendly company and save money, too.

Impact of the project on students' employability skills

It has been noted in several recent articles and reports (Boxhall, 2016; Confederation of British Industry (CBI), 2015; Ipsos MORI, 2010; UK Commission for Employment and Skills (UKCES), 2016) that graduates from UK universities do not always have the soft skills that employers require. These include team-work, time management and communications (Prospects, 2015; TARGETjobs, 2016). In an ideal world, *all* undergraduates would participate in some form of relevant work experience – a summer internship or a year-long work placement, for example – exposing them to the world of work, thereby helping them to develop both soft and hard skills. However, this is not always possible and projects within the curriculum can help to ensure that work-integrated learning takes place. Case studies and business simulations go some way to develop such skills, but doing real-life consultancy, such as the GHG project, allows the students to work together as a team and develop appropriate communication skills, as they need to procure information from the client, then report back, explaining clearly the implications of their analysis. Further skills are developed as the teams need to plan the project carefully and ensure they allow sufficient time, while juggling other final year research, reading and assessments. This necessitates or helps build good organisation skills.

The time frames are quite tight as this is part of just one of the six modules during the students' final year as an undergraduate at NBS. The technical aspects first need to be understood (so hard skills are developed) before the students can start to gather, collate and analyse the data from the organisation in order to make appropriate recommendations. The lack of ability of graduates to analyse complex data has been identified by the UKCES (2016), in their Employer Skills Survey, as being a particular challenge to UK businesses. This project also helps the students to develop this ability.

While it could be argued that using GHG management is just a vehicle for the students to practise their consultancy skills, the reality is that they are also developing a good knowledge of energy usage (SDG #13) and how careful management of this can benefit an organisation in terms of cost savings. The UK low-carbon economy is now worth around £26 billion per year, and there is a growing skills shortage of carbon-literate graduates (Autio and Webb, 2015).

The NBS initiative ensures there is a pipeline of graduates entering into the marketplace with a good understanding of the opportunities in the low-carbon economy. The consultancy they carry out allows the students, in a very practical way, to start to understand some of the bigger issues of climate change and sustainability. This will be invaluable if they are to be responsible leaders in the future. Increasingly, topics relating to sustainability are being discussed at recruitment events. Students have returned from assessment centres reporting that their participation in the GHG project has really helped them to stand out in such interviews. A number of students have also been offered intern-ships with the businesses they have supported. One NBS student has even changed her career plans entirely and, on graduating, has moved into environ-mental management.

Concluding remarks and recommendations

This chapter has illustrated the operationalisation of Principles 3 (Method) and 5 (Partnership) of PRME and the UN's SDG #13 (Climate Action) in a partnership between a business school (NBS) with a local organisation (NetPositive Ltd). This partnership model is replicable in other universities and is especially suitable for SDG #13 , as practically all businesses and organisations worldwide have the potential to reduce their carbon footprint. This project could also be set up by an individual lecturer (as it was in the case study described); the only institutional support needed is the permission of senior management to include it in one module/course.

As described above, in this case the lecturer needs to find the businesses to take part, which is time-consuming. The same model (on an individual base or in partnership) could also be used to engage businesses in relation to other SDGs, especially the other environmental ones, for example, resource efficiency and waste management, as these will again be common to most businesses/ organisations. However, students can also contribute to other SDGs such as SDG #1 (No Poverty), #2 (Zero Hunger) and #11 (Inclusive Communities) by partnering up, for example, with local organisations such as Superkitchen[5] and FareShare[6] to provide nutritious meals from surplus food in impoverished areas (Molthan-Hill *et al.*, 2016).

The GHG project described in this chapter has had an impact on the low-carbon economy local to NTU. It could be replicated by other universities all over the country or further afield to have an even broader national and international impact. It is especially suitable for business schools, although in other disciplines, such as architecture, students could provide a similar service by screening existing buildings of local organisations with regard to heat loss, insulation and other improvements to reduce energy consumption. Furthermore, interdisciplinary projects could be designed, joining the expertise of business students and students of architecture, for example.

As this project is more time-consuming for students than a desk-based activity, it is important that the business school/university attaches the right amount of credits. It is also more suitable for the core curriculum than as an elective, since in the latter case, the number of students needs to be known well in advance in order to source enough suitable clients. Based on the experience with the project described in this chapter, the optimal number is four students per organisation. The project is not suitable for first years as students need some basic understanding of business/management studies, but the content of the module can be adapted to all other levels, including Master's. The authors of this chapter can provide more information and help on setting up a similar project at another university.

NetPositive Ltd can also help to set up a similar partnership along with the not-for-profit accreditation scheme: iiE in other locations. The university/ business school could also work directly with client organisations. However, the benefits of working with an external party to help source suitable clients and prepare them to work effectively with the students should not be underestimated. While, in this example, NetPositive runs the franchise as a privately owned limited company and social enterprise, it would be possible for this to be a university spin-off, or a student-run enterprise. Linking the exercise to the iiE accreditation also attracts more SMEs rather than it just being an 'academic' exercise, which might be seen as too time-consuming for the client organisation, with fewer benefits. However, ensuring the students are not overburdened with the extra work required for the accreditation is important, as this might make them resentful and less likely to cooperate fully. Academic institutions, students and external organisations can all gain multiple benefits that the project offers, and last but not least, *everyone* will also benefit from the consequent reduction in carbon emissions on this planet.

Notes

1 www.netpositive.org.uk (at the time of this book's publication, the franchise has been bought by another company).
2 www.pect.org.uk
3 www.gov.uk/guidance/erdf-programmes-progress-and-achievements#annual-implementation-reports
4 www.nottinghammeansbusiness.com/
5 www.superkitchen.org/uploads/1/1/1/5/11155553/super_kitchen_brochure_2015.pdf
6 www.fareshare.org.uk/about-us/

Suggested further reading

1 Dharmasasmita, A., Kennedy, E., Puntha, H. and Holmes, R. (2014) 'Climate change and greenhouse gas management' in Petra Molthan-Hill (ed.), *The business student's guide to sustainable management*, 1st edn, Sheffield, UK: Greenleaf Publishing, 276–320. This chapter provides some of the teaching material used in the project described above but also further ideas on how to teach Climate Action (SDG #13) in business studies.
2 Molthan-Hill, P. (ed.) (2014) *The business student's guide to sustainable management*, 1st edn, Sheffield, UK: Greenleaf Publishing. This book features several teaching methods such as fully developed seminars, and suggested projects similar to the one above, which address different SDGs and principles of PRME. This will be made more explicit in the second edition, which will be published in July 2017.

References

Association to Advance Collegiate Schools of Business (AACSB). (2006a) *A world of good: Business, business schools, and peace*, Tampa, FL: AACSB.

Association to Advance Collegiate Schools of Business (AACSB). (2006b) *Business and business schools: A partnership for the future*, Tampa, FL: AACSB.

Association to Advance Collegiate Schools of Business (AACSB). (2011) *Globalization of management education*, Tampa, FL: AACSB.

Autio, E. and Webb, R. (2015) 'Engineering growth – enabling world-class entrepreneurship in the low-carbon economy'. Available online at http://papers.ssrn.com/sol3/papers.cfm?abstract_id=2609726 (accessed 21 April 2016).

Boxhall, M. (2016) 'How can the UK overcome a national skills shortage? Think local', *The Guardian Online*, 8 February 2016. Available online at http://theguardian.com/higher-education-network/2016/feb/18/uk-skills-shortage-universities-employers-industry (accessed 27 February 2016).

Brayshaw, M. and Gordon, N. A. (2008) 'Inquiry-based learning in computer science teaching in higher education', *Innovations in Teaching and Learning in Information and Computer Sciences*, 7(1): 22–33.

Chartered Management Institute (CMI) (2014) *21st century leaders: Building practice into the curriculum to boost employability*, London: CMI. Available online at www.managers.org.uk/21CLeaders (accessed 21 April 2016).

Confederation of British Industry (CBI). (2015) *Inspiring growth: CBI/Pearson education and skills survey 2015*, London: CBI/Pearson. Available online at http://news.cbi.org.uk/reports/education-and-skills-survey-2015/education-and-skills-survey-2015/ (accessed 27 February 2016).

Department for Business, Innovation and Skills (BIS). (2012) 'Leadership & management in the UK – The key to sustainable growth'. Available online at https://gov.uk/government/uploads/system/uploads/attachment_data/file/32327/12-923-leadership-management-key-to-sustainable-growth-evidence.pdf (accessed 21 April 2016).

Dharmasasmita, A., Kennedy, E., Puntha, H. and Holmes, R. (2014) 'Climate change and greenhouse gas management' in Petra Molthan-Hill (ed.), *The business student's guide to sustainable management* (1st edn), Sheffield, UK: Greenleaf Publishing, 276–320.

The Environmental Association for Universities and Colleges (EAUC). (2016) 'The Green Gown Awards'. Available online at http://eauc.org.uk/green_gown_awards (accessed 11 March 2016).

European Commission (EC). (2010) 'Europe 2020: A strategy for smart, sustainable and inclusive growth'. Available online at http://eur-lex.europa.eu/LexUriServ/LexUriServ.do?uri=COM:2010:2020:FIN:EN:PDF (accessed 14 April 2015).

European Commission (EC). (2013) 'Overview of work-based learning in Europe, deliverable 6: Work-Based Learning as an Integrated Curriculum (WBLIC)'. Available online at http://wblic.org.uk/wblhe/files/WBLIC_Overview_of_WBL_in_Europe.pdf (accessed 27 February 2016).

Gentiles, M. (2016) 'Giving voice to values'. Available online at http://darden.virginia.edu/ibis/initiatives/giving-voice-to-values/ (accessed 17 November 2016).

Ipsos MORI. (2010) 'Skills for a sustainable economy: The business perspective'. Available online at https://ipsos-mori.com/Assets/Docs/Publications/skills-for-a-sustainable-economy-the-business-perspective_170610.pdf (accessed 20 April 2016).

LiFE (Learning in Future Environments). (2016) 'Welcome to LiFE'. Available online at http://eauc.org.uk/life/home (accessed 3 March 2016).

Lingl, P., Carlson, D. and the David Suzuki Foundation. (2010) *Doing business in a new climate*, Abingdon, UK: Earthscan.

McBain, R., Ghobadian, A., Switzer, J., Wilton, P., Woodman, P. and Pearson, G. (2012) *The business benefits of management and leadership development*, London: CMI.

Molthan-Hill, P., Puntha, H., Dharmasasmita, A., Hunter, K. and Lawe, B. (2016) 'Addressing food waste: Collaborative student and community projects' in W. Leal Filho, L. Brandli, J. Newman, P. Castro (eds), *Handbook of theory and practice of sustainable development in higher education* – Volume 1, Springer: Cham, Switzerland.

People and Planet. (2015) 'People & Planet University league table'. Available online at https://peopleandplanet.org/university-league/2015/tables (accessed 10 April 2016.

Principles for Responsible Management Education (PRME). (2007) 'The principles for responsible management education'. Available online at www.unprme.org/the-6-principles/ (accessed 7 August 2015).

Principles for Responsible Management Education (PRME). (2015a) *Partner with business schools to advance sustainability: Ideas to inspire action,* New York, NY: UN Global Compact Office.

Principles for Responsible Management Education (PRME). (2015b) 'Shaping the future business leader: State of sustainability in management education'. Available online at http://unprme.org/resource-docs/SFBLStateofSustainabilityEducationOverview.pdf (accessed 4 September 2015).

Prospects. (2015) 'What skills do employers want?' Available online at https://prospects.ac.uk/careers-advice/applying-for-jobs/what-skills-do-employers-want (accessed 27 February 2016).

The Quality Assurance Agency for Higher Education (QAA). (2008) 'The framework for higher education qualifications in England, Wales and Northern Ireland'. Available online at http://qaa.ac.uk/academicinfrastructure/fheq/ewni/default.asp (accessed 3 March 2016).

The Quality Assurance Agency for Higher Education (QAA). (2014) 'Education for sustainable development: Guidance for UK higher education providers'. Available online at http://qaa.ac.uk/en/Publications/Documents/Education-sustainable-development-Guidance-June-14.pdf (accessed 3 March 2016).

Siebert, S., Mills, V. and Tuff, C. (2009) 'Pedagogy of work-based learning: The role of the learning group', *Journal of Workplace Learning, 21*: 443–454.

Starkey, K., Hatchuel, A. and Tempest, S. (2004) 'Rethinking the business school', *Journal of Management Studies, 41*(8): 1521–1531.

Syvertsen, C. (2008) 'What is the future of business schools?' *European Business Review, 20*(2): 142–151.

TARGETjobs. (2016) 'The skills consulting recruiters are looking for in 2016'. Available online at https://targetjobs.co.uk/career-sectors/management-consulting/412766-the-skills-consulting-recruiters-are-looking-for-in-2016 (accessed 27 February 2016).

Thomas, K. (2015) 'Business partnership category: Winner and runners up', *The Guardian Online,* 19 March 2015. Available online at www.theguardian.com/higher-education-network/2015/mar/19/business-partnership-category-winner-and-runners-up (accessed 28 August 2016).

UK Commission for Employment and Skills (UKCES). (2016) 'Employer skills survey 2015: UK results, January 2016.' Available online at https://gov.uk/government/uploads/system/uploads/attachment_data/file/498890/UKCESS_2015_Report_-_v4_for_web.pdf (accessed 27 February 2016).

United Nations (UN). (2016a) 'United Nations global compact'. Available online at https://unglobalcompact.org (accessed 11 February 2016).

United Nations (UN). (2016b) 'Sustainable development goals: 17 goals to transform our world'. Available online at http://un.org/sustainabledevelopment/sustainable-development-goals/ (accessed 14 January 2016).

United Nations Economic Commission for Europe (UNECE). (2013) 'Implementing the United Nations Economic Commission for Europe strategy for education for sustainable development post 2015'. Available online at https://unece.org/fileadmin/DAM/env/esd/8thMeetSC/ece.cep.ac.13.2013.6e.pdf (accessed 21 April 2016).

Dr. Petra Molthan-Hill PFHEA, PhD, MBA, MDiv
Petra leads the Green Academy at Nottingham Trent University, developing curricular and extra-curricular activities in Education for Sustainable Development. Petra has won the Sustainability Professional Award in the Green Gown Awards 2016. Petra is also the Academic Lead for PRME in Nottingham Business School and the module leader for the Greenhouse Gas Management Project, which features in this chapter and has won the Guardian University Award 2015 in Business Partnership.

petra.molthan-hill@ntu.ac.uk

Fiona Winfield PG Cert, Dip CESEM, BA
Fiona is a Principal Lecturer and Nottingham Business School's Employability Coordinator, liaising between the University's Student Employability & Enterprise Team and Business School colleagues. Her role is to ensure relevant skills and attributes are embedded within the curriculum, plus offer a wide range of extra-curricular activities. In 2012, she developed the capstone Leadership & Employability module across the undergraduate platform, one version of which features in this chapter.

fiona.winfield@ntu.ac.uk

Jerome Baddley MIEMA, CEnv, PGCE, BSc
Jerome is a Chartered Environmentalist and Director of NetPositive Ltd. Over the last decade he has supported low-carbon sector growth across Nottinghamshire and Derbyshire. His roles have included 'Low Carbon Sector' Chair of the Local Enterprise Partnership and Sustainability Chair of the East Midlands Chamber of Commerce. He is currently National Head of the NHS (National Health Service) Sustainable Development Unit.

jerome.baddley@nhs.net

Susan Hill FHEA, MSc, MBA
Susan is Nottingham Business School's United Nations Principles for Responsible Management Education (PRME) Coordinator. Her role is to support colleagues in the development of sustainability and corporate responsibility within management education, including methods and activities for the inclusion of PRME-related issues within the curriculum, along with extra-curricular activities.

susan.hill2@ntu.ac.uk

The authors would like to thank Nottingham Business School (NBS) Dean, Baback Yazdani, Deputy Dean, Melanie Currie, Academic Team Leader, John Buglear, Course Leader, Jan Lincoln, Director of Future Factory, Lynn Oxborrow, and other colleagues at NBS for their continuing support of this project.

15

AIM2Flourish

Students connecting with businesses doing good for our own good

Guénola Nonet

Nova Southeastern University, USA

Maria Petrescu

Nova Southeastern University, USA

Abstract

This story is about two professors, of Management and Marketing respectively, who helped their students learn about sustainability and responsible leadership, and developed the appropriate mindset to innovate for a better world. In 2015, the authors of this chapter decided to join the pioneering AIM2Flourish initiative hosted by Case Western Reserve University and supported by the Principles for Responsible Management Education, the Globally Responsible Leadership Initiative and the Association to Advance Collegiate Schools of Business. The authors discovered the inspiring impact of this program on students and began to share their experiences with other educators. AIM2Flourish has had powerful beneficial impacts on business curricula and their learning outcomes in that it helps connect students with business innovators using Appreciative Inquiry to celebrate business innovations aligned with the United Nations Sustainable Development Goals.

What is the good news when it comes to business?

What is the good news when it comes to businesses' impacts on our communities and on planet Earth? What gets our entrepreneurs inspired to start businesses that are both profitable and progressive? What are these profitable enterprises around the world that are investing for a better world? Those are not the typical topics we read in the newspapers. How much space is dedicated to businesses doing well versus businesses doing badly for the environment and its communities? Very little space is left for good news. Does this reflect the world we live in? Where are the inspiring stories about entrepreneurs who want to make this world a better place to live, a more just society and a more sustainable environment for all beings?

With these questions in mind, the AIM2Flourish pilot initiative was launched in March 2015, bringing together thirty-two professors from nineteen countries, who got their students involved in submitting 'Business for Good' stories. The AIM2Flourish was later affirmed by the United Nations (UN) as an 'agent of world benefit' in a UN declaration (United Nations Principles for Responsible Management Education (UN PRME), 2015). By the end of 2016, AIM2Flourish counts close to 1,600 members, including 150 professors and a community that spans fifty-seven countries. Close to 400 examples of diverse and inspiring business innovation stories have been published by December 2016.

AIM2Flourish's mission demonstrates to the world that for-profit businesses can be financially profitable as well as socially responsible and beneficial to their communities:

> AIM2Flourish celebrates and catalyzes business innovation as part of a global learning challenge. We are inspiring the next generation of business leaders to build a better world by discovering new ways of doing business that are both profitable and progressive: Businesses that do good and do well.
>
> (AIM2Flourish, 2016)

The creators of AIM2Flourish are David L. Cooperrider, Ron Fry, Chris Laszlo, Roger Saillant and Roberta Baskin of the Weatherhead School of Management's Fowler Center for Business as an Agent of World Benefit (Case Western Reserve University, USA). Founded by Case Western Reserve University, Principles for Responsible Management Education (PRME), Globally Responsible Leadership Initiative (GRLI) and Flourishing Leadership Institute, and endorsed by the Association to Advance Collegiate Schools of Business (AACSB), AIM2Flourish seeks 'to create a more hopeful future' (Weatherhead School of Business, 2016). AIM2Flourish looks at businesses through the lens of the UN's seventeen Sustainable Development Goals (SDGs). It brings professors, students and businesses together in partnership, responding to PRME's principles of innovating in classrooms, connecting stakeholders for responsible management and inspiring current and future leaders to work together for a better world.

AIM2Flourish and the classroom curricula

The AIM2Flourish initiative is a valuable tool to help university students connect with business leaders and managers who have successfully integrated their business practice with sustainability, global ethics and social responsibility values. It is often a grassroots initiative, adopted by professors who see the value of these projects for their students. Twenty-two professors have already formally integrated AIM2Flourish as a mandatory element in their core course curricula, while others have encouraged their students to write an AIM2Flourish story as an elective. According to the professors' profiles, AIM2Flourish is used across a range of business disciplines, including management, leadership, entrepreneurship, marketing, economics, finance, corporate social responsibility, ethics and strategy.

AIM2Flourish provides a unique platform for professors who want their students to create uplifting stories about how to make the world a better place with a focus on great business initiatives. Students learn the skills of Appreciative Inquiry and use them to interview business leaders or managers whose organizations make a contribution to one or more of the UN's seventeen SDGs. Appreciative Inquiry recognizes the full worth of what the business wants to grow. It does so by creating a strengths-based interview built upon the successes developed by the company and the interviewee. Using Appreciative Inquiry to conduct AIM2Flourish interviews helps the students stimulate a conversation in which the interviewee talks about his/her true motivations, passions, successes (even minor successes), ambitions and lessons that can be learnt from his/her experience.

The AIM2Flourish process is as follows: professors and students from universities around the world work to identify innovations in the for-profit business world that fit a set of sustainability criteria (described in next section). Students are asked to interview key business leaders and then work with their professors to write stories about what these businesses are accomplishing and how. The selection criteria are aligned with the UN's seventeen SDGs to showcase business innovations for good, e.g. ending poverty, supporting environmental regeneration, boosting sustainable economies and creating more human dignity.

The more creative the students are in their documentation and analyses of their projects, the better the class experience. Videos, audio recordings and interviews with chief executive officers (CEOs) and employees, pictures and drawings, recordings of the students help amplify the narratives of the case studies. The final story is then submitted to the AIM2Flourish editorial team, called 'Story Stewards' for publication. Once accepted, it is published on the AIM2Flourish website (see Figure 15.1), and by so doing helps to develop awareness about the businesses featured, their innovations, the students who wrote the stories as well as supervising professors and their schools.

The purpose of AIM2Flourish is to help connect 'students, business leaders, management schools, media makers and investors across geographies,

FIGURE 15.1 **AIM2Flourish innovators webpage snapshot**

Accessed on January 12 2016

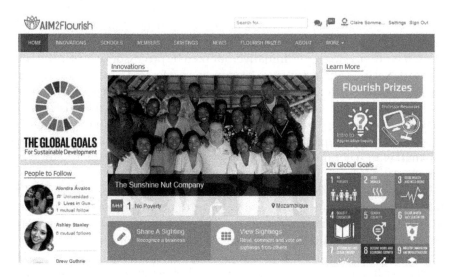

generations and industries', (AIM2Flourish, 2016) and to share their innovation stories and help inspire and engage others. The 'best-of-the-best business innovations' (AIM2Flourish, 2016) will be celebrated for the first time in June 2017 at the 4th Global Forum for Business as an Agent of World Benefit with the awarding of the inaugural seventeen Flourish Prizes.

Benefits for students and educators

The AIM2Flourish experience invites students to develop an inquisitive mind-set. They first learn about the various challenges we are facing regarding sustainability and the UN's seventeen SDGs. For a business to be accepted for publication on the AIM2Flourish platform, it must meet the following criteria:

- Be a for-profit business corporation

- Have sustained operations for at least two years

- Help achieve one or more of UN's SDGs

- Have developed a full product or service, or its entire strategy, based on serving its community and/or the environment in a more sustainable way

Encouraging students to go out in the field to interview businesses that have developed their strategy for a social and/or environmental sustainability has multiple benefits. The following sections describe some benefits acknowledged by students and professors involved in the initiative described in this section.

Enhance the university's/school's network

During the past year, professors who encouraged their students to conduct an Appreciative Inquiry with local or international businesses fitting the AIM2Flourish's criteria saw their network expand in several ways. Some professors are using AIM2Flourish as a required component of their curricula: Dr. Amelia Naim Indrajaya, teaching at IPMI International Business School, (Indonesia), and Dr. Guénola Nonet, visiting professor at Nova Southeastern University (NSU, Florida, USA) have integrated the AIM2Flourish experience in their courses. In total, fifty-two innovation stories have already been published under the leadership of these two professors: half of them were written by students from IPMI, and the other half by students from NSU.

Due to the AIM2Flourish project, IPMI has now expanded its network to the following sectors: water management, access to food and water, insurance, apparel, lightning, marine and fish habitat, actuaries, hearing-impaired employment, agriculture, supply chain management, alternatives to plastic bags, social empowerment, chemical industry, education, energy and waste management. As a result of the AIM2Flourish projects, NSU has expanded its network to the following sectors: counselling, food services, education, medicine, financial literacy, sport and health, waste management, hair dressing, architecture, food distribution and supermarket retail, car industry, car wash, sanitation, therapeutic services, growing food and fish, lighting and cutlery. Most stories are written about local and regional companies.

These expanded networks bring a new potential for the school, including collaborative research projects, subsidies, participation in events such as Earth Day, Global Citizen Day and other events, and internships (PRME Principles 4: *Research*, 5: *Partnerships* and 6: *Dialogue*).

The following sections describe a range of benefits that emerged from these projects. They highlight several schools around the world and their students' experiences (details about the schools, the students and their professors can be found in the Appendix).

Increase student understanding of local and international issues and the UN SDGs

By having the responsibility of finding and presenting an innovative and sustainable business, students are likely to develop a deeper understanding of local and international issues, including those covered by the ten UN Global Compact Principles and the seventeen SDGs. 'The information I gathered through my research and in class has awakened awareness of challenges that affect the environment, and human life', commented Sharon Sims, who interviewed a Nutrition Smart Manager as part of her learning experience about the UN's SDGs. Another student, Yick Yan Hung Janet, interviewed Fuji Xerox leaders in Hong Kong. Fuji Xerox provides measurement software, usage reports and education related to customers' energy-using habits. This combination is expected to reduce energy consumption and influence more sustainable worker behaviours through direct data about their use of energy. Yick Yan Hung Janet reported about her experience:

> Looking back, what I most enjoyed about the research process for AIM2Flourish was researching what are the SDGs. At the beginning, I had no idea about SDGs, or I could say I hadn't heard anything about it before. The reason is that when professors taught about sustainable development, they would only mention that we should focus on three angles, 'Social, Economic and Environmental'. Thus, as a student, even when we had initiatives to conduct further research about sustainable development, we would only focus on those three angles. Hence, when I knew that 17 SDGs were established in these few years, I was excited about them and I wanted to find out more about them.

Get familiarized with real-life business and leadership challenges

From this exercise, students also learn about the different functions and difficulties of running a business: from the obstacles they encounter in finding financing and suppliers to the creativity necessary when dealing with international market regulations and cultures. For example, MBA student Sebastian

FIGURE 15.2 **Groasis inventor Pieter Hoff**

Garcia researched Groasis Tech, an environment-friendly Dutch company whose objective is to plant degraded and eroded land with trees.

The Groasis Waterboxx is a planting device that can be used to grow trees in dry and rocky areas because it produces water via artificial condensation. In his story, Sebastian noticed the importance of teamwork and reliable suppliers:

> Mr. Hoff told us during the interview that 'Maybe I am the one who had the inspiration and main idea. But it was made by all the people who I work with in my company, a group of reliable suppliers and many users who sent ideas. Maybe I did 20 per cent and the rest [contributed] over 80 per cent of the ideas. Our product is the fruit of combined thinking of many people who worry about water scarcity. In fact, that was the best quote for us because through his sentences we noticed that he was proud to have contributed to the creation of these new technologies without forgetting the hard work of his teams.

Acquire applied learning experience

Unlike in a traditional case study, a practical project of this type requires students to acquire information about a company, perform different hands-on research activities, including interviewing business leaders and reading news and stories about the company (Weber and Englehart, 2011). It helps them acquire applied

FIGURE 15.3 **The Sunshine Nut Company**

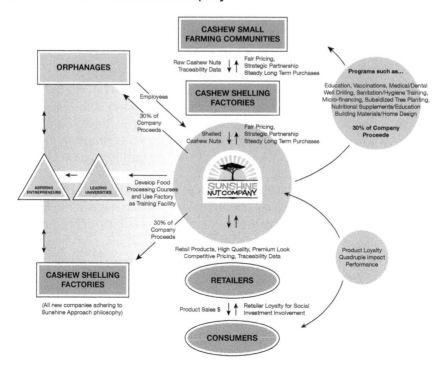

learning experiences to create new knowledge and skills. Sandra McCants researched The Sunshine Nut Company in Mozambique, a company created in 2011 by Don Larson. Sunshine's purpose is to develop a profitable market for small growers. Sandra explained the experience she gained:

> [T]ransforming the lives of the poor and orphaned in sub-Saharan Africa. [This experience] allows for a wide flow (of) thoughts and ideas. The experience is not just a yes or no. It is not simply in a text book. I have grown because I was allowed to think, not just read a text book.

The AIM2Flourish participants do research to find innovative businesses, interview entrepreneurs and analyze company strategies. These efforts lead to greater student engagement and can transform them to lead responsibly. MBA student Sophia Nicholson studied the strategy of ALDI (Albrecht Diskont, German grocery stores challenging the typical retail business model by offering over 1,400 of the most commonly purchased grocery and household products at a lower price). ALDI employs a three-pronged strategy to ensure business success, which aligns with the triple bottom line concept. It is a holistic view of doing business that attempts to balance people, profit and the planet. After her interview, Sophia explained:

> I do recommend the AIM2Flourish experience. This is an engaging way of bringing awareness of both social and environmental challenges. But most of all, exploring the many fixes was a positive experience. I believe it should also be offered through schools in Caribbean Islands where the awareness and discovery of solutions would offer hope.

Develop critical thinking for sustainability

One of the most important benefits of teaching AIM2Flourish as a class project is the possibility of immersing the students in the business world in order to analyse and evaluate sustainable innovations. Research has found that this approach motivates students to become more critical thinkers and more interested in sustainability in their organizations; it also encourages them to look for more information regarding sustainability in the business world (Canto de Loura, 2014; Christiensen *et al.*, 2007; Dickson *et al.*, 2013; Mather *et al.*, 2011). Students also become aware of what it takes to become an innovative business leader who is also able to keep sustainability in focus. Students learn from the practical experience of looking in the marketplace for businesses responding to some of the UN's seventeen SDGs.

Increase students' awareness of environmental, social and humanitarian issues

Using this global initiative as a teaching tool (PRME, Principle 3: *Method*) exposes students to a more international context, with the potential of expanding their view of the world and making them more tolerant and more focused on ethics

FIGURE 15.4 **Hotel Posta de Pumamarca**

and sustainability in global society. Claudia Riviera researched Sseko Designs, a footwear and accessory brand currently employing fifty women in Uganda and having already enabled sixty women to continue on to university:

> The organization that I ultimately decided to research was based in Africa. I knew from staying abreast of current events and my studies in political science and international relations about the issues that are faced in the region and efforts that are made by other countries. However, to see the actual statistics behind the social challenges was new and astounding for me.

The AIM2Flourish experience helps increase our students' level of awareness on social, environmental and humanitarian issues. Laura Banzer Godefroy researched the Hotel Posta de Pumamarca in Jujuy, Argentina, a certified Ecohotel that has promoted over ten years the principles of sustainable tourism. The hotel's mission is to provide distinctive and high quality service following a program of Corporate Social Responsibility based on its commitment to respecting the architectural and cultural heritage, supporting community development, protection of the environment and good business practices. Laura says this experience totally changed her understanding of social/environmental/humanitarian issues:

> I did have a certain level of awareness before working for this project. But seeing how others do big things with small changes (that everyone can do) showed me that you can always do more, and that there is no valid excuse for not taking care of what's important. No matter how small you are, or your business is, you can change the world inch by inch, and it's not just a phrase, it's a REALITY, that you can see in all the amazing businesses participating in AIM2Flourish.

Find inspiration to make a difference in the world

Conducting research for AIM2Flourish shows students that the two concepts of financial success and social/environmental sustainability are not mutually exclusive (PRME, Principles 1: *Purpose,* 2: *Values* and 4: *Research*). This was also highlighted by some of the participating students. Mariana Morimura reviewed an innovative business in Brazil, a country where water shortage is an issue in some areas, and where an engineer from the state of São Paulo, Pedro Ricardo Paulino, developed a technology that produces drinking water from the air. The Wateair condenses the air, purifies, sterilizes and mineralizes the water so that it becomes suitable for human consumption. This equipment only needs a 10 per cent level of humidity and to be connected to electric power, and the more humid the immediate atmosphere, the more water it produces. In 2010, Paulino patented his invention and started to manufacture the machine in different models, with the capability to produce between 4 gallons and 500,000 gallons per day. The smaller version of the equipment costs about $2,000. Mariana commented upon her AIM2Flourish experience:

> Students may gain new perspectives of the business world. They see it is possible to have a successful business considering social, environmental and humanitarian challenges. There is always a solution to make the world a better place without stopping the company's growth.

Moreover, students found sources of inspiration and motivation that can enhance their future work performance, creativity and innovation. MBA student Mariely Acevedo reviewed LuminAID, which offers a unique way of illuminating an area during an emergency through a small packet that can inflate to diffuse light like a lantern. The packet lasts up to 16 hours, and it is waterproof and floatable. After reporting about an interview with a business entrepreneur, Mariely said the following:

> The quote that Anna Stork left me with was one by Scott Belsky which states: 'It's not about ideas, it's about making ideas happen.' I believe that this quote will probably follow me in my thoughts for many years to come. Simply thinking about something is nothing until you make it happen. The most interesting factor of their story to me was the fact that they got the opportunity to help so many people. I am a giving person and feel that when you give selflessly you receive twice as much back as a blessing. Although their idea may have only been a small idea to them at first, it has evolved into what is now seen as an innovative product that may have inspired many more like me to follow in their footsteps. This was honestly an incredible experience.

AIM2Flourish, an invaluable experience for students, educators and business leaders

Researchers and practitioners have highlighted the importance of incorporating sustainability in business education in order to prepare business leaders for responsible management practices (Alcaraz and Thruvattal, 2010; Association to

Advance Collegiate Schools of Business (AACSB), 2013; Dickson *et al.*, 2013; Exter *et al.*, 2013). Moreover, research has noted that sustainability needs to be addressed through both substance and process in order to expand students' views of the world and to develop professional skills (Mather *et al.*, 2011).

The use of AIM2Flourish's global initiative as a class project teaches students about profitable innovation and sustainability and about the benefits of paying attention to the world around them. They also immerse students in the business community and puts them in direct contact with business innovators, underlining the benefits and challenges of entrepreneurship. This global initiative represents a practical tool to help students acquire business skills and knowledge for different disciplines as well as to find inspiration in their communities. It has been endorsed by the UN Global Compact, PRME and the GRLI, as it is the first tool in higher education helping students research and identify an innovation, interview a leader using the lens of the UN SDGs, learn first-hand from business leaders and publish their stories on AIM2Flourish.com

References

AIM2Flourish. (2016) 'Executive summary'. Available online at https://weatherhead.case.edu/centers/fowler/aim2flourish/about (accessed 27 September 2016).

Alcaraz, J. M. and Thruvattal, E. (2010) 'An Interview with Manuel Escudero. The United Nations' principles for responsible management education: A global call for sustainability', *Academy of Management Learning & Education*, 9(3): 542–550.

Association to Advance Collegiate Schools of Business (AACSB). (2013) 'Business accreditation standards'. Available online at http://aacsb.edu/accreditation/standards/2013-business (accessed 15 February 2016).

Canto de Loura, I. (2014) 'Dilemmas in sustainability. A pedagogical approach to raise awareness on the key role businesses play to practice and promote sustainability', *Journal of Management Development*, 33(6): 594–602.

Christiensen, L. J., Peirce, E., Hartman, L. P., Hoffman, W. M. and Carrier, J. (2007) 'Ethics, CSR, and sustainability education in the Financial Times top 50 global business schools: Baseline data and future research directions', *Journal of Business Ethics*, 73(4): 347–368.

Dickson, M. A., Eckman, M., Loker, S. and Jirousek, C. (2013) 'A model for sustainability education in support of the PRME', *Journal of Management Development*, 32(3): 309–318.

Exter, N., Grayson, D. and Maher, R. (2013) 'Facilitating organizational change for embedding sustainability into academia: A case study', *Journal of Management Development*, 32(3): 319–332.

Mather, G., Denby, L., Wood, L. N. and Harrison, B. (2011) 'Business graduate skills in sustainability', *Journal of Global Responsibility*, 2(2): 188–205.

United Nations Principles for Responsible Management Education (UN PRME). (2015) 'PRME global forum responsible management education statement'. Available online at http://unprme.org/resource-docs/2015PRMEGlobalForumforResponsibleManagementEducationOutcomeStatementFINAL.pdf (accessed 15 February 2016).

Weatherhead School of Business. (2016) 'AIM2Flourish'. Available online at https://weatherhead.case.edu/centers/fowler/AIM2Flourish/ (accessed 12 September 2016).

Weber, J. W. and Englehart, S. W. (2011) 'Enhancing business education through integrated curriculum delivery', *Journal of Management Development*, *30*(6): 558–568.

Dr. Guénola Nonet was a visiting professor/scholar in residence during 2 years 2015–2017 to help develop responsible and sustainable management at Nova Southeastern University, Florida. Guénola is now full time Assistant Professor in Business Administration at Jönköping International Business School, Sweden. Guénola has a PhD in Management from University of Montpellier France and she graduated from Erasmus University – Rotterdam School of Management, The Netherlands.

guenola.nonet@gmail.com

Dr. Maria Petrescu is an Assistant Professor of Marketing. Maria has a PhD in Business Administration and Marketing from Florida Atlantic University and a M.B.A. from Nova Southeastern University. Contact detail: mpetresc@nova.edu
Our special gratitude goes to our AIM2Flourish colleagues, to all the students who contributed to this story by sharing their experiences, to Claire Sommer, AIM2Flourish Director and to Roberta Baskin, AIM2Flourish Executive Director for their guidance.

mpetresc@nova.edu

Appendix: Participants' list

The following table presents the different stories written by students. Eight students from NSU (Florida, USA) were quoted: five did their project under the guidance of Dr. Guénola Nonet and three worked with Dr. Maria Petrescu. One student from Hang Seng M. College (Hong Kong) did her research supported by Dr. Yeung Mo Ching, and one student from Universidad Catolica (Argentina) did her research with Dr. Aleandra Scarfati.

Company	Company's headquarters	Student	Professor	School	School's country
ALDI	Germany	S. Nicholson			
Nutrition Smart	USA	S. Sims	Dr. G. Nonet		
Sanergy	Kenya	D. Whitley-Bowman		Nova Southeastern University, HCBE	USA
The Sunshine Nut C.	Mozambique	S. McCants			
Ssesko Designs	Uganda	C. Riviera			
Groasis Tech	The Netherlands	S. Garcia			
The Wateair	Brazil	M. Morimura	Dr. M. Petrescu		
LuminAID	USA	M. Acevedo			
Fuji Xerox	China	Y. Yan Hung Janet	Dr. S. Yeung Mo Ching	Hang Seng M. College	China
Hotel the Pumamarca	Argentina	L. Banzer Godefroy	Dr. A. Scafati	Universidad Catolica	Argentina

16

Orange

The colour of responsibility and inclusion[1]

Michael John Page
Bentley University, USA

Dianne Lynne Bevelander
Erasmus University Rotterdam, The Netherlands

Abstract

This chapter investigates the extent to which ING Group has moved beyond values as written in their Orange Code and their ING Diversity Manifesto to the values being embedded by employees. It argues that a *virtuous spiral* set by *tone at the top* encouraged, and empowered, a committed change agent in the organisation to develop and expand education programs oriented to transforming the gender paradigm of the Group. The spiral begins with statements of intent by senior executives that are taken on board by one or more change agents who take action on these statements. This results in the change agent(s) influencing peers and subordinates who then internalize these values themselves. Survey research conducted among participants and non-participants provided evidence of the virtuous spiral. After a total of eight programs or workshops, the evidence finds that respondents are positive about diversity practices at ING. The core proposition of the chapter is that committed change agents can play a key transformative role if the tone at the top is appropriate, and if sponsors come to the fore with the needed emotional and financial resources. Virtuous spirals, such as the one illustrated in the chapter, offer interesting insight as to how values and behaviours can be influenced over time through a development agenda, and thereby position enterprises to better practice the principles of the UN Global Compact.

Introduction

ING Group formally launched the Orange Code – named after the banking group's corporate colour – in 2015 as the articulation of the values and behaviours expected of all employees in their relationships with one another as well as with clients and other external stakeholders. The Code, developed with input from over 15,000 employees (Knaapen, 2016), reaffirmed ING's commitment to integrity and accountability, and immediately became part of the performance assessment of senior leaders within the Group. The undertaking was made to integrate it into performance assessment for all employees a year later (ING Group 2016a, p. 11).

Beyond its consistency with the Netherlands Bankers Oath[2], the Orange Code makes an implied commitment to the UN Global Compact principles of elimination of discrimination, freedom of association and rejection of corruption[3]. However, in spite of the fact that the Orange Code is referred to twenty-five times in the Group's 2015 Annual Report, the journey from espoused ideas and values to observed behaviours is often a long one. As has been reported in popular and academic literature, value and mission statements are sometimes seen as window dressing rather than as reflections of what entities and their employees really believe and strive to practice (Bartkus *et al.*, 2000; Sebastian *et al.*, 2011). Similarly, commitment to ethical and transparent behaviour underlying codes of conduct of the type required by the Netherlands Bankers Oath has been questioned (Aitken, 2014; Banks, 2003; Pieters, 2016; Vermaelen, 2009).

This chapter examines the extent to which ING Group has moved beyond stated values to transformed behaviours. It suggests that a virtuous spiral was seeded by 'tone at the top' that encouraged and empowered committed change agents – who can be viewed as early believers in the Group's commitment to its stated values – to develop and expand programs that impacted employees experiences of the expressed values and began to change their behaviours. Specifically, this issue is addressed here within the context of ING's commitment to gender diversity – a commitment that has been recognized by its inclusion in Bloomberg's recently launched Financial Services Gender-Equality Index[4].

The empirical research undertaken for the chapter advances the understanding of how the internal dynamics of an organisation can enhance social and economic values. As such, it aligns with the fourth Principle ('Research') of the UN Global Compact's Principles for Responsible Management Education (PRME). The case was developed in dialogue with key personnel at ING Bank, and the lessons learned are being explored with other companies partnering with the Erasmus Centre for Women and Organizations (Principles 5 'Partnership' and 6 'Dialogue'). Furthermore, the ING transformation process can be used as a pedagogical tool to expand students' understanding of sustainable and socially responsible business practices consistent with requirements specified for academic institutions related to purpose (Principle 1) and values (Principle 2).

Mission, values and organisational changes

Much has been written about the difficulties organisations face when trying to innovate and transform. Most also acknowledge that change is essential and practically continuous, given the current global hyper-competitive business landscape – one that is continuously buffeted by rapid technological change and continually evolving economic, political and social environments (Brown and Eisenhardt, 1997; Prastacosa *et al.*, 2002; Sirkin *et al.*, 2008). It has been argued that credible statements of purpose – values and mission – become even more important in such environments. They give direction beyond the immediacy of task and serve as key internal and external signals to stakeholders. Internally, they provide clarity about the organisation's ethical stance and raison d'etre, which can frame employee choice and influence employee behaviour (Davies and Glaister, 1997). Externally, they signal identity, and position the organisation against its competitors with respect to its choice of activities and the relationship it wishes to hold with its wider stakeholders (Hartley, 2002; Short and Palmer, 2008).

The complexity of organisational change is often described along the continuum from incremental to transformative (Bartunek and Moch, 1987; Gersick, 1991; Morgan and Zeffane, 2003; Nadler, Shaw, Walton and Associates, 1995; Nadler and Tushman, 1990). On the incremental side, improvement occurs within established organisational structures and value systems. In contrast, transformational change often involves amending value systems and re-examining the appropriateness of existing organisational form (Seo, 2003). External environmental factors that extend considerably beyond the historical competitive landscape place banking and financial services company change agendas well along the continuum towards transformative change. Under these circumstances, Pascale and Sternin's (2005, p. 74) 'positive deviants' approach has a lot to recommend it. Rather than being seen as predictable and controllable, this approach delivers on the change agenda through utilizing innovators within the organisation who take ownership and act. Further, they contend that 'disbelief and resistance are easier to overcome' (Pascale and Sternin, 2005, p. 74) with the active support of 'change agents' embedded within the existing organisation.

As Nadler and Tushman (1990, p. 77) have stated: 'Charismatic leadership must be bolstered by institutional leadership' and 'responsibility for managing in turbulent environments must be institutionalized'. Change agents – whether formal managers or informal leaders – take on this responsibility. They push the change agenda forward and expand the cadre of employees committed to its success. Their embedded location within the organisation can help rebuild trust and identification with the customer base (Morgan and Zeffane, 2003).

The Orange Code and ING's Diversity Manifesto

Officially launched in early 2015, ING's Orange Code expresses a set of three values and three behaviours oriented to placing *integrity above all* for employees.

Developed following broad employee consultation across over forty countries, the Code re-emphasises corporate values and describes desired behaviours that are considered key to building customer trust and to ensuring that the Group engages responsibly with broader society (ING Group, 2016a, p. 3). Knaapen (2016), chief human resources (HR) officer of ING Group, suggests that the Code describes '2/3rd of who we are and 1/3rd of who we want to be' and that the aspirational aspects are more oriented to improving inclusion and personal accountability. The three values of honesty, prudence and responsibility are considered to be long-held non-negotiable promises made to one another and to the world at large[5]. In turn, they inform behaviours that reflect a commitment to individual action and accountability that *makes things happen, helps others be successful* and looks to innovate and stay *a step ahead.*

The Orange Code's potential to impact employee practices was further enhanced with the subsequent launch of the Group's Diversity Manifesto (ING Group, 2016b). It strives to ensure that ING attracts and retains top talent – talent needed to adapt and innovate in ways that disrupt existing 'wisdom' and thereby better serve its customers. Both documents recognize that shifts from statement to action require an environment of respect, trust, support and tolerance for different points of view and approaches. Diversity is considered key to the future 'not just because it is the right thing to do' but 'because we cannot deliver on our strategy without it' (ING Group, 2016b). The importance of gender within ING Group's broader diversity aspirations is acknowledged in its 2015 Annual Report (ING Group, 2016a, p. 45) that states: 'In particular, we aim to achieve an increase in the number of women in leadership positions' (Hamers, 2016).

From espoused to lived values and aspirations

While the above statements articulate commendable values and express executive leadership's desire for transformation, are the desired behaviours being adopted by the broader employee base of the Group? The chapter argues in the affirmative and demonstrates that this is being achieved through the *virtuous spiral* presented in Figure 16.1. The spiral begins with statements of intent by senior executives that are seen as credible because of actions by these same executives. This 'tone at the top' is considered a necessary first step for a committed change agenda and for the development of pervasive ethical values throughout the enterprise (Becker, 2008; Cameron, 2007; Pickerd et al., 2015; Schwartz et al., 2005). The second step is that key connected actors – change agents – take action based upon their belief in the sincerity of statements made by executive leadership. These change agents are important initiators of the action sequence because of their closer proximity to the broader base of employees either as peers or as line managers (Pickerd et al, 2015). Their social networks, commitment and tenacity drive the release of resources necessary to deliver on the change agenda (Seibert et al., 2001). The third step occurs when the behaviours and actions of the change agent influence peers and subordinates, lending credence to the

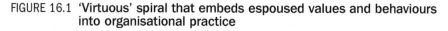

FIGURE 16.1 'Virtuous' spiral that embeds espoused values and behaviours into organisational practice

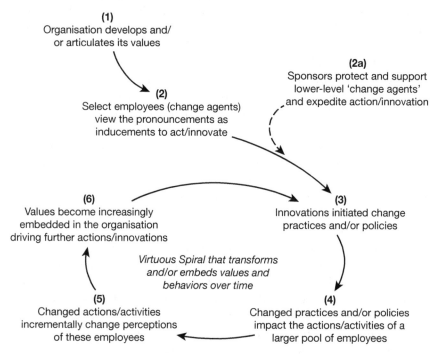

previously heard statements by executives, providing demonstrable evidence of the change commitment. This expands the pool of employees who internalize the values and commit to actions needed to realize the longer-term strategic goals.

Unfortunately, the spiral described above is not always virtuous – something most recently illustrated during the US Senate Hearing into the unauthorized opening of two million accounts by Wells Fargo employees[6]. Senator Elizabeth Warren's questioning of CEO John Stumpf clearly suggests that 'tone at the top' induced early initiators lower down in the ranks to engage in unethical practices designed to meet unrealistic targets[7]. The resultant spiral ultimately resulted in over 5,000 employees being fired.

Achieving ING Group's diversity aspirations: The case of gender

ING's Diversity Manifesto makes the case for diversity of 'gender, age, background, sexual orientation, physical ability and religious beliefs' (ING Group,

2016, p. 5) and provides clarity about what is expected on processes such as hiring, career development and communications. The motivations provided in the document mirror those suggested in the academic literature and in policy directives. Namely, diversity increases the range of contributions and the collective intelligence of teams (Woolley and Malone, 2011), because it draws from the widest pool of talent available (Ely and Thomas, 2001), and because it increases access to customers (European Commission, 2015).

Knaapen (2016) justified ING leadership's emphasis on gender in the shorter-term from two perspectives. First, in common with the state sector and academia, current statistics for the corporate sector lag considerably behind what might be expected for contemporary society. ING Group is no exception to this. As Bevelander (2016, p. 10) has argued, indicators and statistics 'present a dismal picture of gender equality for the corporate sector, for government, and for academia', and that human capital development approaches as well as retention and promotion practices need to be changed. Second, discussions and pro-clamations at national and international levels suggest that companies must become proactive to avoid regulations that may hamper rather than support corporate efforts to correct existing diversity shortcomings. Illustrations of recent legislative changes include the introduction of gender quotas across Belgium, Iceland, Italy, the Netherlands and Spain following their 2003 introduction in Norway (*The Economist*, 2014), and the 2012 European Commission (2015, p. 5) directive that proposes 'a quantitative objective of a 40 per cent presence of the under-represented sex among non-executive directors of companies listed on stock exchanges by 2020.'

There are a number of diversity initiatives offered through ING's HR division, and ING is working hard at addressing any diversity deficiencies. However, this chapter will focus on one of the initiatives for improving gender performance that involved working with the Rotterdam School of Management's Erasmus Centre for Women and Organisations. This relationship started in early 2015 as a single mid-level workshop for women in wholesale banking's finance depart-ment and subsequently grew to include multiple offerings for middle level personnel across retail and wholesale banking, all eleven support divisions of the Group, for senior managers of both genders, and senior women specifically. By November 2016, approximately 200 employees had attended one of the eleven workshops, and approval had been granted to begin a research program to assess the short- and long-term efficacy of the program.

ING's virtuous spiral

Although ING Group's efforts to increase recruitment, retention and promotion of women predate the release of the Orange Code and the Diversity Manifesto, they added significantly to diversity dialogue within Group. Knaapen (2016) believes that dialogue about gender equity from a business and societal perspective has increased over the last two years[8]. He argues that 'increased diversity across the employee base – across divisions and organisation levels – enables the Group to better understand its varied customer base as well as other interested external stakeholder groups.'

The emerging emphasis on diversity coincided with Izabela Csontos attending an Erasmus Centre for Women and Organisations workshop in Fall 2014. The event had a profound impact on her, as she came to appreciate that her eastern European and Nordic gender experiences were not universal[9]. In her estimation, women in the Netherlands 'hit the glass ceiling even before reaching the middle management level' (Csontos, 2016). As the person responsible for organisational development within the finance division of ING wholesale banking, Izabela decided to build the case for how 'customers, society and the company would win by building a more gender-balanced organisation'. With a measure of tenacity, she brought her ideas to the attention of management and secured the chief financial officer (CFO) of wholesale banking, Lars Kramer, as a primary sponsor and champion of the initiative to bring the Centre's Women in Leadership open program into her division[10]. Approval and funding for the first workshop was given. Twenty-six women employed in the finance division of wholesale banking (principally in the Netherlands) attended and their feedback was so overwhelmingly positive that the workshop was repeated and expanded to other divisions and internationally. To date, a further five middle-level workshops have been run, two have been run for senior-level[11] women, and three senior-level workshops have been run for men and women oriented to 'making the business case for gender diversity'. Two middle-level workshops were planned for 2016.

The above description reflects a *virtuous spiral* for transforming the gender paradigm at ING. A change agent – Izabela Csontos – is inspired by the articulated values and behaviours expected of employees. She proceeds to execute on what she believes to be an institutional mandate for innovation and change. With the support of sponsors, she initiates an intervention that impacts others and induces them to become co-champions of the initiative. This growing enthusiasm feeds into the organisation stimulating further demand. In doing so, it increases perceptions of the veracity of the articulated values and behaviours for more employees. What might have been viewed as espoused beliefs become embedded practices because of the bottom-up and lateral engagement of the change agent or founding champion.

When asked what factors led her to feel that she could succeed in driving forward a sizeable gender initiative, Csontos (2016) cited her passion for the topic and courageous personality as well as finding 'senior managers in ING to be approachable and willing to find time to listen to employees'. She also recorded that she considers the Orange Code as a foundation for inspiring continuous change by stating the following: 'The values and behaviours framed by the Orange Code encourage us to take initiatives to make things better.'

Assessing employee perceptions

Research on perceptions of the efficacy of the initiative involved surveying a sample of employees, including some who had not yet attended one of the workshops. If the central proposition that the process was creating a virtual spiral is correct, both attendees and non-attendees should have a net favourable impression of their employer following almost eighteen months of interventions. Consequently, the core hypothesis was that female employees had a positive impression of the Orange Code and the gender diversity initiatives underway across the Group. It was also postulated that past participants would have a stronger belief in the ING's commitment to transformation than non-attendees, but that this difference would be relatively small given the transference effect of the 'spiral'. Similarly, it was proposed that senior personnel would have only slightly stronger positive beliefs than junior personnel. Therefore, the secondary hypotheses were that workshop attendees and senior personnel would have marginally higher positive perceptions than those who had not yet attended and the junior colleagues respectively.

Developing and administering the survey instrument

The administered questionnaire consisted largely of questions drawn from previously validated instruments. Areas covered included diversity climate, integration of differences and sense of similarity (Chung *et al.*, 2015; Harrison *et al.*, 1998; Nishii, 2013), inclusion (Mor Barak, 2014; Nishii, 2013), distributive, interactional and procedural justice (Niehoff and Moorman, 1993), assertiveness and self-efficacy (Goldberg, 1992), organisational identification (Mael and Ashford, 1992) and social capital (Kouvonen *et al.*, 2006). Further, Likert-scale perceptual questions were asked about the embedded nature of the Orange Code and the commitment of executive leadership to gender diversity. Finally, while continuing to respect the confidentiality of respondents, a few demographic questions were asked about gender, division, nationality, level (contributor, manager and manager-of-managers) and workshop attendance. The Likert-scale questions asked, and their source, are presented in the Appendix. Group permission was given for employees to be surveyed prior to the questionnaire being administered using SurveyMonkey (https://surveymonkey.com/).

One hundred and one employees responded to the questionnaire. Fifty-seven had attended one of the workshops and forty-four had not; forty-two were managers and fifty-nine were contributors[12]; and seventy-five were Dutch nationals and the remainder were nationals from twelve other countries. Instrument reliability is presented in Table 16.1. All of the instruments were found to have Cronbach's alpha between 0.65 and 0.90[13].

TABLE 16.1 **Reliability measures and instrument statistics**

Instrument[1]	Source	No. of items	Alpha	Mean	SE	t-stat.	p value[4]
(a)	(b)	(c)	(d)	(e)	(f)	(g)	(h)
Assertiveness	Goldberg, n.d.	6	0.652	0.847	0.040	21.36	0.000
Self-efficacy	Goldberg, n.d.	6	0.676	1.063	0.035	30.22	0.000
Self-to-other similarity	Harrison et al., 1998	6	0.706	0.454	0.057	7.93	0.000
Social capital	Kouvonen et al., 2006	8	0.870	0.755	0.059	12.90	0.000
Justice	Niehoff and Moorman, 1993	8	0.824	0.579	0.053	10.96	0.000
Diversity climate	Chung et al., 2015	7	0.729	0.513	0.055	9.36	0.000
Inclusion–exclusion	Mor Barack, 2014	5	0.685	0.402	0.063	6.33	0.000
Inclusion in decision-making	Nishii, 2014	5	0.814	0.347	0.058	5.95	0.000
Integration of differences	Nishii, 2014	5	0.784	0.568	0.053	10.74	0.000
Executive leadership[2]		4	0.659	0.220	0.061	-3.61	1.000
Organisational identification	Mael and Ashford, 1992	4	0.809	0.485	0.069	7.00	0.000
Orange Code acceptance[3]		4	0.772	0.807	0.060	13.47	0.000

1 Mean values and standard errors (SE) are computed after each item is centred on zero by deducting 3 and then the items are averaged to create the composite scale. This transformation of each instrument allows for easier visual interpretation without changing statistical significance in any way. Items that were reverse scaled in the questionnaire were transposed – subtracted from 6 – prior to analysis.

2 Items extracted and amended to suit the current study (Cukier, 2009; Cukier and Smarz, 2012).

3 Orange Code items developed for the current study.

4 p value is for the probability of getting a value greater than the observed mean value if the true mean value is zero.

Results and analysis

The primary hypothesis of the research was that female employees had a positive impression of the Orange Code and the gender diversity initiatives underway across the Group. Formally, this hypothesis was established as follows:

$H_O^{(1)}$: Female employees do not have a favourable impression of (each of the validated instruments).

$H_A^{(1)}$: Female employees have a positive impression of (each of the validated instruments).

The results presented in columns (g) and (h) of Table 16.1 strongly reject the null for 11 of the 12 measures, and it can be concluded that female employees:

- See themselves as assertive and confident they have the ability to produce needed results – reflected in the *assertiveness* (1) and *self-efficacy* (2) measures;

- Identify with those they work with, feel personally included, identify with ING and believe that they are integrated into the social capital of the Group – reflected in the *self-to-other similarity* (3), *inclusion–exclusion* (7), *organisational identification* (11) and *social capital* (4) measures;

- Believe that ING respects diversity and seeks the input of its employees, operates with integrity by treating employees fairly, honestly and with dignity, and by considering their opinions – reflected in the *diversity climate* (6), *integration of differences* (9), *inclusion in decision-making* (8) and *justice* (5) measures;

- View the Orange Code positively and integrated into the value system of the Group – reflected in the *ING Orange Code* (12) measure.

The null hypothesis is not rejected for the *executive leadership* (10) measure. Additionally, this is the only measure where respondents had a statistically significant negative perception. A deeper analysis of the four constituent items of the measure is contained in Table 16.2. The pattern of responses shows that the overall measure is heavily influenced by the factually correct perception that senior leadership does not reflect the composition of the ING workforce. This is recognized by executive leadership (ING Group, 2016a, p. 77). The next two questions that account for the overall negative perception concern communication. Respondents believe that considerably more can be done to 'market' the importance of gender diversity for ING Group. Interestingly, what is perceived positively by respondents is the Board's concern for gender diversity. Only 12.9 per cent of respondents felt that the Board did not consider 'gender diversity

TABLE 16.2 **Distribution of responses for items of the executive leadership instrument**

	Strongly disagree and disagree[1]	**Neutral**	**Agree and strongly agree**
1 The ING Board considers gender diversity important when identifying and developing people	13 12.9%	43 42.6%	45 44.6%
2 Senior executive proactively communicates the importance of gender diversity inside and outside the organisation	41 40.6%	33 32.7%	27 26.7%
3 Leadership of ING bank reflects the composition of the workforce	70 69.3%	17 16.8%	14 13.9%
4 The business case for gender diversity is widely communicated	45 44.6%	34 33.7%	22 21.8%

1 A five-point Likert scale was employed for all questions, where: 1 = strongly disagree; 2 = disagree; 3 = neutral; 4 = agree and 5 = strongly agree.

important when identifying and developing people'. Clearly, the multi-faceted nature of the *executive leadership* measure means that it should be interpreted with caution!

The secondary hypotheses of the research relate to the efficacy of the workshops and the transference effect of the *virtuous spiral*. They concern the extent to which junior employees and employees who have not attended Centre for Women and Organisation workshops lag behind those of senior employees and employees who have attended them. Although no causal interpretation can be drawn, a lag in sentiment across the portfolio of diversity measures is consistent with what a *loop effect* would produce where the positive sentiments of senior personnel and employees who have attended workshops transfer to others over time, thereby enhancing the latter's perceptions of the gender diversity efforts of ING.

Specifically, the following hypotheses are tested concerning employee impressions of each of the validated instruments across (1) senior employees – managers and managers-of-managers; (2) contributors – those without management responsibilities; (3) those who have attended a workshop; and (4) those who have not yet attended a workshop.

$H_O^{(2)}$: The selected subset of employees does not have a favourable impression of (each of the instruments).

$H_A^{(2)}$: The selected subset does have a positive impression of (each of the instruments).

$H_O^{(3)}$: Aggregate impressions across the portfolio of instruments is independent of rank/attendance.

$H_A^{(3)}$: Aggregate impressions of senior employees/attendees are more positive than for junior employees/non-attendees.

Table 16.3 presents the results of the hypotheses tests. Columns (b), (c), (e) and (f) show that the null hypothesis is rejected for eleven of the twelve measures, indicating that managers, contributors, workshop attendees and non-attendees have a favourable impression of ING Group's diversity efforts. The single measure where this is not the case across the four groups is *executive leadership*, for the reasons described earlier. Columns (d) and (g) show that the null hypothesis of sentiment equivalence between managers and contributors and the null hypothesis of sentiment equivalence between program attendees and non-attendees cannot be rejected for eight and four of the twelve cases respectively. The percentage of measures for which managers scored higher on average than employees and attendees scored higher than non-attendees are 100 per cent and 83 per cent respectively[14].

Columns (h), (i) and (j) in Table 16.3 find that international participants have as favourable an impression of the diversity initiatives as do the Dutch participants who represented approximately 75 per cent of the respondents. It can be concluded that there is no domestic bias in the sentiments of employees concerning the issue of gender diversity.

TABLE 16.3 Comparison of instruments across rank, participation and nationality

Instrument[1]	Managers	Contrib.	p value[2]	Attendee	Non-attend.	p value[2]	Dutch	Internat.	p value[3]
Number of respondents	42	59		57	44		75	26	
	Mean	Mean		Mean	Mean		Mean	Mean	
(a)	(b)	(c)	(d)	(e)	(f)	(g)	(h)	(i)	(j)
Assertiveness	0.960 **	0.766 **	0.005 **	0.915 **	0.758 **	0.025 #	0.851 **	0.833 **	0.825
Self-efficacy	1.099 **	1.037 **	0.192	1.059 **	1.068 **	0.948	1.071 **	1.039 **	0.699
Self-to-other similarity	0.544 **	0.390 **	0.090 +	0.488 **	0.409 **	0.254	0.431 **	0.519 **	0.475
Social capital	0.875 **	0.670 **	0.029 #	0.792 **	0.707 **	0.240	0.712 **	0.880 **	0.179
Justice	0.691 **	0.500 **	0.038 #	0.643 **	0.497 **	0.088 +	0.585 **	0.563 **	0.851
Diversity climate	0.667 **	0.404 **	0.007 **	0.597 **	0.406 **	0.045 #	0.461 **	0.665 **	0.115
Inclusion–exclusion	0.771 **	0.139 #	0.000 **	0.509 **	0.264 **	0.030 #	0.363 **	0.515 **	0.238
Incl. in decision-making	0.381 **	0.322 **	0.312	0.400 **	0.277 **	0.155	0.331 **	0.392 **	0.631
Integration of differences	0.681 **	0.488 **	0.034 #	0.607 **	0.518 **	0.213	0.528 **	0.685 **	0.172
Executive leadership	-0.143	-0.275	0.136	-0.276	-0.148	0.654	-0.263	-0.096	0.251
Org. identification	0.607 **	0.398 **	0.068 +	0.535 **	0.421 **	0.204	0.470 **	0.529 **	0.746
Orange Code acceptance	0.893 **	0.746 **	0.111	0.811 **	0.801 **	0.467	0.810 **	0.798 **	0.927

1 +Significant at 10% level; #significant at 5% level; **significant at 1% level.

2 The p value is the probability of getting the observed difference or greater if the two true mean values are equal (one-tailed test) based upon an unequal variance assumption.

3 The p value is the probability of getting the absolute value of the observed difference or greater if the two true mean values are equal based upon an unequal variance assumption.

Conclusions and discussion

ING Group's view of human rights as fundamental and universal (ING Group, 2016a, p. 45), its perspective on labour rights and practices (ING Group, 2016), its sustainable development goals (ING Group, 2016a, p. 424) and its zero tolerance policy on bribery and corruption (ING Group, 2016a, p. 22) reflect a comprehensive commitment to all four dimensions of the UN Global Compact.

The extent to which these principles are *lived* is reflected in the behaviour and decisions of employees across all ranks. The chapter argues that the ING Orange Code and the ING Diversity Manifesto – in their content and through the *tone at the top* displayed following their launch in 2015 and 2016 respectively – played a key enabling role in moving ING further along the labour dimension of the UN Global Compact. It is further argued that champions can help transform *espoused values and behaviours* into *lived values and behaviours* in a bottom-up fashion. Similar to the ripples that radiate out when a stone is thrown into a pool, the initial actions of the change agent create a *virtuous spiral* that expands over time throughout the organisation.

The case study presented in this chapter demonstrates how the virtuous spiral has operated to expand the appreciation of gender diversity and the importance of gender transformation at ING Group. It provides confirmatory evidence to support Pascale and Sternin's (2005, p. 72) contention that 'somewhere in your organisation, groups of people are already doing things differently and better. To create lasting change, find these areas of positive deviance and fan their flames.'

While acknowledging that categorical statements are not possible on the basis of the exploratory research conducted, leadership of companies wishing to make transformational change seek out *embedded* change agents and provide them with the space, resources and sponsorship to act. As Morgan and Zeffane (2003) have argued, their capacity to push the change agenda is enhanced because their peer status can help rebuild internal trust and subsequent identification with the customer base.

The difference between espoused and enacted values across the business and government sectors has been subjected to considerable research (Howell *et al.*, 2012; Morand, 1995; Schuh and Miller, 2006; Simons, 2002) with some suggesting that alignment between the two is often less than that might be desired. It is argued here that achieving alignment is a process. Committed change agents can play a key role in this if the *tone at the top* is appropriate and if sponsors come to the fore with the needed emotional and financial resources. *Virtuous spirals*, such as the one illustrated in the chapter, offer interesting insight as to how values and behaviours can be influenced over time through a development agenda and position enterprises to better live the principles of the UN Global Compact.

Business school academics will find the ING case a rich platform for discussing complex leadership and management issues (PRME 3 'Method'). The scope of the issues addressed – tone at the top, organisational value, personal motivation, sponsorship etc. – means that an instructor can use the case as a grounding supplement to a more theoretically oriented course of study or as a stand-alone inductive teaching tool. Courses that may find the case beneficial for both peda-gogical approaches include change management, diversity management, human resource management, leadership and change, organisational development and corporate governance.

Notes

1 The authors would like to express their appreciation to Izabela Csontos and Hein Knaapen for their assistance. Beyond being the principal protagonist in the case, Izabela provided invaluable support throughout the development of the chapter. The interview with Hein Knaapen was instrumental in setting the context. While acknowledging their contribution, the authors take the responsibility for any errors of analysis and interpretation.
2 See, Orange: www.nvb.nl/publicaties-standpunten/publicaties/3565/bankierseed-bank ers-oath-toekomstgericht-bankieren.html, accessed 2 October 2016, 2:30 PM CET.
3 ING Group has had a human rights statement for employees since 2006 that articulates its commitment to international labour rights standards. See, www.ing.com/ING-in-Society/Sustainability/Human-Rights.htm, accessed 2 October 2016, 10:00 PM CET.
4 See, www.ing.com/Newsroom/All-news/ING-among-top-ranked-companies-in-Bloom bergs-gender-equality-index-.htm, accessed 8/16/2016, 11:18 AM CET.
5 See, www.ingdirect.com.au/about-us/careers-our-values.html, accessed 7/27/2016, 9:00 AM CET.
6 US Senate Committee on Banking, Housing and Urban Affairs hearing examining of 9/20/2016 into Wells Fargo's opening of unauthorized accounts and the regulatory response needed.
7 A lawsuit by one fired branch manager claims that she was instructed by a district manager to make employees reporting to her open unauthorized accounts. See, http://money.cnn.com/2016/09/26/investing/wells-fargo-fake-accounts-before-2011/, accessed 10/3/2016, 1:55 PM CET.
8 Further impetus for this dialogue may have been the recognition of Hein Knaapen as an annual OUT-standing Top 100 LGBT executive in the 3rd annual Financial Times Top 100 LGBT executive list in 2015 (see, https://ing.com/Newsroom/All-news/Hein-Knaapen-included-among-top-global-2015-LGBT-executives.htm accessed 10/3/2016, 5:28 PM CET.
9 Progression of women to the highest level within business entities is significantly better in many eastern European and Nordic countries than elsewhere across Europe (European Commission, 2015)
10 Over time, Juultje van der Wijk (head of Trade & Commodity Finance Rotterdam) became a second sponsor and key player in attracting participants from other business areas and all continents.
11 Senior level refers to employees who are managers of managers and to those who might be described as Board potential.
12 ING uses the term 'contributors' for employees who do not have responsibility to manage others.
13 0.65 is considered minimum Alpha for a scale to be considered internally consistent while numbers above 0.90 are considered to contain redundant items. For a fuller discussion of appropriate values for Cronbach's Alpha and an interpretation of the measure see, http://data.library.virginia.edu/using-and-interpreting-cronbachs-alpha/, accessed 9/26/2016, 4:40 PM CET.
14 Significantly above the 50 per cent expected if the two groups' perceptions are the same.

References

Aitken, R. (2014) 'Dutch bankers swearing an oath to god. . .whatever next?' *Forbes*, 23 December 2014, *10*: 24. Available online at http://forbes.com/sites/rogeraitken/2014/12/23/dutch-bankers-swearing-an-oath-to-god-whatever-next/#2409155d8987 (accessed 9/30/2016).

Banks, S. (2003) 'From oaths to rulebooks: A critical examination of codes of ethics for the social professions', *European Journal of Social Work*, 6(2): 133–144.

Bartkus, B., Glassman, M. and McAfee, R. B. (2000) 'Mission statements: Are they smoke and mirrors?' *Business Horizons*, 43(6): 23–28.

Bartunek, J. M. and Moch, M. J. (1987) 'First-order, second-order, and third-order change and organizational development interventions: A cognitive approach', *Journal of Applied Behavioral Sciences*, 23: 483–500.

Becker, K. (2008) 'Tone from the top', *Strategic Finance*, July: 22–23.

Bevelander, D. L. (2016) '*The 8th summit: Women's ascent of organizations*', Inaugural address, Erasmus University Rotterdam, 5 February 2016.

Bevelander, D. L. and Page, M. J. (2011) 'Ms. trust: Gender, networks and trust – implications for management and education', *Academy of Management Learning and Education*, 10(4): 623–642.

Brown, S. L. and Eisenhardt, K. M. (1997) 'The art of continuous change: Linking complexity theory and time-paced evolution in relentlessly shifting organizations', *Administrative Science Quarterly*, 42: 1–34.

Cameron, A. (2007) 'Tone at the top', Transparency International Australia AGM. Available online at http://transparency.org.au/wp-content/uploads/2012/07/2007-AGM-speech-Alan-Cameron1.pdf (accessed 3 October 2016).

Caprio, Jr., G. (2013) 'Financial regulation after the crisis: How did we get here, and how do we get out?' LSE Financial Markets Group, special paper series 226. Available online at http://lse.ac.uk/fmg/workingPapers/specialPapers/PDF/sp226.pdf (accessed 13 September 2016).

Chung, Y., Liao, H., Jackson, S. E., Subramony, M., Colakoglu, S. and Jiang, Y. (2015) 'Cracking but not breaking: Joint effects of fault-line strength and diversity climate on loyal behavior', *Academy of Management Journal*, 58(5): 1495–1515.

Claessens S. and Kodres, L. (2014). 'The regulatory responses to the global financial crisis: Some uncomfortable questions', IMF working paper, WP14/46. Available online at www.imf.org/external/pubs/ft/wp/2014/wp1446.pdf (accessed 13 September 2016).

Csontos, I. (2016) 'Document of personal reflections concerning the development of the ING women in leadership programs'. Created 26 September 2016.

Cukier, W. (2009) 'Attracting, retaining, and promoting women: Best practices in the Canadian tech sector'. Canadian Advanced Technology Alliance Women in Technology Forum.

Cukier, W. and Smarz, S. (2012) 'Diversity assessment tools: A comparison', *International Journal of Knowledge, Culture and Change Management: Annual Review*, 11(6): 49–63.

Davies, S. W. and Glaister, K. W. (1997) 'Business school statements: The bland leading the bland', *Long Range Planning*, 30(4): 594–604.

The Economist. (2014) 'The spread of gender quotas for company boards', 25 March 2014 blog posting. Available online at http://economist.com/blogs/economist-explains/2014/03/economist-explains-14 (accessed 6 October 2016).

Ely, R. J. and Thomas, D. A. (2001) 'Cultural diversity at work: The effects of diversity perspectives on work group processes and outcomes', *Administrative Science Quarterly*, 46(2): 229–273.

European Commission. (2015) 'Gender balance on corporate boards: Europe is cracking the glass ceiling'. Available online at http://ec.europa.eu/justice/gender-equality/files/women onboards/factsheet_women_on_boards_web_2015-10_en.pdf (accessed 6 April 2016).

Gersick, C. J. G. (1991) 'Revolutionary change theories: A multilevel exploration of the punctuated equilibrium paradigm', *Academy of Management Review*, 16(1): 10–36.

Goldberg, L. R. (1992) 'The development of markers for the Big-Five factor structure', *Psychological Assessment*, 4(1): 26–42.

Hamers, R. (2016) 'CEO statement: A step ahead', in *ING group annual report 2015*, pp. 2–4.

Harrison, D. A., Price, K. H. and Bell, M. P. (1998) 'Beyond relational demography: Time and the effects of surface- and deep-level diversity on work group cohesion', *Academy of Management Journal*, 41(1): 96–107.

Hartley, M. (2002) *A call to purpose: Mission-centered change at three liberal arts colleges*, New York, NY: Routledge.

Howell, A., Kirk-Brown, A. and Cooper, B. K. (2012) 'Does congruence between espoused and enacted organizational values predict affective commitment in Australian organizations?' *International Journal of Human Resource Management*, 23(4): 731–747.

ING Group. (2016a) 'ING Group Annual Report 2015: A step ahead'. Available online at https://www.ing.com/Investor-relations/Annual-Reports.htm (accessed 23 June 2016).

ING Group. (2016b) 'ING diversity manifesto'. Available online at www.ing.com/About-us/Diversity-and-Inclusion.htm (accessed 23 June 2016).

International Bar Association. (2010) 'A survey of current regulatory trends', *Financial Crisis Task Force Report*. Available online at www.davispolk.com/files/uploads/FIG//Financial_Crisis_Report_IBA.pdf (accessed 30 September 2016).

Knaapen, H. (2016) 'Interview with the chief HR officer of ING group', 15 July, 2016, ING Headquarters, Bijlmerplein 888, 1102 MG Amsterdam, The Netherlands.

Kouvonen, A., Kivimaki, M., Vahtera, J., Oksanen, T., Elovainio, M., Cox, T., Virtanen, M., Pentti, J., Cox, S. J. and Wilkinson, R. G. (2006) 'Psychometric evaluation of a short measure of social capital at work', *BMC Public Health*, 6: 251–261.

Luckerath, M. (2015) 'The Dutch female board index'. Available online at www.tias.edu/docs/default-source/Kennisartikelen/femaleboardindex2015.pdf (accessed 2 October 2016).

Mael, F. and Ashforth, B. E. (1992) 'Alumni and their alma mater: A partial test of the reformulated model of organizational identification', *Journal of Organizational Behavior*, 13(2): 103–123. Available online at http://doi.org/10.1002/job.4030130202

Morand, D. A. (1995) 'The role of behavioral formality and informality in the enactment of bureaucratic versus organic organizations', *Academy of Management Review*, 20(4): 831–872.

Mor Barak, M. E. (2014) *Managing Diversity: Towards a Globally Inclusive Workplace*, 4th edition, Thousand Oaks, CA: SAGE Publications.

Morgan, D. and Zeffane, R. (2003) 'Employee involvement, organizational change and trust in management', *International Journal of Human Resource Management*, 14(1): 55–75.

Nadler, D. A., Shaw, R. B., Walton, A. E. and Associates (1995) *Discontinuous change: Leading organizational transformation*, San Francisco, CA: Jossey-Bass.

Nadler, D. A. and Tushman, M. L. (1990) 'Beyond the charismatic leader: Leadership and organizational change', *California Management Review*, 32(2): 77–97.

Niehoff, B. P. and Moorman, R. H. (1993). 'Justice as a mediator of the relationship between methods of monitoring and organizational citizenship behavior', *Academy of Management Journal*, 36(3): 527–556.

Nishii, L. H. (2013). 'The benefits of climate for inclusion for gender-diverse groups', *Academy of Management Journal*, 56(6): 1754–1774.

Pascale, R. T. and Sternin, J. (2005) 'Your company's secret change agents', *Harvard Business Review*, 83(5): 72–81.

Pickerd, J. S., Summers, S. L. and Wood, D. A. (2015) 'An examination of how entry-level staff auditors respond to tone at the top vis-à-vis tone at the bottom', *Behavioral Research in Accounting*, 27(1): 79–98.

Pieters, J. (2016) 'Banker's oath ineffective, two-thirds don't believe in it', *NL Times*, 8 March 2016. Available online at http://nltimes.nl/2016/03/04/bankers-oath-ineffective-two-thirds-dont-believe-in-it/ (accessed 19 September 2016).

Prastacosa, G., Söderquist, K., Spanosa, Y. and van Wassenhove, L. (2002) 'An Integrated framework for managing change in the new competitive landscape', *European Management Journal*, 20(1): 55–71.

PwC. (2014) 'The future shape of banking: Time for reformation of banking and banks?' Financial Services Report. Available online at www.pwc.com/financialservices.

Schuh, A. M. and Miller, G. M. (2006) 'Maybe Wilson was right: Espoused values and their relationship to enacted values', *International Journal of Public Administration*, 29(9): 719–741.

Schwartz, M. S., Dunfee, T. W. and Kline, M. J. (2005) 'Tone at the Top: An ethics code for directors?', *Journal of Business Ethics*, 58(1–3): 79–100.

Sebastian D., Prinzie, A. and Decramer, A. (2011) 'Looking for the value of mission statements: A meta-analysis of 20 years of research', *Management Decision*, 49(3): 468–483.

Seibert, S. E., Kraimer, M. L. and Liden, R. C. (2001) 'A social capital theory of career success', *Academy of Management Journal*, 44(2): 219–237.

Seo, M. (2003) 'Overcoming emotional barriers, political obstacles, and control imperatives in the action-science approach to individual and organizational learning', *Academy of Management Learning and Education*, 2(1): 7–21.

Short, J. and Palmer, T. (2008) 'Mission statements in US colleges of business: An empirical examination of their content with linkages to configurations and performance', *Academy of Management Learning and Education*, 7(4): 454–470.

Simons, T. (2002). 'Behavioral integrity: The perceived alignment between managers' words and deeds as a research focus', *Organization Science*, 13(1): 18–35.

Sirkin, H. L., Hemerling J. W. and Bhattacharya A. K. (2008) 'Globality: Challenger companies are radically redefining the competitive landscape', *Strategy & Leadership*, 36(6): 36–41.

Vermaelen, T. (2009) 'Why MBAs should not sign the Harvard Business School oath', *INSEAD Knowledge*. Available online at http://knowledge.insead.edu/leadership-management/why-mbas-should-not-sign-the-harvard-business-school-oath-1444 (accessed 19 September 2016).

Woolley, A. and Malone, T. W. (2011) 'Defend your research: What makes a team smarter?' *Harvard Business Review*, June 2011.

Michael Page MBA (Cape Town), PhD (Cape Town) is Professor of Finance and Management at Bentley University in the United States. He serves on the Advisory Boards of several international business schools and on the governing boards of the European Foundation for Management Development (EFMD), the Association to Advance Collegiate Schools of Business (AACSB International), and South Africa Partners.

mpage@bentley.edu

Dianne Bevelander MBA (Cape Town), PhD (Lulea) is Professor of Management Education at Rotterdam School of Management, Erasmus University in the Netherlands. Currently she is leading the drive for women empowerment at the Rotterdam School of Management, and increasingly within the broader Erasmus University. Dianne is the Executive Director of the recently established Erasmus Centre for Women and Organizations.

dbevelander@rsm.nl

Appendix: Likert-scale questions and the source of the instruments

1 Assertiveness – Goldberg, n.d.

- I don't like to draw attention to myself (scale reversed).
- I take charge.
- I try to lead others.
- I can talk others into doing things.
- I seek to influence others.
- I take control of things.

2 Self-efficacy – Goldberg, n.d.

- I complete tasks successfully.
- I excel in what I do.
- I handle tasks smoothly.
- I am sure of my ground.
- I come up with good solutions.
- I know how to get things done.

3 Self-to-other similarity – Harrison *et al.*, 1998

- I feel similar to my departmental colleagues with respect to age.
- I feel similar to my departmental colleagues with respect to gender.
- I feel similar to my departmental colleagues with respect to cultural background.
- I feel similar to my departmental colleagues with respect to education background.
- I feel similar to my departmental colleagues with respect to personal values.
- I feel similar to my departmental colleagues with respect to attitudes about work.

4 Social capital at work – Kouvonen *et al.*, 2006

- Our manager treats us with kindness and consideration.
- Our manager shows concern for our rights as an employee.

- We have a 'we are together' attitude in the team.

- People keep each other informed about work-related issues in the team.

- People feel understood and accepted by each other.

- Members of the team build on each other's ideas in order to achieve the best possible outcome.

- People in the team cooperate to help develop and apply new ideas.

- We can trust our manager.

5 Justice – Niehoff and Moorman, 1993

- I consider my work load to be fair (distributive).

- I feel that my job responsibilities are fair (distributive).

- Our manager makes sure that all employee concerns are heard before job decisions are made (procedural).

- Our manager clarifies decisions and provides additional information when requested by employees (procedural).

- Employees can challenge or appeal job decisions made by our manager (procedural).

- When decisions are made about my job, my manager treats me in a truthful manner (interactional).

- When decisions are made about my job, my manager treats me with respect and dignity (interactional).

- My manager explains very clearly any decision made about my job (interactional).

6 Diversity climate – Chung *et al.*, 2015

- I receive many opportunities to work with diverse teams.

- I have the same opportunities for career growth as my co-workers.

- My co-workers help me feel like an important part of team.

- My co-workers appreciate my background and perspective.

- My manager always treats me like a valued member of the team.

- ING's actions demonstrate complete commitment to diversity with inclusion.

- Capable people succeed at all levels in ING, regardless of the group that they belong to (gender, nationality, race).

7 Inclusion Exclusion – Mor Barak, 2014

- I have influence in decisions taken by my work regarding our tasks.
- I am able to influence decisions that affect my division.
- I am usually among the last to know about important changes in my division (R).
- I am often invited to participate in meetings with management higher than my immediate supervisor.
- I am invited to actively participate in review and evaluation meetings with my supervisor.
- My manager does not share information with me (R).

8 Inclusion in decision-making – Nishii, 2013

- ING has a climate for healthy debate.
- Employee input is actively sought.
- ING clearly perceives employees input as a key to success.
- People's ideas are judged based on their quality and not based on who expresses them at ING.
- Top management at ING believes that problem-solving is improved when input from different roles, ranks and functions is considered.

9 Integration of differences – Nishii, 2013

- ING employees are comfortable being themselves.
- Gender diversity awareness is a priority at ING.
- People's differences are respected at ING.
- People at ING often share and learn from one another as people.
- ING has a culture in which employees appreciated the differences that people bring to the workplace.

10 Executive leadership – (DAT)

- The ING Board considers gender diversity important when identifying and developing people.
- Senior executive pro-actively communicates the importance of gender diversity inside and outside the organisation.
- Leadership of ING bank reflects the composition of the workforce.
- The business case for gender diversity is widely communicated.

11 Organisational identification – Mael and Ashford, 1992

- When someone criticizes ING, it feels like a personal insult.
- When I talk about ING, I usually say 'we' rather than 'they'.
- ING's success is my success.
- When someone praises ING, it feels like a personal compliment.

12 ING Orange Code

- The Orange Code is part of ING work culture.
- The Orange Code has been explained and discussed in my division.
- I am proud of the ING Orange Code.
- ING has empowered us to act according to the Orange Code without fear of reprisal.

17

Management faculty opening
Males preferred

Cubie L. L. Lau
University College Dublin, Singapore

John F. Hulpke
University College Dublin, Singapore

Abstract

Gender equity is important. It is a major principal advocated by the United Nations Global Compact (UNGC). Despite attention to this issue, women are still under-represented in business leadership and business faculties. The issue is related to hiring practices in business schools. Management-area faculty job announcements often look for candidates with publications in top-tier journals. Using the articles in four top management journals of 2014 and 2015, this chapter demonstrates how a seemingly gender-neutral policy favours males over females. To move towards gender equity, as suggested by UNGC Principle 6, there should be less emphasis on top-tier publications in faculty employment decisions. Longer-term, gender equality in academia and in business would benefit from more female professors and administrators in management education. The chapter concludes with some recommendations for making this a reality.

Global Compact: Towards a better world

One of the United Nations Global Compact (UNGC) goals is the elimination of gender discrimination. However, today there are relatively few females in top business positions. This chapter looks at one factor contributing to this imbalanced world: business schools dominated by males. This can occur if faculty hiring policies, even unconsciously, favour males. As of today, employment decisions that tend to emphasize 'top-tier publications' work to the detriment of female candidates. This chapter looks at low numbers of women in top jobs in business and business schools, and then specifically looks at faculty publications. Finally, the chapter suggests ideas to help academia move closer to the UNGC goal of gender equality (UNGC, 2016a, 2016b), looking beyond top-tier publications to understanding and supporting the environment in which female faculty can better thrive and succeed.

One persistent managerial challenge relates to the UNGC Principle 6: 'The elimination of discrimination in respect of employment'. Men still reach higher positions than women, and the UNGC recognizes this. In reaching the UNGC goals, 'Business schools and national schools are such an important part . . . that's the future of the Global Compact.' (Moody-Stuart, 2015).

With this understanding, the UNGC established Principles for Responsible Management Education (PRME). At a PRME gathering in New York in 2015 professors were reminded that: '. . . business exists to make the world a better place and those who educate business leaders have the fundamental responsibility of educating the types of business leaders who get that.' (Cabrera, 2015: 30).

Gender equality is a worthy goal in and of itself, but some suggest that having more women leaders may facilitate achievement of all ten UNGC principles, as 'there seems to be a very strong connection between being female and holding a solid ethical view' (Haski-Leventhal *et al.*, 2015: 1). One survey of more than 1,200 business students found that 'female students placed a higher value on ethical responsibilities than male students' (Haski-Leventhal *et al.*, 2015: 1). Maudal and Fossen-Brainwells (2016) offer their opinion that more female decision makers in business will lead to a better world.

Female business leaders: Low numbers

In 2015, the Fortune 500 companies were led by 476 male and 24 female chief executive officers (CEOs) (Fairchild, 2015). The respective number of female CEOs in 2005 and 1995 were nine and zero respectively (Zahidi, 2015). Some studies look more comprehensively at management positions in addition to the CEO-level appointments. Scholars say women 'continue to remain grossly under-represented at the highest levels' (Joshi *et al.*, 2015: 1516), and are 'dramatically under-represented in top leadership positions' (Brady *et al.*, 2011: 85). Some research suggests that gender equity can also be good for business. A McKinsey study says, companies where women are included in top management perform better on both organizational and financial performance: these firms 'tended to have operating margins . . . twice as high . . . Companies with three or more women in senior management functions score more highly, on average' (Desvaux *et al.*, 2007: 12, 13).

A UNGC book entitled *Impact: Transforming Business, Changing the World* reports that 'companies with a higher representation of women at the most senior levels deliver stronger organizational and financial performance' (UNGC, 2015: 142).

Over four decades ago, the Associated Press (1971) highlighted that while CEOs are chosen by a firm's board of directors, most directors have typically been males. As one female board member said, 'With a lot more qualified people to choose from down the road, you will see a lot of changes in the make-up of boards'(*Business Week*, 1977). The same article quoted another female board member, from IBM: 'Give it 25 years'. Apparently 25 years was not enough. One detailed study showed that 'in both 2012 and 2013, less than one-fifth of companies had 25 per cent or more women directors, while one-tenth (fifty firms) had no women serving on their boards' (Catalyst, 2013). A 2016 update by the same organization shows that boards are still predominantly male, and women hold only 12 per cent of the world's board seats as of 2015 (Catalyst, 2016). In 2014, on average women held 21.3 per cent of board seats at European stock index companies, including fourteen countries, and 19.2 per cent of Standard & Poor 500 firms (Catalyst, 2014).

Women in business schools: Far from equality

The pool of candidates for management jobs depends in part on who studies business. The percentage of female business school graduates is impacted also by the gender of business faculty and leaders who serve as role models for business school students and aspiring entrepreneurs. Most business deans, faculty and students are males (Baron, 2015; Flynn *et al.*, 2015; Lavelle, 2013). The percentage of females serving as business professors and deans is expected to increase, as more females earn PhD degrees in business. But other factors, such as hiring practices and publication expectations, can impede progress towards equality.

Publications required

'For this business school faculty position, preference will be given to male candidates,' while no academic institution says this directly, some universities are doing this indirectly, and possibly inadvertently. Some schools are unintentionally signalling in their job postings that preference will be given to males.

An analysis of management-area faculty job announcements illustrates the importance of publications for faculty positions. The Academy of Management (AoM) website placement section in mid-2016 listed tenure-track faculty openings in fifty-three schools. This chapter presents the results of analysis of these announcements with respect to expectations regarding publications. The idea is not new: as Cadez (2013: 6885) points out, 'the "publish or perish" convention has a long tradition'. Today, it seems to get in the door one should have published. Numerous announcements call for applicants with publications in top journals. Of the fifty-three job postings studied, twenty-six make specific reference to publications in 'top-tier', 'premier', 'high-quality', 'high-impact' or 'top' journals. Twenty-four of the fifty-three job postings mention research with an adjective such as 'strong', 'exceptional' or 'high quality'. If more articles in top journals were authored by males than females, it could have a gender-related outcome. Males would more likely pass the initial curriculum vitae (CV) screening process. This leads to the question whether publications in top-tier journals are more likely to be written by males than by females.

Top-tier journal articles

Articles published in the *AoM Journal* (AMJ), *AoM Review* (AMR), *Strategic Management Journal* (SMJ) and *Administrative Science Quarterly* (ASQ) were reviewed. In 2014 and 2015, these four 'top' management journals published a total of 584 articles, with a total of 1,434 authors. Of these authors, 72 per cent (1,031) were males, and 28 per cent (403) were females.

Management faculty percentages of females are increasing as detailed below. But males who as a group have been playing the publish-or-perish game longer have an edge in publication statistics. Management faculty hiring decisions today will impact faculty composition for the next generation. Publications today will facilitate hiring tomorrow, which will impact faculty composition and publication records decades ahead. Gender-blind hiring, given current requirements, will inadvertently tilt faculty composition, with more males than females, well into the future.

Why fewer females?

As in any complex issue, there are many factors. Women entering graduate school may have learned to read from children's books where women stayed at home and men worked (Association for Library Service to Children (ASLC), 2016; Bem and Bem, 1973). Long before selecting universities or academic majors, women learn 'appropriate' roles (Calogero and Jost, 2011; Wilson, 1992). Women who pursue traditional goals may find life smoother than females who look towards businesses.

Things have changed dramatically since 1970 when only 8.7 per cent of graduates earning business and management degrees at the bachelor's level were females and 3.6 per cent at the master's level. By 2009, these figures for females were 48.9 per cent and 45.4 per cent, respectively, at the bachelor's and master's degree levels. In 2009, there were also still more males earning US business doctoral degrees than females; however, the female share of such degrees rose from 1.6 per cent to 38.7 per cent between 1970 and 2009 (all data in this paragraph are from Flynn *et al.*, 2015: 38). But until 50 per cent of PhD graduates are females, one should not look for 50 per cent female publication ratio in top journals.

One factor slowing the shift to equal numbers of female business doctoral students might be whether a person entering university can see female role models among professors. A female entering Harvard might be subconsciously influenced by the fact that more than half (59 per cent) of education faculty are females (Harvard Graduate School of Education, 2016) but only about a quarter of business faculty are females (Wittenberg-Cox and Symons, 2015). Similar observations are made in many fields, not only in business, and not only for Harvard (Aspelund and Bernhard, 2015). One study puts it this way:

> It is a phenomenon that has been grasping academics for decades: there are too few women... women continue to be in a minority position among university teachers and researchers, and are severely under-represented at the top. (Van den Brink, 2010: 1)

A 2015 source looked at the schools on the *Financial Times* list of top 100 MBA programs. Only one of those business schools had above 30 per cent female faculty and full one-third of them had less than 20 per cent female faculty (Wittenberg-Cox and Symons, 2015).

One might ask, why in 2016 there are still relatively few female faculty members in business at, for example, Harvard Business School (HBS)? A news report in 1997, which interviewed the then HBS dean Kim Clark, noted that 'recent efforts (prior to 1997) to hire more female faculty ... haven't turned things around' (Rosenberg, 1997: 82). Those efforts in the late twentieth century to improve the status of females continued, but not enough according to current dean Nitin Nohria, who 'pledged to pursue a feminist makeover at the school when he was appointed in 2010' (Young, 2013). Nohria had previously researched gender equity issues as an associate dean, and had found that at HBS, women 'were not succeeding at the same rate as the men' (Pazzanese, 2015, citing studies done by Nohria prior to 2010). Despite taking the job in 2010 pledging to work on gender issues, four years later in what was called 'an unusual apology', dean Nohria again said that Harvard would do more to admit female students and hire more women, saying that (HBS) must do better (Byrne, 2014). Things have changed and are changing at Harvard, but a 2016 review showed that 'unbeknownst to the school, the Business School had been hiring men at the assistant level at twice the rate of women' (Debenedictis, 2016: 4).

How can it be that this one school, which was already making 'efforts to hire more female faculty' prior to 1997, followed by promises of dean Kim Clark in the latter years of the twentieth century, then by dean Nitin Nohria in 2010 and again in 2014, can show such limited progress? This is the main point of this chapter: the gender-neutral practice of putting emphasis on top-tier publications favours males.

Increasing gender equality

To move towards gender equity, two paths seem worthy of consideration: (1) have more females as authors of publications in top-ranked journals, and (2) place less emphasis on top-tier publications in employment decisions. Having more top-tier articles published by females will require multi-faceted long-term efforts. Modifying faculty hiring practices can begin immediately.

Seventy-two per cent of the authors in these AMJ/AMR/ASQ/SMJ samples were males, and 28 per cent were females (see Table 17.1). This is substantial improvement from the ratios of 1975 or 1980 when 94 per cent of authors were males and 6 per cent were females (AMJ/AMR/ASQ data from 1975, SMJ data from 1980 when SMJ began publishing). However, there is a long way to go to reach gender equality in this area.

More females are receiving PhDs in business, thus the pool of those likely to submit articles is increasing. Of the four journals studied here, two of the six chief-editors are females, which might be seen as a positive sign. Historically, most existing articles have been authored by males. This pattern has been found across many fields, including natural sciences, law, engineering, technology, medicine and humanities (Bell, 2010; Bell and Chong, 2010; Cecchi-Dimeglio, 2015; Mukherjee *et al.*, 2006; Rorstad and Aknes, 2015). Thus, males have a better chance when faculty openings occur if published articles are expected. This is particularly significant when higher-level positions are open, such as those for associate or full professors (Hancock and Baum, 2010).

TABLE 17.1 Male/Female Authorship in Four Top Management Journals, 2014–2015

	Total articles	Total authors	Male authors	Female authors
AMJ	164	488	68%	32%
AMR	77	185	71%	29%
ASQ	97	134	59%	41%
SMJ	247	627	78%	22%
Grand total	587	1,434	72%	28%

AMJ = *Academy of Management Journal*
AMR = *Academy of Management Review*
ASQ = *Administrative Science Quarterly*
SMJ = *Strategic Management Journal*

Breaking in

Some females do get published. One study of six of the world's best journals, including two in management, suggests that females and males have equal productivity 'when the percentage of women participating in the academic workforce is factored in' (Tower *et al.*, 2007: 23). Factors affecting journal publication include previous record of publishing, institutional research support, time allowed or allocated for research, longevity in the professorial job, connections to associations which sponsor journals and the productivity rate of key mentors (Ryazanova and McNamara, 2016). Having the right mentor counts (Hyers *et al.*, 2012; Tsui and O'Reilly, 1989). None of these factors are necessarily gender-related but the end result may again favour males. Faculty with stronger research records and better mentors are likely to be males (Ragins and Cotton, 1991; Ragins and Scandura, 1994). Females are typically more junior, less experienced as researchers and less connected.

Another study by Hatfield and Webb (2015: 229) notes that in the finance area,

> [w]omen continue to make up less than 20% of those advancing to associate professor and less than 10% being promoted to full professor. Research productivity is a primary determinant for promotion, so it appears that many women are not publishing enough or of sufficient quality.

Fewer female role models can negatively impact the number of females choosing business as a major, and thus the number of female business school graduates, and ultimately the number of female high-level executives in business. Looking beyond the hiring process of business schools, in the tenure and promotion process, publications are often given more weight than teaching (Balkin and Mallo, 2011). The end result is a disproportionately larger number of males in associate and full professorships and in leadership positions. A 2015 study looked at the *Financial Times*' list of top 100 MBA programs, focussing on the best twelve schools on that list. These schools all had male deans (Wittenberg-Cox and Symons, 2015).

Editorial boards: Important

Editorial boards might be another leverage point. The concept of editorial board has developed over time, beginning with a small number of assistant editors, to the present where a typical journal may have more than a hundred editorial board members. Being on an editorial board gives members opportunity to see how the publishing game is played (Metz and Harzing, 2009). Hatfield and Webb (2015: 230) state that 'if women do not have proportional representation on editorial boards, then it would certainly impact what is being published'. A look at two representative management journals suggests the same (see Table 17.2).

TABLE 17.2 Editorial boards and article authorship in two management journals, 1976 and 2015

	AMJ				AMR			
	1976		2015		1976		2015	
	Male	**Female**	Male	**Female**	Male	**Female**	Male	**Female**
Editorial board membership	9	**0**	235	**90**	3	**0**	100	**48**
Gender authorship	116	**3**	184	**83**	100	**3**	82	**26**

AMJ = *Academy of Management Journal*
AMR = *Academy of Management Review*

For example, the number of female authors in AMJ went up to eighty-three in 2015 as compared to only three in 1976. At the same time, female editorial board members of that journal increased from zero in 1976 to ninety in 2015. Similarly, the four management journals studied here also have female associate editors. The AMJ had ten male associate editors and seven female associate editors (May 2016 data); the AMR had six male associate editors and three females; the ASQ had seven males on the editorial board ('associate editors') and three females; and the SMJ had eighteen males as 'associate editors' and seven females. These numbers, with twenty females on the editorial boards, show greater female participation than in the past, but the progress is still slow. In a review of female academic progress in AMJ, Joshi and colleagues (2015) note uneven progress and restate that the goal is to end gender inequality.

One possible point of intervention into this large complex system would be to have more females as faculty members. One way to reach that goal faster might be for schools to place less emphasis on top-tier publications in job announcements and for more schools to say what many recruiting announcements already say: 'Preference will be given to under-represented groups, including women.' Statements referring to publications could be worded carefully in ways less likely to favour males. For example, the phrase 'top-tier publications' could be replaced with 'candidates should demonstrate potential to publish in top-tier journals'. Having more female business school faculty members will facilitate more female authors of journal articles in top-tier publications.

Concluding remarks

Females have not yet reached equality in business schools. The fact that more publication authors are males than females contributes to gender inequality. To help lessen inequality, numerous specific recommendations have been made by those who have studied this area. For example, journals could add more females to editorial boards (Hatfield and Webb, 2015; Metz and Harzing, 2009). Once females are in the faculty ranks, mentorship is important, as covered above (Ryazanova and McNamara, 2016, and others). Business schools could employ a greater number of females in positions of responsibility. Overall, to move closer to the goal in UNGC Principle 6, which includes gender equality, business schools can utilize more gender-balanced criteria for hiring; establish and follow policies to help female faculty members to publish; offer mentoring and peer-support programs as well as networking and co-authoring opportunities for females with PhDs; and seek to create gender-balanced search committees.

Schools that are not yet in PRME could join that effort. One of the PRME key ideas is that faculty should do research that advances understanding about social issues (PRME Principle 4), and the topic of this chapter area fits in this. Additional research is welcome on the issues raised here, including philosophy and employment practices of management development institutions. Much more could be studied about publications, who, when, how, and why gets published. Research could lead to a deeper understanding of the role of gender equality in the university, but also in society at large, especially in the target of the UNGC, the business community.

Increasing the chances for research to make a difference in the real world is addressed in PRME Principle 6, which encourages 'dialog and debate among educators, students, business, government, consumers, media, civil society organizations and other interested groups and stakeholders on critical issues' (PRME, 2017: 1).

These ideas and suggestions merit continued attention. The key contribution of this chapter is to link relatively fewer top-tier publications by females to faculty hiring. Now is the time to look at how to increase the number of females publishing in top journals, and time to decrease the emphasis on top-tier journal authorship in academic employment-related decisions.

There is an increasing awareness that gender equality is necessary for positive social and economic outcomes (UNGC, 2016b). So far, the female representation in business and in faculty and leadership positions in management education has been somewhat low. Gaps remain. To achieve the UNGC goals as stated in Principle 6 in promoting equality, many things could be done as suggested above. To have a better world, things need to keep moving towards equality.

References

Association for Library Service to Children (ASLC). (2016) 'Caldecott Medal Winners, 1938–Present'. Available online at www.ala.org/alsc/awardsgrants/bookmedia/caldecott medal/caldecottwinners/caldecottmedal.

Associated Press. (1971) 'Black woman new IBM director'. *San Francisco Chronicle*, 26 May 1971.

Aspelund, K. M. and Bernhard, M. P. (2015) 'Among Harvard's faculty, "women are still pioneers"', *Harvard Crimson*, 6 May 2015.

Balkin, D. B. and Mello, J. A. (2011) 'Facilitating and creating synergies between teaching and research: The role of the academic administrator', *Journal of Management Education*, *36*(4): 471–494.

Baron, E. (2015) 'A historic gathering of female B-school deans tackles gender inequality, poets and quants web page, February 12'. Available online at http://poetsandquants. com/2015/02/12/a-historic-gathering-of-female-b-school-deans-to-tackle-gender-inequality/2/.

Bell, R. L. (2010) 'The relative frequency of faculty's publications: A content analysis of refereed business journals'. *Academy of Educational Leadership Journal*, *14*(2): 59–84.

Bell, R. L. and Chong, H. G. (2010) 'A caste and class among the relative frequency of faculty's publications: A content analysis of refereed business journals'. *Journal of Leadership, Accountability and Ethics*, *8*(1): 65–89.

Bem, S. L. and Bem, D. J. (1973) 'Training the woman to know her place: The power of a nonconscious ideology', in Leavitt, H. J. and Pondy, L. R. (eds), *Readings in Managerial Psychology*, 2nd edn, Chicago, IL: University of Chicago Press, pp. 142–155.

Brady, D., Isaacs, K., Reeves, M., Burroway, R. and Reynolds, M. (2011) Sector, size, stability, and scandal: Explaining the presence of female executives in Fortune 500 firms. *Gender in Management: An International Journal*, *26*(1): 84–105.

Business Week. (1977) 'The corporate women: A big jump in the ranks of corporate directors', 10 January 1977, pp. 49–50.

Byrne, J. A. (2014) 'HBS dean makes an unusual public apology', *Poets and Quants.* Available online at http://poetsandquants.com/2014/01/28/hbs-dean-makes-an-unusual-public-apology/ (quote from tape at 6:30).

Cabrera, A. (2015) 'Speech at UNGC global forum for responsible management education – 6th PRME Assembly, New York'. Available online at www.youtube.com/watch?v= TqqzhQhCKsM.

Cadez, S. (2013) 'Social change, institutional pressures and knowledge creation: A bibliometric analysis', *Expert Systems with Applications*, *40*(17): 6885–6893.

Calogero, R. M. and Jost, J. T. (2011) 'Self-subjugation among women: exposure to sexist ideology, self-objectification, and the need to avoid closure', *Journal of Personality and Social Psychology*, *100*(2): 211–228.

Catalyst. (2013) 'Catalyst census: Fortune 500 appendix 4 – Companies with zero women directors'. Available online at www.catalyst.org/knowledge/2013-catalyst-census-fortune-500-appendix-4-companies-zero-women-directors.

Catalyst. (2014) 'New global 2014 catalyst census: Women board directors'. Available online at http://catalyst.org/media/new-global-2014-catalyst-census-women-board-directors

Catalyst. (2016) Statistical overview of women in the workforce. Available online at http://catalyst.org/knowledge/statistical-overview-women-workforce.

Cecchi-Dimeglio, P. (2015) 'Legal education and gender equality', in P. M. Flynn, K. Haynes and M. A. Kilgour, *Integrating gender equality into business and management education: Lessons learned and challenges remaining*, Sheffield, UK: Greenleaf.

Debenedictis, J. E. (2016) 'Gender inequality at HBS: A case study', *Harvard Crimson*, 4 May 2016. Available online at www.thecrimson.com/article/2016/5/4/tacking-gender-inequality-at-hbs/.

Desvaux, G., Devillard-Hoellinger, S. and Baumgarten, P. (2007) *Women matter: Gender diversity, a corporate performance driver*, Paris, France: McKinsey.

Fairchild, C. (2015) 'Why so few women are CEOs', *Fortune*, 14 January 2015. Available online at fortune.com/2015/01/14/why-so-few-women-ceos/.

Flynn, P. M., Cavanagh, K. V. and Bilimoria, D. (2015) 'Gender equality in business schools: The elephant in the room', in P. M. Flynn, K. Haynes and M. A. Kilgour, *Integrating gender equality into business and management education: Lessons learned and challenges remaining*, Sheffield, UK: Greenleaf.

Hancock, K. J. and Baum, M. (2010) 'Women and academic publishing: Preliminary results from a survey of the ISA membership', The International Studies Association Annual Convention, New Orleans, Louisiana. Available online at www.hks.harvard.edu/fs/mbaum/documents/ISA_Hancock_Baum_WomenPub.pdf.

Harvard Graduate School of Education. (2016) 'Faculty directory'. Available online at www.gse.harvard.edu/faculty-directory.

Haski-Leventhal, D., Pournader, M. and McKinnon, A. (2015) 'The role of gender and age in business students' values, CSR attitudes, and responsible management education: Learnings from the PRME international survey', *Journal of Business Ethics*, (11). Available online at link.springer.com/article/10.1007/s10551-015-2936-2.

Hatfield, P. and Webb, S. (2015) 'Gender analysis in editorial boards of finance journals', The Clute Institute International Academic Conference Munich, Germany, 2014, pp. 229–231.

Hyers, L., Syphan, J., Cochran, K. and Brown, T. (2012) 'Disparities in the professional development interactions of university faculty as a function of gender and ethnic under-representation', *The Journal of Faculty Development*, *26*(1): 18–28.

Joshi, A., Neely, B., Emrich, C., Griffiths, D. And George, G. (2015) 'Gender research in AMJ: An overview of five decades of empirical research and calls to action thematic issue on gender in management research', *Academy of Management Journal*, *58*(5): 1459–1475.

Joshi, A., Son, J. and Roh, H. (2015) 'When can women close the gap? A meta-analytic test of sex differences in performance and rewards', *Academy of Management Journal*, *58*(5): 1516–1545.

Lavelle, L. (2013) 'Even with a female dean, most MBAs are still men', *Bloomberg Businessweek*, 13 March 2013. Available online at https://bloomberg.com/news/articles/2013-03-13/even-with-a-female-dean-most-mbas-are-still-men.

Maudal, K. and Fossen-Brainwells, E. (2016) 'Will female leaders make a better world?' *Huffpost Business*, 9 January 2016. Available online at www.huffingtonpost.com/kristine-maudal-even-fossen-brainwells/will-female-leaders-make-_b_6184526.html.

Metz, I. and Harzing, A. W. (2009) 'Gender diversity in editorial boards of management journals, *Academy of Management Learning & Education*, *8*(4): 540–557.

Moody-Stuart, M. (2015) 'Speech at UNGC global forum for responsible management education – 6th PRME Assembly, New York'. Available online at www.youtube.com/watch?v=TqqzhQhCKsM.

Mukherjee, T. K., Farhat, J. and Cotei, C. (2006) 'Factors explaining the results of job search by 2002 FMA job applicants: A survey', *Journal of Financial Education*, *32*(1): 1–22.

Pazzanese, C. (2015) '"I had this extraordinary sense of liberation": Nitin Nohria's exhilarating journey', *Harvard Gazette* 29 April 2015. Available online at http://news.harvard.edu/gazette/story/2015/04/i-had-this-extraordinary-sense-of-liberation/.

PRME. (2017) 'Principles for responsible management education – about us – six principles'. Available online at http://unprme.org/about-prme/the-six-principles.php.

Ragins, B. R. and Cotton, J. L. (1991) 'Easier said than done: Gender differences in perceived barriers to gaining a mentor', *Academy of Management Journal*, *34*(4): 939–951.

Ragins, B. R. and Scandura, T. A. (1994) 'Gender differences in expected outcomes of mentoring relationships', *Academy of Management Journal*, *37*(4): 957–971.

Rorstad, K. and Aknes, D. W. (2015) 'Publication rates expressed by age, gender and academic position – A large-scale analysis of Norwegian academic staff', *Journal of Informetrics*, *9*(2): 317–333.

Rosenberg, D. (1997) 'Getting down to cases: Some of Harvard B-school's influential case studies will finally feature women executives', *Newsweek*, 22 December 1997, p. 52d.

Ryazanova, O. and McNamara, P. (2016) 'Socialization and proactive behavior: Multilevel exploration of research productivity drivers in US business schools', *Academy of Management Learning & Education*, *15*(3): 525–548.

Streuly, C. A. and Maranto, C. L. (1994) 'Accounting faculty research productivity and citations: Are there gender differences?' *Issues in Accounting Education*, *9*(2): 247.

Tower, G., Plummer, J. and Ridgewell, B. (2007) 'A multidisciplinary study of gender-based research productivity in the world's best journals', *Journal of Diversity Management – Fourth Quarter*, *2*(4): 23–32.

Tsui, A. and O'Reilly, C. (1989) 'Beyond simple demographic effects: The importance of relational demography in superior–subordinate dyads', *Academy of Management Journal*, *32*: 402–423.

UN Global Compact. (2015) *Impact: Transforming business, changing the world*', New York, NY: UN Global Compact and DNV GLAS.

UN Global Compact. (2016a) 'What is UN global compact?' Available online at www.unglobal compact.org/what-is-gc.

UN Global Company. (2016b) 'Gender equality'. Available online at https://unglobalcom pact.org/what-is-gc/our-work/social/gender-equality.

Van den Brink, M. (2010) *Behind the scenes of science: Gender practices in the recruitment and selection of professors in the Netherlands*. Amsterdam, the Netherlands: Amsterdam University Press.

Wilson, F. (1992) 'Language, technology, gender and power', *Human Relations*, *45*(9): 883–904.

Wittenberg-Cox, A and Symons, L. (2015) 'How women are faring at business schools worldwide', *Harvard Business Review*, 27 April 2015. Available online at hbr.org/2015/04/how-women-are-faring-at-business-schools-worldwide.

Young, C. (2013) 'Gender engineering at Harvard business school', *Minding the Campus* (Web page), 10 September 2013. Available online at www.mindingthecampus.org/2013/09/gender_engineering_at_harvard_/.

Zahidi, S. (2015) 'Where are the women in global leadership?' *World Economic Forum Agenda*, 14 January 2015. Available online at agenda.weforum.org/2015/01/where-are-the-women-in-global-leadership-7-charts/.

Cubie L.L. Lau, PhD, is a faculty member for University College Dublin based in Singapore. She was educated in the UK, Hong Kong, and Ireland. She has held academic posts in Ireland, Hong Kong, and Singapore. She has published in journals such as *Strategic Management Journal, Journal of Business Ethics,* and *Social Responsibility Journal.*

cubie.lau@ucd.ie

John F. Hulpke received his doctorate at the University of California, Berkeley. He has taught in many universities in the US and Asia. He has lectured to business leaders and students in 12 cities in China. He has published in the *Journal of Applied Management Studies, Public Administration Review* and other journals.

john.hulpke@ucd.ie

We wish to thank Lester S.B. Jiang for research and data analysis.

Concluding remarks

Patricia M. Flynn
Bentley University, USA

Tay Keong Tan
Radford University, USA

Milenko Gudić
Refoment Consulting and Coaching, Serbia

Business schools and other providers of management education can play key roles in integrating sustainability into the curriculum, into research, and into organizational practices, as they prepare current and future business professionals to challenge the ways in which success has traditionally been defined. Highlighting the non-prescriptive nature of the UNGC and PRME principles, this book demonstrates a variety of strategies and programs that can be effective across disciplines, organizations and countries. The authors demonstrate how management educators collaborating with business practitioners and civic organizations can be change agents for a better world.

These concluding remarks focus on the lessons learned from the case studies, innovations and perspectives that contribute to the advancement of social responsibility and sustainability. Challenges making such changes difficult are then assessed, followed by discussion of the longer-term implications for responsible management education.

Lessons learned

The chapters provide a wealth of information on strategies and guidance for integrating sustainability into management education. All of the PRME principles come into play.

With respect to the PRME Principles 1 ('Purpose') and 2 ('Values'), for instance, several new frameworks are proposed for thinking about responsible management education and how best to measure success. Anninos (Chapter 2) calls upon faculty to understand and incorporate aspects of neuroscience into management education. He demonstrates how the integration of self-awareness, empathy and mindfulness helps to develop an ethical mindset, thus generating sensitive and responsible individuals eager to become change agents. He encourages management educators to create stress-free and immersive learning environments, which will foster critical and meaningful decision-making that will benefit the planet. Ciccmil, Ecclestone and Colins (Chapter 3) propose a new 4E (ethics, economy, ecology and epistemology) framework that challenges assumptions, and encourages respect for differences in values, backgrounds and perspectives. Through a participatory approach students become active and equal partners in the creation and development of knowledge. In Chapter 4, Hope provides a new blueprint, the PRME Curriculum Tree, for creating innovative courses on ethics, responsibility and sustainability that engage students across all disciplines. The Curriculum Tree also helps faculty integrate responsible management concepts into existing courses and structures, thereby fostering the buy-in of faculty in a timely fashion.

Innovative perspectives and approaches (PRME 3, 'Methods') are critically important as the traditional ways of teaching, and topics for research can constrain the capacity to deliver new courses, programs and strategies in these areas. A common theme highlighted by many of the authors is the value of getting students out of the classroom. In particular, several case studies demonstrate the importance of engaging students in projects that provide them access to business professionals (PRME 5, 'Partnerships' and PRME 6, 'Dialog') who deal with responsible management issues on a daily basis. Field trips around these topics (Chapters 6 and 8) show that in addition to students gaining key knowledge and skills on sustainability, they are being exposed to businesses, working professionals and possible future job opportunities in organizations that highly value individuals with these skills and attributes. One case study (Chapter 15) demonstrates the wide range of benefits that accrue to students who go out into the field and interview business managers and innovators who have been instrumental in integrating sustainability, business ethics and social responsibility into their organizations. Another outside-the-classroom option involves students directly applying their new skills on consulting teams (Chapter 14), thereby effectively helping businesses that may lack expertise in these areas. Such exposure increases student awareness of these key issues well beyond textbooks. In addition to being recipients of knowledge and skills, students can become vital contributors to the practice of responsible management. Student interviews, internships, consulting assignments and other work-based projects, all relate to the critical roles of 'Partnerships' (PRME 5) and 'Dialog' (PRME 6) in implementing responsible management education, and in developing future employees and business leaders eager to influence economic and societal metrics.

Beyond fostering business skills and expertise, out-of-classroom projects help develop critical thinking skills as well as proficiency in terms of communication, team building and time management (Chapters 14 and 17). The hands-on problem-solving skills the students acquire in these activities are found to be put into practice in their own daily lives almost immediately (Chapter 14), and students in these courses are inclined to sign up for related events, such as Earth Day activities and internships (Chapter 15). Having direct contact and exposure to leadership and its challenges can also inspire students to become advocates for sustainability practices across the globe.

In addition, the case materials highlight the value of 'Research' (PRME 4) in providing context and understanding of the key issues and challenges of sustainability. Having students as well as faculty conduct meaningful research on these critical topics helps demonstrate and understand the results of past practices and strategies that can lead the way to overcoming barriers to incorporating sustainability into courses. Assignments involving local companies provide excellent opportunities for student research projects. In preparation for field trips or internships, for instance, students can be asked to collect data, both quantitative and qualitative, on these organizations (Chapter 9). Such exercises foster development of skills useful in a variety of other contexts as well. Moreover, students engaged in the AIM@Flourish projects (Chapter 15) have opportunities to publish their research on the project website.

Research can also be a critical link and motivator for engaging faculty in sustainability issues in management education. This aspect is effectively demonstrated in the case study of a business school long focussed primarily on teaching (Chapter 9). The author explains how responsible management education and student-initiated research projects can be instrumental in demonstrating the importance of change given evolving environmental issues. Moreover, student engagement through research projects both on and off campus can be a key driver of institutional change in business schools and other providers of management education even where tradition and a risk-averse culture might have previously hindered innovation.

Several of the chapters advocate for the integration of the UNGC and PRME principles at the institutional level rather than just focussing on one or two departments or faculty members, thus addressing the so-called PRME 7, i.e. 'The Importance of Organizational Practice'. The nature of research and out-of-classroom projects has the potential to bring together students, faculty, administrators and members of the university board (Chapter 9). Chapter 17 makes the case that institution-wide change is necessary to overcome the current biases in hiring and promotions if gender inequality is to be addressed in management education. A case study on business schools in the Philippines (Chapter 11) highlights the importance of a multi-level approach if transformational change is to take place. And, Chapter 10 demonstrates how one business school integrated the PRME principles throughout the organization. Looking well beyond curricular innovation, responsible management practices were sought of all relevant parties (students, faculty, staff and administration) in terms of courses, research, campus life and outreach to the community.

Beyond the PRME principles, numerous chapters also provide lessons and insights on responsible business management as highlighted in the UNGC principles and the more recently developed Sustainability Development Goals (SDG). Chapter 1 provides the historical underpinnings of the origins of the UNGC and PRME, and their relationships to the SDGs. As the student work-based assignments in Chapter 14 focus on the Greenhouse Gas Management project, it addresses SDG 13 on climate change. In tackling gender issues in faculty hiring decisions in business schools, Chapter 17 focusses on the UNGC principle of eliminating discrimination in employment (Principle 6). Chapter 16 also addresses diversity issues, with the case study on ING Group demonstrating the critical role of change agents in transforming business institutions to better foster responsible management for all workers (Principle 7). Virtuous spirals that involve, for instance, tone at the top, personal motivation and sponsorship are shown to provide key insights on values and behaviours that can be influenced to better incorporate the principles of UNGC and PRME. The issues in Chapter 7, which address managerial and legal aspects of human rights, directly or indirectly relate to all ten of the UNGC principles.

Another lesson learned involves the benefits of interdisciplinary approaches taken to address sustainability and responsible management education. A case study in Brazil, for instance (Chapter 8), demonstrates the value of bringing faculty from different disciplines to the table to tackle the multi-faceted nature of the issues at hand. In this particular instance, business school and law school faculty collaborated on the development of a joint elective course addressing human rights. The case study on integrating AIM2Flourish (Chapter 15) also successfully brought faculty together from different departments in case management and marketing to the benefit of students, faculty and local businesses.

Challenges to Integrating the UNGC and PRME Principles

Innovative change and implementation of the PRME and UNGC principles are not without their challenges. Several chapters, for instance, flag the lack of relevant information in textbooks, research and case studies as a major hindrance in the integration of sustainability into management education. In emerging market and developing countries, these shortfalls are especially critical.

Faculty are cited in many chapters as part of the problem rather than the solution in integrating sustainability into management education. A lack of awareness of sustainability issues and of UNGC and PRME was not uncommon. And, beyond the lack of relevant textbook content and other relevant resources, the interdisciplinary nature of responsible management, sustainability and Corporate Social Responsibility (CSR) issues can generate additional barriers to faculty. Another obstacle to the adoption of new curricular offerings on sustainability is the already crowded field of established courses; new ones addressing issues of sustainability often have to compete with incumbent courses in order to be given space.

Faculty buy-in for such integration is imperative but may be slow in coming. Academia is not known for its rapid pace of change. Moreover, as demonstrated above, significant changes are often involved in the successful integration of the PRME and UNGC principles. The focus on work-based learning, changing priorities and partnerships with business professionals requires thinking outside the box for many faculties. Moreover, beyond getting buy-in, incorporating field-based learning projects into a course is relatively time-consuming compared to in-class lectures. Arranging contacts in the community and generating the particular assignments take considerable time prior to the start of such courses. Then, once the course is up and running, on-going oversight and guidance of the students in the field is quite time-consuming.

A related challenge is picking the right business partners for student projects and longer-term relationships. The case studies demonstrate the value of having faculty and students working with business leaders and managers who have demonstrated success in integrating social responsibility and CSR into their business practices. Interaction with SMEs, entrepreneurs, and not-for-profit institutions offer potential benefits for students as well. Location of the academic institutions influences the availability and nature of relevant and constructive projects. Business schools in developing countries have to further address relative disadvantages in terms of infrastructure, technology, communication and unstable economies.

The good news is that numerous chapters and case studies in this book demonstrate that the challenges that exist in integrating sustainability into management education can successfully be overcome. Doing so usually requires academics to think creatively and be willing to do things differently than in the past.

Implications for responsible management education

The widespread lack of background and sample materials on sustainability across numerous academic disciplines and countries makes clear the need to develop and disseminate additional case studies, relevant textbook material and research so that students, faculty and business professionals can learn about the myriad issues involved and benefit from the experiences of others. This was one of the key drivers for developing this book as well as its earlier companion volume, *Beyond the Bottom Line: Integrating Sustainability into Business and Management Practice.*

Some key archives already exist of case studies, curricula material and research findings for faculty teaching management education; these need to be given widespread visibility and attention. As described in Chapter 1, for example, the SDG Industry Matrix[1], a resource being developed in partnership with UNGC and KPMG, offers academics numerous industry-specific examples and corporate initiatives related to the SDGs. Another resource is the Global Repository[2] created by the PRME Working Group on Gender Equality to help faculty integrate gender issues into their courses, and assist businesses in reducing gender inequalities at the workplace. The Repository, accessible on the UN PRME website[3], includes a wealth of case studies, syllabi, research studies and contacts on gender-related issues across fifteen business-related disciplines. Faculty and other researchers should be encouraged to share their findings and outputs through this resource.

Additional relevant theoretical and conceptual insights, case studies, inspiration stories and practical guidance resources have been developed in recent years by members of the three PRME working groups that subsequently collaborated on the current book. For instance, the Anti-Corruption Working Group created an online anti-corruption toolkit to aid educators in incorporating integrity and governance issues into their curricula. This toolkit is available at no charge at actoolkit.unprme.org. Publication of the book, *Anti-Corruption: Implementing Curriculum Change in Management Education*, followed[4].

The PRME Working Group on Poverty has conducted and published a global survey series on management education and poverty alleviation, including one on Fighting Poverty through Management Education: Challenges, Opportunities and Solutions[5]. Following this, two books were published: *Socially Responsive Organizations and the Challenge of Poverty*[6] and *Responsible Management Education and the Challenge of Poverty*[7].

The PRME Working Group on Gender Equality, noted above, produced two books to encourage and assist management educators and business prac-titioners addressing gender inequality: *Integrating Gender Equality into Business and Management Education: Lessons Learned and Challenges Remaining*[8] and *Overcoming Challenges to Gender Equality in the Workplace: Leadership and Innovation*[9].

Many more innovative course materials and research projects are needed to accelerate the integration of sustainability across disciplines, organizations and countries – resources that will provide theoretical and practical rationales; documented experiences and best practices; and success stories on how to overcome critical challenges in the process.

Greater attention is also needed in the cultivation of faculty to get many more on board and excited about delivering responsible management education. Training and development programs for faculty; collaborations with academics in other institutions that are further along in the process of incorporating such change; and mentoring and sponsorship programs for faculty have all been shown to be successful drivers of creating faculty change agents. And, we should not underestimate the value of global networks and international exchanges (such as UNGC and PRME) for scholars that provide for the exchange of ideas, methodologies and teaching materials. Global, regional and local conferences of scholars interested in teaching and researching sustainability can also go a long way in promoting best practices in pedagogy, joint research and collaboration on various fronts.

Business schools themselves and other providers of management education can learn how they, too, can become more effective change agents in the quest for social responsibility and sustainability. This is essential if they are to prepare current and future leaders as advocates for global social responsibility. Addressing institutional barriers and breaking down silos between academic departments will facilitate the shift to greater responsible management education and also motivate more faculty and administrators to become actively involved.

While numerous challenges remain in the integration of sustainability in management education, we hope that this book provides guidance and inspiration to students, faculty, administrators and business practitioners in tackling these issues and contributing to the future we all want.

Notes

1 www.unglobalcompact.org/library/3111
2 http://prmegenderequalityworkinggroup.unprme.wikispaces.net/Welcome+to+the+ Wikispace
3 http://prmegenderequalityworkinggroup.unprme.wikispaces.net/Resource+Repository
4 Amann, W., R. Berembeim, T. K. Tan, M. Klenhempel, A. Lewis, R. Nieffer, A. Stachowicz-Stanusch and S. Tripathi, 2015. *Anti-Corruption: Implementing Curriculum Change in Management Education*, UK: Greenleaf Publishing, ISBN 978-1-78353-546-0.
5 Gudić, M., A. Rosenbloom, and C., Parkes 2012: *Fighting Poverty through Management Education: Challenges, Opportunities and Solutions* (June) www.unprme.org/resource-docs/FightingPovertythroughManagementEducationChallengesOpportunitiesand Solutions.pdf.
6 Gudić, M., A. Rosenbloom, and C. Parkes, (Eds.) 2014: Socially Responsive Organizations and the Challenge of Poverty, UK: Greenleaf Publishing, ISBN 978-1-78353-059-5.
7 Gudić, M., C. Parkes, and A. Rosenbloom (Eds.) 2015: Responsible Management Education and the Challenge of Poverty, UK: Greenleaf Publishing, ISBN 978-1-78353-257-5.
8 Flynn, P., K. Haynes, and M. Kilgour (Eds.) 2015 *Integrating Gender Equality into Business and Management Education: Lessons Learned and Challenges*, UK: Greenleaf Publishing, ISBN 978-1-78353-225-4.
9 Flynn, P., K. Haynes, and M. Kilgour (Eds.) 2016. *Overcoming Challenges to Gender Equality in the Workplace: Leadership and Innovation*, UK: Greenleaf Publishing, ISBN 978-1-78353-546-0.

About the editors

Patricia M. Flynn, PhD, is Trustee Professor of Economics and Management at Bentley University, USA, where she served as Dean of the McCallum Graduate School of Business for 10 years. Her research focuses on corporate governance, women in business and technology-based economic development. She has served on numerous corporate, mutual fund and non-profit boards, and testified before Congress on the impacts of technological change on jobs and workers. Patricia serves as co-chair of the PRME Working Group Gender Equality. In 2016, she became the inaugural recipient of the Distinguished Women Leader in Business Education Award given by the Women Administrators in Management Education at AACSB-International; the award now bears her name. In 2017, Pat was awarded one of the first Principles for Responsible Management Education (PRME) Pioneer Awards for 'Thought Leadership – Translating PRME into Action'.

pflynn@bentley.edu

Tay Keong Tan is Director of International Studies and Leadership Studies, and an Associate Professor in the Department of Political Science at Radford University, USA. His research interest is on integrity systems and global sustainability. He has headed public and non-profit organizations in Singapore, Israel, and the United States, and for more than a decade worked in development projects on governance and anticorruption in more than 20 countries. He is a member of the PRME Working Groups on Sustainability and AntiCorruption.

ttan2@radford.edu

Milenko Gudić is Founding Director of Refoment Consulting and Coaching, Belgrade, Serbia, and visiting lecturer at University Donja Gorica, Montenegro. He has worked as a consultant, researcher and lecturer at the Economics Institute, Belgrade, as a visiting lecturer in several countries, and as a speaker in over 30 countries. He has been engaged as a consultant to OECD, UNDP, UNIDO, etc., on various entrepreneurship, regional, rural and public management-development projects. Milenko was Founding and Managing Director (2000–2014) of the International Management Teachers Academy (IMTA), while also leading CEEMAN's major international research and educational leadership capacity building projects. He was Program Chair of EURAM 2008. Since 2008 he has been co-coordinating the UN Global Compact PRME Working Group on Poverty, a Challenge for Management Education. In 2017, Milenko was awarded one of the first (PRME) Pioneer Awards for 'Thought Leadership – Translating PRME into Action'.

milenko.gudic@gmail.com